REAL ESTATE BY THE NUMBERS

REAL ESTATE BY THE NUMBERS

A Complete Reference Guide to
DEAL ANALYSIS

J Scott and Dave Meyer

BiggerPockets®
PUBLISHING
Denver, Colorado

EARLY PRAISE FOR
REAL ESTATE
BY THE NUMBERS

"J and Dave are two of the best analytical minds in real estate. Together, they have put together a book that is both highly detailed and easy to understand—a perfect combination for novice and experienced investors alike."

—Joshua Dorkin, Founder of BiggerPockets.com

"When people ask me if they should buy a certain property they've identified, I often reply, 'Let the numbers be your guide.' However, many new investors don't know how to analyze the numbers and are left guessing...This book changes all that. You'll be able to make decisions like a pro and easily determine which deals meet your unique financial goals. A big shout-out to J and Dave for sharing their brilliance!"

—Kathy Fettke, Cofounder of the RealWealth Network

"If financial literacy and real estate investing are ever taught in schools, this should be the textbook! Everyone should know how to build a personal financial statement, read a balance sheet, and create a profit and loss statement. J and Dave break down these concepts with easy-to-understand examples and charts. This book should be required reading for every high school student and up!"

**—Henry Washington, Cohost of
the BiggerPockets *On the Market* podcast**

Real Estate by the Numbers: A Complete Reference Guide to Deal Analysis
J Scott and Dave Meyer

Published by BiggerPockets Publishing LLC, Denver, CO
Copyright © 2022 by J Scott and Dave Meyer

Publisher's Cataloging-in-Publication Data
Names: Scott, Jason, 1971-, author. | Meyer, Dave, 1987-, author.
Title: Real estate by the numbers : a complete reference guide to deal analysis / J. Scott and Dave Meyer.
Description: Includes bibliographical references. | Denver, CO: BiggerPockets Publishing, LLC, 2022.
Identifiers: LCCN: 2022940032 | ISBN: 9781947200210 (paperback) | 9781947200241 (ebook)
Subjects: LCSH Real estate investment. | Real estate investment--Rate of return. | Real estate business--Mathematics. | BISAC BUSINESS & ECONOMICS / Real Estate / Mortgages | BUSINESS & ECONOMICS / Business Mathematics | BUSINESS & ECONOMICS / Investments & Securities / Real Estate | BUSINESS & ECONOMICS / Personal Finance / Investing | BUSINESS & ECONOMICS / Real Estate / General
Classification: LCC HD1375 .S36 2022 | DDC 332.6/324--dc23

Published in the United States of America
Printed in Canada on recycled paper
MBP 10 9 8 7 6 5 4 3 2 1

DEDICATION

Dave

To my dad, for teaching me that everything—from sandwich toppings to investing decisions—deserves a deep and thoughtful analysis.

J

To my fifth-grade math teacher, Mr. Cozzolino. Thank you for awakening a passion and talent in me that nobody else recognized. For anyone this book might help, much of the credit goes to you. I'm only sorry that it took me forty years to properly thank you.

TABLE OF CONTENTS

PART 3
THE KEY RETURN METRICS

PART 4
FUNDING AND FINANCING DEALS

PART 5
MAKING IT WORK FOR YOU

INTRODUCTION

Growing up, I (J Scott) was taught that knowledge is all about having the answers. From a young age, we learn our ABCs, take spelling tests, study multiplication tables, and memorize state capitals. We spend years going over the names and dates of notable people and events throughout history. We memorize formulas to solve chemistry and physics problems.

If we do a good job of remembering the answers, we get good grades—maybe even accolades and awards. If we're fortunate, those grades give us a chance to go to college, where our task is to memorize more facts and continue to build our repository of answers. And if we can accomplish that successfully, we're rewarded with a job that pays us money to start learning answers to new and seemingly more important questions.

Our whole lives, we're trained that success comes from having the answers. The more answers we have, the more successful we'll be.

This was me. I was "the smart kid." Remembering answers always came easy to me. I breezed through elementary, middle, and high school. I went to college and got an engineering degree, which also came easily; I realized early on that if I applied the right formula at the right time, the solution would present itself. I got a corporate job, went back to school to get my MBA, and continued to thrive on my ability to study the facts and formulas, and to always have the answers people were looking for.

As I advanced through my career, I continued to find myself intrigued by the idea of investing as a profession. In my mind, investors were the epitome of success—I set my sights on becoming a full-time investor. So, when I met Evan back in 2006, I saw an opportunity. Evan was a co-worker, but he was also an investor. I was fascinated to learn that Evan ran a nine-figure real estate fund outside of his corporate job.

Weren't investment funds the realm of CEOs and billionaires? How did a co-worker of mine come to control hundreds of millions of dollars in real estate? And as a side job, no less!

This was my chance. I was determined to learn from Evan. Over the next couple of months, we became better friends, and I finally got up the courage to ask him to mentor me. In my attempt not to be too much of an imposition, I simply asked if he'd be willing to let me take him to lunch once a week (his choice of restaurant, of course) and let me ask him questions.

Not only did he agree, but he even seemed enthusiastic about it.

At our first lunch, I was prepared. I pulled out my list of questions and started by asking him about how he analyzes his deals. What formulas did he use to determine if a property was worth buying for his fund?

Before I could get through my first question, he stopped me. Without even a hint of humor or sarcasm, he said, "You're a smart guy. Why are you asking dumb questions? Do you think investing is simply about plugging numbers into formulas and getting rich?"

He proceeded to lecture me for several minutes, explaining that there's no system, no magic formula, no step-by-step guide to becoming a successful investor. Any investor who simply plugs numbers into a formula will eventually find themselves losing money, he insisted. In Evan's words, "A pilot who only knows how to fly in perfect conditions can be destroyed by even a small storm."

Over the next few months of lunches, Evan helped me realize that great investors aren't great simply because they can memorize and apply formulas. Great investors understand the rules of finance and money. They recognize the relationships within and between markets. They appreciate the forces that drive asset values up (and down). And they recognize that, in many cases, the difference between a good deal and a bad deal is nothing more than *time*.

Most importantly, Evan helped me realize that great investors aren't great simply because they have all the answers. They're great because they know what questions to ask. Knowing the answers might make you smart, but knowing the questions to ask makes you wise.

As investors, our goal is to ask the right questions. The right questions will lead us down a path to decisions that will ultimately make us money. The wrong questions will lead us down a path of confusion and uncertainty. Long story short, the better the questions we ask—and the better we are at answering those questions—the more successful we will be as investors.

In some situations, the right question might simply be "Is this a profitable deal?"

In other situations, we might need to know "How profitable is it?"

In still other situations, the right question is "How much is this asset worth?" (Which, by the way, is a completely different question than "How much should I be willing to pay for it?")

Oftentimes, our questions revolve around "Should I pursue investment #1 or investment #2?" And that answer is likely to change depending on the question, "What am I trying to optimize for?" or "What types of returns should I be trying to maximize?"

More importantly, once we make the decision to invest, we will need to ask the question "How do I make the most money off this deal that I've chosen?"

Sometimes we specifically want to know "*Should* I sell this asset that I own?" If the answer is "yes," then we may want to know "*When* exactly should I sell it to maximize my profits?" Or perhaps we should be asking "*How* should I sell it to maximize my returns?"

The first goal of the book is to help you determine which questions to be asking, and when. The second goal is to help you answer those questions. We will provide you with an arsenal of concepts and methodologies that you can use to formulate the right questions to ask in any situation. And then we will provide you with the formulas and metrics you can use to lead to answers that are meaningful.

If you're new to investing, you'll likely want to read this book from the beginning. Each part and each chapter builds on what came before, so new investors—or those who don't have a strong math background—will find a cover-to-cover read-through the best way to build a solid foundation. However, each section is written so that it can stand alone, so if you're already a successful investor—and/or if you have a decent understanding of real estate finance—you can read only what serves you best. If you're looking to refresh your memory on financing options, want to study up on the time value of money, or are trying to remember the purpose and definition of a particular metric, feel free to skip around.

This five-part book is meant to be both a comprehensive guide to real estate math and a reference guide that investors can come back to time and again over the course of their investing journey.

In Part 1, "Personal and Business Performance," we discuss simple ways to organize and understand your finances—both your personal finances and the finances of your business. This section will walk you through the process of calculating your net worth, help you determine what investable assets you have, give you the tools to track the performance of your (real estate) business, and provide you with a framework to start thinking about analyzing investments. Even if you don't yet have a business or an investment, understanding these concepts will help you be a better investor and set you up to better apply the lessons learned later in the book.

In Part 2, "The Concepts," we walk step-by-step through some of the most important ideas behind making successful investments. From the basics (like how interest works) to one of the most important financing concepts there is (the time value of money), this part of the book will likely both challenge and enlighten you. These are the concepts that separate the good investors from the great investors, and if you put in the effort to learn them, you will soon find yourself far ahead of most of the competition.

In Part 3, "The Key Return Metrics," we delve into the ten most common metrics we use to evaluate investment performance. Not only do we discuss how these metrics are used, but we also walk you through them in a very specific order, providing insight into why some metrics are more versatile and powerful than others. Even if you know your real estate performance metrics, we have a feeling you'll start looking at them differently after reading this part.

In Part 4, "Funding and Financing Deals," we dig into how we buy and finance our investments. From how capital stacks work to discussions of debt, equity, loan structuring, leverage, and more, we answer all your questions about how deal funding works. And at the end of this part, we delve into the important discussion of when the right time is to sell or refinance your investments—a topic that we don't see addressed nearly enough.

Finally, in Part 5, "Making It Work for You," we walk through some of the most important frameworks for those who are looking to build wealth through real estate investing. The first half of this part will hopefully change the way you think about wealth building and the benefits of real estate. Then, in the second half, we dive deep, using the lessons taught throughout the book to analyze the various types of deals you're likely to encounter in the real world.

Because this book is about asking the right questions, we have chosen to start each chapter with the question or questions the chapter hopes to answer. Many chapters also include sample problems at the end to test your understanding of those concepts.

Finally, because real estate finance is such a vast topic, we expect that this book will likely spawn a lot of questions that it doesn't answer. If—and when—this is the case, we hope you'll jump onto the BiggerPockets forums and ask. We're always here to answer!

—J Scott & Dave Meyer

PART 1
PERSONAL AND BUSINESS PERFORMANCE

Most people think of financial statements as something only Fortune 500 companies use. That couldn't be further from the truth. In reality, financial statements are a valuable tool to any investor or business owner.

As a real estate investor, you may already be using financial statements in your life and business. If you're not, it's probably safe to say you will be at some point.

Financial statements have many uses:

- They help you to analyze potential investments.
- They are required by many lenders who provide you financing.
- They give you and your tax professional information that can be used to reduce your tax burden.
- They provide insight into the health of your investments.
- They allow you to track your financial goals.
- They are a warning system for when you or your business face potential cash flow issues.
- They often serve as documentation for your buyers when selling your investments.

Financial statements are so important to investors and their businesses that we've decided to devote the entire first section of this book to the topic. We know it might sound dry and boring, but we have a feeling that you'll walk away from this part of the book with a new appreciation for how serious investors think about their businesses and financial lives.

This part is broken up into four chapters. In the first, we'll walk through financial statements and calculations that apply to you as an individual: the Personal Financial Statement, your savings rate, and your investable assets. These concepts will help you assess your finances as they stand today and help you plot a course to reach your financial goals.

In the second and third chapters, we'll turn our attention to each of the major financial statements. These statements are similar to those discussed in Chapter 1, but they are applied to businesses instead of individuals. We'll teach you how to construct the individual statements' more formal business equivalents: the balance sheet and the profit and loss statement. We will talk about how these statements will be used to benefit your business, and we will provide a concrete example of how each is created and applied.

Lastly, Chapter 4 will demonstrate how financial statements are used in real estate. We'll cover a few terms unique to the real estate investing industry and show how to use financial statements to analyze potential deals and track your existing portfolio.

As you read through Chapter 1 ("Your Personal Financial Statement"), remember that the concepts you're learning will be almost the same as the concepts in Chapter 2 ("The Balance Sheet") and Chapter 3 ("The Profit and Loss Statement (P&L)"). Your Personal Financial Statement is basically just a balance sheet for your life. Calculating your burn rate is just making a profit and loss statement for your spending habits. There are just a few simple concepts to learn.

By learning these concepts, you'll always be able to keep an eye on the big picture. You'll be able to take advantage of investing opportunities, know with perfect clarity how your businesses are performing, and understand how your efforts impact your personal finances and net worth.

CHAPTER 1
YOUR PERSONAL FINANCIAL STATEMENT

Chapter 1 will help answer the questions:
- What is my net worth?
- How much money do I have to invest?
- What strategies should I consider given my personal financial situation?

If we were to ask you what your personal net worth is, would you know the answer? Would you even know what we were referring to?

To understand the concept of net worth, think of it this way: If you could magically convert all the stuff you own and control—your investments, your house, your car, and all your other belongings—into its cash value, and then use that cash to pay off all your debts, how much money would you have left?

#1   **Net worth** = Total value of assets − Total value of liabilities (debts)

Now, if we asked, would you know your savings rate? In other words, do you know how much your net worth is growing (or shrinking) each month, given how much you earn and how much you spend?

Your savings rate is simply how much money you have "coming in," how much you have "going out" toward essentials or luxuries, and how much is ultimately being saved to grow your net worth. As an investor, these concepts are important, as they indicate how much money you could reasonably and responsibly commit to a real estate deal if a great one came along.

If you know the answers to these questions, you're well ahead of the game. We know a lot of people—including a lot of successful businesspeople—who aren't this attuned to their personal financial situation.

But if you cannot yet answer these questions, don't fret. That's what this book is for! We're going to walk you through exactly how to calculate these numbers and what the results mean.

At this point, just know that these two concepts—net worth and savings rate—are metrics every adult should know how to calculate to evaluate their current financial picture and plan out their financial future.

As an investor, having this information at your fingertips is important for many reasons:

- It ensures you are investing responsibly and not taking on more risk than is advised or necessary.
- It provides a mechanism to monitor your financial health and ensure that you continue to make progress toward your financial goals. If you don't know how much you were worth last year, how do you know if you're better or worse off today? Or whether you will be better or worse off next year?
- It can indicate whether you are spending your money in ways that move you closer to—or further from—your financial goals.
- It can offer insight into whether you should pay off debt or use debt in more strategic ways.
- It can help you decide whether you should pursue a deal now or save up additional money to get a higher-priced property.
- It offers information to others you'll work with who will need this information. Lenders often ask you to provide a breakdown of your personal financial life before extending personal or business credit. Investors want to know whether you are financially solid before investing in your deals. Your tax professional and attorney may need to assess your financial situation when helping you make business and tax decisions.

To be a successful investor, it's vital to have a good grasp on your personal financial situation. Luckily, understanding your personal finances is not difficult. We've broken it down into three simple concepts: the *Personal Financial Statement (PFS)*, which tracks your net worth; your *savings rate*, which shows how your finances are performing on a monthly basis; and your *investable assets*, which will help newer investors understand how to invest with an appropriate level of risk.

CALCULATING YOUR NET WORTH

Calculating your net worth is important—and luckily, it's also relatively easy. The Personal Financial Statement (PFS) is the tool we use that allows you to do that (a PFS is also known as a "Net Worth Statement" or a "Personal Balance Sheet").

A PFS is built on two sets of information: assets and liabilities.

These two concepts are fundamental to all financial statements, and we'll be revisiting them later when discussing how to construct a balance sheet, a profit and loss statement, and an income statement for your business.

INVESTOR STORY
J's Launchpad

What was the single biggest thing I ever did to put myself on the path to financial freedom?

One day, about twenty years ago, I created a PFS to calculate my net worth. I knew I was in debt, but I didn't know how bad it was. It was scary to see a big negative number staring back at me.

But it also gave me the motivation to start changing things.

Ever since, I've looked at my financial situation as a game—a game that I try to win every single day.

My first day playing the "game," I sold a few things on eBay and that negative net worth number moved a couple dollars closer to zero. (Win!) And within about eighteen months, that net worth number hit zero. (Big win!)

I did this by asking myself every day: *What can I do to increase that number by tomorrow?* And you know what? The number started going up. I started to make small, daily changes to boost my income and minimize my expenses.

Next, I started asking myself what I could do to increase that number over the next month. And you know what? The number started going up faster. I started to think about the larger financial decisions I could make that would impact my financial situation.

Soon, I was asking myself what I could do to increase that number over the next year. The number started going up even faster. By now, I was asking myself the important life questions that ultimately drive financial success over long periods of time.

These days, I ask myself the question: *What can I do to make that number go up over the next five years? Or ten years?*

And as you might guess, the number continues to go up faster and faster.

One day, perhaps I'll be smart enough to start asking myself what I can do to make that number go up over the next twenty or thirty years. I have a pretty good idea of what would happen if I targeted my net worth that way.

I'm not saying that what worked for me will necessarily work for you...but it probably will. The PFS is an incredibly powerful tool—not just as a tracking device, but also as a motivator. If you're having trouble getting yourself to be more financially diligent, why not try treating it like a game? See if you can achieve a new "high score"!

Assets

Assets are, simply put, things of value that you own or control. More specifically:

 Assets are resources owned or controlled by you or your business that can be measured in dollars and will provide some future value.

Some examples of personal assets include cash, investments, land or "real property," retirement accounts, automobiles, jewelry, collectibles, furniture, and the cash value of life insurance policies.

Let's imagine a typical investor—we'll call him John. If John were to capture all his personal assets on a spreadsheet, it might look something like this:

ASSETS	Estimated Value
CASH OR CASH EQUIVALENT	
Cash on Hand	$200.00
Bank - Checking Account	$20,000.00
Money Owed from Bill Jones	$5,000.00
RETIREMENT ACCOUNTS	
Self-Directed IRA	$54,500.00
INVESTMENTS	
Stocks	$3,200.00
Bonds	$800.00
BUSINESS INTERESTS	
ABC Properties, LLC	$65,000.00
REAL/PERSONAL PROPERTY OWNED	
Personal Residence	$185,000.00
2013 Honda CRV	$7,000.00
Furniture and Household Goods	$5,000.00
Jewelry	$2,000.00
ASSETS TOTAL	**$347,700.00**

Quick Tip | **PFS**

It's important to know that every PFS will look a little different. Everyone will have different categories, amounts, and organizational structure. So don't get caught up in trying to mimic our exact PFS in the example above—just focus on learning the concepts and you'll be well on your way.

You'll notice that the assets list is broken up into sections, with each section containing assets that are similar in nature. John's list of assets includes both liquid assets (those assets that are easily turned into cash, like stocks and bonds) and nonliquid assets (assets that aren't easily turned into cash, like his retirement account).

#3	**Liquid assets** are assets that are easily turned into cash, such as stocks, bonds, and—of course—actual cash.

Notice that John has an interest in a business (ABC Properties, LLC) that's worth $65,000. Keep this in mind; we'll come back to it in the next chapter to discuss how we arrived at that asset's value.

Also notice that John has included his personal residence in his list of assets. You may be wondering how that number might change if John had a mortgage or a loan against his house. The answer is that it wouldn't—that $185,000 is the market value of John's house, or the price at which John believes he could reasonably sell the property. Asset values don't change simply because we have a loan against the asset. That said, we'll deal with any mortgage or loan against the house in the next section.

Finally, at the bottom of the list, we add up all the assets and arrive at a total. In theory, if John were to convert all his assets to cash at their fair market value (the value at which he'd be able to find buyers for each asset), he should have a little under $348,000.

Before we move on, there are two important concepts about assets that we want to clarify.

Is an Asset Always an Asset?

Many industry "gurus" will tell you that certain things—like cars, or even a personal residence—are not really assets. They believe that something that loses value over time or doesn't directly generate cash should not be considered an asset. They say this in attempt to steer their students away from buying assets that aren't good long-term investments. While we believe they have the best interests of their students in mind when saying this, from a finance perspective, they are wrong.

It may be true that for most people, an expensive car isn't a smart asset to own; however, it's still an asset. Remember, the word "asset" has no judgment associated with it—a good asset for me might not be a good asset for you, and vice versa. The "right" assets for any person will change over time as their financial situation develops. For example, some people would say that only cash-flowing assets (assets that generate cash flow every month) are good, but there are many situations where non–cash flowing assets are better at helping us achieve our goals.

As an extreme example, let's say an investor friend of ours owns a yacht. It doesn't generate any income for him, and it is very expensive to own, operate, and maintain. Not to mention that it is going down in value every year. Among other things, our friend uses his yacht to wine, dine, and entertain his private-money investors, and he has raised tens of millions of dollars thanks to this depreciating and non–cash flowing asset. In other words, his yacht has made him a lot more money than it has cost him. From this perspective, it's hard to argue that it's not an asset.

And while it's true that a boat, a car, your personal home, or any of the rest of your "stuff" doesn't directly generate cash, these things do have value. You can sell these things today for cash that you can use to pay bills, purchase investments, or put into your business. More importantly, many of these things are used to help you generate income. For example, for anyone who doesn't work from home 100 percent of the time, a car is a necessary part of ensuring that you can commute to your job and continue to earn income.

Remember, by definition, any asset can be converted to any other type of asset. You can sell an asset for cash, and then use that cash to buy a different asset. So, while you may not have considered a car an asset (until now), consider that you can sell that car and use the cash to buy a rental property. Do you consider a rental property an asset? If so, then the car was also an asset, just in another form. It's just like ice, water, and steam—all the same substance, just in different forms.

If others in the industry want to change the definition of asset to provide a different perspective on the things we should be spending our money on, they can of course do so. But in this book, our definition of asset is going to be more in line with how most businesspeople and financial professionals use the term.

If it has cash value—if it can be converted to cash—it's an asset.

 #4   **Appreciating assets** are assets that tend to increase in value over time. **Depreciating assets** are assets that tend to decrease in value over time.

APPRECIATING VERSUS DEPRECIATING ASSETS

A lot of the confusion about whether a car is an asset or not comes from the difference between appreciating assets (assets that gain value over time) and depreciating assets (assets that lose value over time). Certainly, almost all cars are depreciating assets (collector cars being the exception), but they are still assets because they have a cash value. Whether an asset is going up or down in value does not change its status as an asset.

That said, as smart investors, our goal should be to have as many of our assets as possible be appreciating assets. Over time, you should try to fill your PFS with assets like real estate, dividend-paying stocks, and other things that will likely be worth more tomorrow than they are today. Sure, any given property or stock can lose value. But it also has the potential to grow, which is what we want. Further, many asset classes (for example, the overall stock market and the overall real estate market) tend to appreciate over the long run. Cars, on the other hand, almost never appreciate.

Even if It's Encumbered?

In the investment world, the term "encumbered" simply means that an asset has a loan against it. If I buy a house and get a mortgage, my house is encumbered. If I buy a car and get a car loan, the car is said to be encumbered until that loan is paid off.

Just because something of value might be encumbered doesn't mean it is any less of an asset. If you own your house outright—meaning you paid for it with cash and don't have a loan on it—and your house is worth $100,000, your house is a $100,000 asset. Even if you purchased that same home with a $100,000 loan, the house is still a $100,000 asset.

If this concept is confusing, keep reading.

Liabilities

Liabilities are the opposite of assets. They are the debts and financial obligations you and/or your business are saddled with.

#5   **Liabilities** are legal debts and obligations that reduce future financial value.

Some examples of personal liabilities include a mortgage on your personal residence, student loan debt, loans owed against a car, and money owed to family or friends.

Remember when we mentioned that an encumbered asset is still an asset? That's true, and here's an example that demonstrates why.

If a house is encumbered (has a loan against it), the house is still an asset—with the same value as if it didn't have the mortgage—but it has a corresponding liability that goes along with it. For example, if you own the aforementioned house worth $100,000 with a $100,000 mortgage, you now have both a $100,000 asset (the house) and a $100,000 liability (the mortgage).

Sometimes we use the term "paired" when referring to an asset and a liability. A house (the asset) is paired with the mortgage (the liability). They are separate things that are coupled together. If the liability goes away (e.g., the loan is paid off), the asset remains. If the asset goes away (e.g., a huge storm destroys the house), the liability remains. They are *separate* things.

If John were to capture all his personal liabilities on a spreadsheet, it might look like this:

LIABILITIES	
	Estimated Value
LOANS	
Mortgage - Personal Residence	$138,200.00
School Loan	$26,300.00
Car Loan	$3,200.00
REVOLVING DEBT	
Credit Cards	$6,800.00
OTHER	
Estimated Taxes Owed on April 15	$18,000.00
LIABILITIES TOTAL	**$192,500.00**

Once again, John's various liabilities are grouped according to the type of liability. That said, there are no absolute groupings you must follow. Feel free to organize your assets and liabilities in whatever way makes sense to you.

At the bottom, we add up all the liabilities and arrive at a total. This is the total amount John would need to pay to clear himself of all future financial obligations.

In this example, that would be $192,500.

Net Worth

As we defined above, net worth is the difference between your assets and your liabilities. To pull together the concepts of assets and liabilities, we can use the following net worth equation:

#6 The Personal Financial Statement (PFS) Equation:
Net Worth = Assets – Liabilities

In the previous sections, we captured John's personal assets and personal liabilities. By putting those side by side, the equation above captures John's total net worth.

And we can use all that information to create John's PFS.

PERSONAL FINANCIAL STATEMENT: John Robinson
As of December 31, 2022

ASSETS	Estimated Value	LIABILITIES	Estimated Value
CASH OR CASH EQUIVALENT		**LOANS**	
Cash on Hand	$200.00	Mortgage - Personal Residence	$138,200.00
Bank - Checking Account	$20,000.00	School Loan	$26,300.00
Money Owed from Bill Jones	$5,000.00	Car Loan	$3,200.00
RETIREMENT ACCOUNTS		**REVOLVING DEBT**	
Self-Directed IRA	$54,500.00	Credit Cards	$6,800.00
INVESTMENTS		**OTHER**	
Stocks	$3,200.00	Estimated Taxes Owed on April 15	$18,000.00
Bonds	$800.00		
BUSINESS INTERESTS			
ABC Properties, LLC	$65,000.00		
REAL/PERSONAL PROPERTY OWNED			
Personal Residence	$185,000.00		
2013 Honda CRV	$7,000.00		
Furniture and Household Goods	$5,000.00		
Jewelry	$2,000.00		
ASSETS TOTAL	**$347,700.00**	**LIABILITIES TOTAL**	$192,500.00
		ESTIMATED NET WORTH: $155,200.00	

In this example, we arrive at John's net worth by subtracting $192,500 (his total liabilities) from $347,700 (his total assets). John's net worth is $155,200.

Notice that John's PFS has a date on it. A Personal Financial Statement is a snapshot of a single point in time, and as such, it will always contain a date so that we know when that snapshot was taken.

FUTURE EXPENSES

If we want to get nitpicky, we can discuss that "Estimated Taxes Owed" line, which some of you are probably wondering about. While not everyone includes future expenses that aren't immediately due, adding information like this helps us get a true understanding of our financial picture. In fact, on my (J's) PFS, I even have a line for "Depreciation Recapture," which is a tax expense I probably won't incur for years (or decades), but which I will eventually have to pay. I also have a line item for "New Roof" on my personal residence, as I know I have this big expense coming up where I'll need a good bit of cash that I won't be able to use for other stuff.

I may not include all of this information when I provide my PFS to the bank for a loan (we want to reflect the highest reasonable net worth possible to the bank), but I like to have it on there when using the PFS for my personal information.

Remember, the PFS is your opportunity to get a true picture of your financial situation, and the goal shouldn't be to try to make your PFS look as impressive as possible. The goal should be to make it look true and accurate.

Now that we understand what a PFS is and how it's created, let's talk about some of the benefits it provides. Why is having a PFS important?

- First, if you are looking to make an investment, real estate or other, knowing your net worth is a great starting point to determine how much capital you have to invest. In the case your net worth is negative or close to zero, building a PFS can help you develop a timeline and game plan for making your next investment.
- If you were to apply for any type of investment loan from a bank or professional lender, there's a high probability that the lender will ask for your PFS. In fact, some lenders will ask for several years of your PFS to see how your net worth has trended.
- If you're just starting out, keeping and updating your PFS can keep you motivated to make progress toward your financial goals. It allows you to track your total net worth over time to determine if it is increasing or decreasing. When net worth is increasing, you are doing something right; when it's decreasing, you may want to reevaluate your financial path—but at least you know what's going on!
- Knowing your net worth will allow you to assess where you might be in relation to retirement. Good investors know how much money is needed to retire comfortably, and the PFS provides a snapshot of where you are relative to that goal.

- Your PFS provides insight into the types of assets you're carrying. You can see how much of your net worth is in assets that will eventually go down in value (like cars, jewelry, and furniture) versus how much is in assets that will likely rise in value (your investments and business interests). Your goal as an investor should always be to have a high percentage of assets that are appreciating (increasing in value) versus depreciating (decreasing in value).
- Your PFS provides insight into the types of liabilities you're carrying. You can see how large a percentage of your liabilities are "good debt" (debt against appreciating assets) versus "bad debt" (debt against depreciating assets). As an investor, your goal should always be to have as little bad debt as possible.
- Finally, if you were to provide your PFS to your accountant, tax professional, and/or attorney (and you should!), there are likely some insights they could provide that would allow you to restructure your assets and liabilities in ways that would provide tax and legal protection.

If you don't currently have a Personal Financial Statement, we highly recommend you download the Excel templates that accompany this book at www.biggerpockets.com/numbersbonus and create your own!

CALCULATING YOUR "INVESTABLE ASSETS"

As we mentioned earlier, one of the primary advantages of developing a PFS is to determine how much capital you have to invest. But to make that determination, we need two important, easy-to-calculate metrics: *liquid assets* and *savings rate*.

Calculating Liquid Assets

Understanding your liquid assets is easy—you already did pretty much all the work when you created your PFS. To determine your liquid assets, simply go back through your PFS and add up all the assets that can easily be turned into cash, like stocks, bonds, or money that you have stored in a savings or checking account. Note that instead of "liquid assets," you may sometimes hear the term "cash equivalents."

Quick Tip | Easy Liquidation

There is no generally agreed-upon time frame for what constitutes an "easy" liquidation of an asset into cash. We believe that anything that can be converted to cash in less than a week should be considered a liquid asset, but if you want to be more relaxed about it and include anything that can be converted to cash within a couple weeks—or if you want to be stricter and say within a couple days—we wouldn't argue.

Continuing our example from above, John has liquid assets of $24,200.

LIQUID ASSETS: John Robinson As of December 31, 2022	
CASH OR CASH EQUIVALENT	
Cash on Hand	$200.00
Bank - Checking Account	$20,000.00
INVESTMENTS	
Stocks	$3,200.00
Bonds	$800.00
TOTAL LIQUID ASSETS	**$24,200.00**

You could turn your car or jewelry into cash relatively easily, but for the purpose of this example, we'll assume that John needs his car and is not interested in selling any of his personal property for his next investment.

Understanding "Savings Rate"

We now know that a PFS is a snapshot of your financial situation at a single point in time. It will help you determine where you stand on the day the PFS is completed or updated. Your liquid assets calculation is also a snapshot in time. But neither of these indicates anything about whether your situation is trending upward or downward. This is why we also need to calculate our savings rate.

#7 | **Savings rate** = Monthly income – Monthly expenses

Calculating our savings rate will help us understand whether our personal assets are growing, shrinking, or staying flat each month. It's very similar to an Income Statement produced by companies (more on that later), but it's simplified for personal use.

Let's return to our friend John to show why you need to know your personal savings rate.

John has $24,200 in liquid assets. $24,200 could be plenty of money to get in on a real estate deal, but it may not be a wise decision if he's spending more than he's saving each month.

For example, if John invests $20,000 in a property that cash-flows $300/month, he might think he's found himself an excellent deal (more on that later). However, if John's expenses exceed his income by $1,000/month, he is still losing money each month—even having found a good deal—and is at risk of running out of cash in six months if something doesn't change.

Let's see why that is.

After John's $20,000 investment, he would have $4,200 in liquid assets remaining.

LIQUID ASSETS: John Robinson As of December 31, 2022	
Starting Liquid Assets	$24,200.00
Investment Amount	$20,000.00
ENDING LIQUID ASSETS	**$4,200.00**

John had been losing $1,000 per month prior to his investment (a savings rate of -$1,000). Since his investment nets him $300 per month, his savings rate has improved and is now -$700. That's a solid improvement, but "saving" negative $700 per month will eat up John's $4,200 within six months after his initial investment. Therefore, even though this deal would improve John's savings rate, John will still have to sell personal property or turn to one of many other undesirable options to cover expenses.

We can break this down by month to see how John's money is running out.

MONTH	SAVINGS RATE	INVESTMENT(S)	LIQUID ASSETS
Month 0	$(1,000.00)	$-	$24,200.00
Month 1	$(700.00)	$20,000.00	$4,200.00
Month 2	$(700.00)	$-	$3,500.00
Month 3	$(700.00)	$-	$2,800.00
Month 4	$(700.00)	$-	$2,100.00
Month 5	$(700.00)	$-	$1,400.00
Month 6	$(700.00)	$-	$700.00
Month 7	$(700.00)	$-	$-
Month 8	$(700.00)	$-	$(700.00)
Month 9	$(700.00)	$-	$(1,400.00)
Month 10	$(700.00)	$-	$(2,100.00)
Month 11	$(700.00)	$-	$(2,800.00)
Month 12	$(700.00)	$-	$(3,500.00)

This scenario would be like pouring water into a leaky bucket. A year after his initial investment, John's liquid assets total -$3,500. He may have found a great deal in this example, but given his personal situation, it would just accelerate his insolvency. Knowing his savings rate could help John avoid this trap.

I (Dave) first started investing around the same time my friend Jason (not his real name) bought his first rental property. One day, Jason told me about this great deal he found, and after looking at his numbers, I agreed—he had found a great property. Jason bought the deal and was generating a strong return. Things looked good at first.

However, problems started to arise about a year into the deal. Although Jason had saved enough money for a down payment and some operating reserves, he was spending more than he made each month.

Jason had a sales job that could be described as "feast or famine." Sometimes he would make a lot of cash; other times his work would dry up. He saved enough money for a down payment while things were good, and he even had enough money to buy a nice car with a high monthly payment. But around the time Jason bought his property, he was not bringing in a lot of income from his job. Jason saw his rental property as a good opportunity to make his income more consistent, which was great in theory. (Rental property investing can do that!) But Jason didn't run the numbers, and he failed to recognize that even after his investment, he would have a negative savings rate.

With high fixed costs (his apartment and fancy car), Jason quickly got in trouble. He ate through his operating reserves and started to rack up credit card debt to pay for everyday expenses. Fortunately, Jason saw the writing on the wall. He knew how dangerous it can be to rack up debt with no plan to repay it, and he decided to cut his losses before things got worse. He sold his car first, but not long after, he also had to sell his rental property to pay off his debt and get his life back in order. Luckily for Jason, this worked, and he is in a good place now. But he put himself in a very dangerous position, and he took losses on a deal that should have been a home run.

Had Jason examined his savings rate prior to his rental property investment, he could have gotten his financial house in order first—before investing—and enjoyed the benefits of the great deal he found.

On the flip side, this knowledge can help people with *positive* savings rates identify the best investment opportunities.

As an example, let's say John has been able to increase his savings rate to $1,000/month (meaning he makes $1,000 more than he spends every month). John finds himself choosing between two investments:

1. To buy a one-bedroom/one-bathroom apartment in his town, John can invest $20,000 and earn $100/month. This is a deal he can afford to do today.
2. To buy a two-bedroom/two-bathroom apartment in his town, John can invest $30,000 and make $300/month. John would have to save for ten months to afford this deal.

For reasons that we'll discuss later in the book, Scenario 2 may be the better invest-ment. But, for now, let's just take a quick look at where John would be in twenty-four months with each of these scenarios.

- **Scenario 1** would earn John $2,400 over two years with a $20,000 investment. This is a 12 percent annual ROI. (If it's not obvious, we'll discuss how we calcu-lated that later in the book.)
- **Scenario 2** would earn John $4,200 over two years with a $30,000 investment, even though he delayed investing by ten months. This calculates to a 14 percent annual ROI.

By understanding his savings rate and patiently growing his investable assets, John can plan ahead and give himself the option of potentially finding a better deal at some point in the near future than he has access to today. We'll talk about comparing scenarios in much more detail and with more sophistication in Part 5 of this book.

Calculating Savings Rate

So how do you determine your own savings rate? It's a very similar exercise to con-structing your PFS; if you've ever set a budget for yourself, you've already done this in essence.

First, add up all your income in a given month. This might be as simple as counting up your paychecks for the month if you have a consistent salary, or each of your salaries if you work multiple jobs.

If your income is variable (i.e., it changes each month), you can use what is known as a "trailing average." Basically, you want to figure out your average monthly income. A good way to do this is to add up everything you've made over the last three months, and then divide the total by three. This will give you your average monthly income.

For example, let's say that John drives for a ridesharing app in addition to his full-time job. Because his income for rideshare driving is variable, he needs to calculate the average of his income for the last three months, which would look like this:

VARIABLE INCOME: John Robinson	
Rideshare Income May	$350.00
Rideshare Income June	$475.00
Rideshare Income July	$675.00
AVERAGE INCOME	**$500.00**

Combined with his W-2 job ($4,500 per month), John's monthly income would look as follows:

	Estimated Value
CASH OR CASH EQUIVALENT	
Monthly Salary	$4,500.00
Ridesharing Income	$500.00
TOTAL INCOME	**$5,000.00**

Next, you need to add up all your expenses: tax withholdings, rent/mortgage, car payments and insurance, groceries, entertainment, etc. Again, if any of your expenses are variable and change a lot month to month, try using an average of your last several months.

Once you have an idea of your monthly expenses, put them all together.

	Estimated Value
EXPENSES	
Tax Withholdings	$1,350.00
Mortgage Payments	$1,150.00
Student Loan Payments	$200.00
Food & Groceries	$400.00
Entertainment	$300.00
Car Loan Payments	$200.00
Gas	$100.00
Misc.	$300.00
TOTAL EXPENSES	**$4,000.00**

Now, simply subtract your expenses from your income, and you have your monthly savings rate.

SAVINGS RATE: John Robinson
As of December 31, 2022

Income		Expenses	
	Estimated Value		Estimated Value
CASH OR CASH EQUIVALENT		**EXPENSES**	
Monthly Salary	$4,500.00	Tax Withholdings	$1,350.00
Ridesharing Income	$500.00	Mortgage Payments	$1,150.00
		Student Loan Payments	$200.00
		Food & Groceries	$400.00
		Entertainment	$300.00
		Car Loan Payments	$200.00
		Gas	$100.00
		Misc.	$300.00
TOTAL INCOME	**$5,000.00**	**TOTAL EXPENSES**	**$4,000.00**
		SAVINGS RATE: $1,000.00	

In this example, John's income is $5,000 per month and his expenses are $4,000. This leaves John with a savings rate of $1,000.

Savings rate = Monthly income – Monthly expenses
Savings rate = $5,000 – $4,000 = $1,000

So, in addition to $24,200 in liquid assets, John has a positive savings rate and is growing his net worth by $1,000 per month.

Quick Tip | Savings Rate as a Percentage

In the personal finance world, as well as at the macroeconomic government level, savings rate is often calculated as a percentage, not a dollar value. Specifically, savings rate is sometimes calculated as:

Savings rate = Total monthly savings ÷ Total monthly income

So, in the example of John above, his savings rate would be:

Savings rate = $1,000 ÷ $5,000 = 0.2 (20%)

John's savings rate is 20 percent.

DIFFERENT STRATEGIES TO CONSIDER BASED ON YOUR PFS AND SAVINGS RATE

No matter what the results of your PFS and savings rate are, it's okay. There are no right or wrong answers here. Remember, this book is all about asking the right questions. The first step toward improving your financial situation is understanding where you are today. Don't be discouraged if your results are low or negative—there is a path forward for everyone. However, the next steps on your investing journey may vary based on the results of your calculations.

Negative Net Worth and Savings Rate

If both your savings rate and net worth are negative, we recommend working to change your savings rate before you do anything else. Living with a negative savings rate is not sustainable; it leaves us at risk for taking on credit card debt, resorting to payday loans, or even winding up in bankruptcy. You need to be making more money than you're spending, regardless of whether you're investing. It will be almost impossible to attract business partners or secure a mortgage if you don't have any assets and are losing money every month.

Now, some of you might be thinking, "I want to invest in real estate to change my savings rate from negative to positive." That's a good thought. There may indeed be some rare scenarios where this is possible, but *it is not the norm*. It will be easier to find success in real estate investing if you start from a position of financial stability—and that starts by having a positive savings rate.

Sometimes fixing a negative savings rate is easy; sometimes it can be a big challenge. Luckily, there are a lot of great resources available to help. We're not going to go into strategies for improving your savings rate in this book, but we recommend *Set for Life*, a great book by Scott Trench, which talks about this in great detail.

Negative Net Worth and Positive Savings Rate

If your net worth is negative (you have more liabilities than assets), that is okay! Most individuals start in this position. It's extremely common for people to have student loans, car loans, or a mortgage that exceeds their assets.

You can still invest in real estate with a negative net worth, so long as your savings rate is positive. In fact, real estate is a great way to leverage the extra income you're generating each month and use it to generate profits and/or cash flow from investments to pay down your debt.

Positive Net Worth and Savings Rate

If your net worth and savings rate are positive—great! You are well-positioned to grow your investment portfolio and should be able to explore a variety of real estate investing strategies in the near future.

DIG DEEP

ACCREDITED INVESTORS

One of the many benefits to measuring your net worth and savings rate is to determine if you qualify as an "accredited investor." The definition of an accredited investor is set by the federal government (the Securities and Exchange Commission [SEC], to be specific), and the current definition is:

A net worth of over $1,000,000, either individually or jointly with a spouse (not including equity in a personal residence).

OR

Greater than $200,000 of personal income (or greater than $300,000 for joint income with a spouse) for the last two years, and the expectation that you'll make as much or more in the current year.

If you qualify as an accredited investor, congratulations! This will allow you to purchase what are known as "unregistered securities." Unregistered securities are investments that are not registered with financial regulatory agencies and are considered inherently riskier than other forms of investments, such as traditional stocks or bonds. Because unregistered securities are considered riskier, the government has put limitations on which investments can be marketed to the general public and which can only be offered to accredited investors. The thinking here is that accredited investors are better positioned to absorb losses from risky investments, and therefore can invest in unregistered securities.

In the world of real estate investing, one of the major benefits of being an accredited investor is being able to participate in syndication deals. These are deals where, for example, a "sponsor" will find a big deal they want to invest in—let's say a hundred-unit multifamily complex. But since the sponsor doesn't have the ability or desire to put up all the money needed to buy this deal, they look to raise money from outside investors. This type of deal is very common in real estate but is considered an unregistered security by the government, so only accredited investors can participate.

By calculating your PFS and savings rate, you'll be able to determine if you qualify as an accredited investor and enjoy the opportunities that come with that designation.

PUTTING IT ALL TOGETHER

Now that we know our liquid assets and our monthly savings rate, we can put it all together and determine our "investable assets." At first glance, it may seem that liquid assets and investable assets are the same thing—but it's not advisable for you to invest 100 percent of your liquid assets, which is where the difference lies.

Budgeting experts recommend that you maintain a liquid reserve of three months' expenses in case of emergency. Perhaps you lose your job. Maybe you need to go on disability. There are a number of unfortunate events that could disrupt your income, so having three months' expenses on hand is an important safety net. If you have children, or if your income is seasonal or highly variable, you might want to keep an even greater reserve—perhaps six months—of expenses.

With that in mind, we can calculate how much of our net worth we can responsibly invest.

All you need to do is multiply your monthly expenses by three (or by six, if you want to maintain a six-month safety net) and subtract that from your total liquid assets. Whatever is left over are your investable assets. If the number is negative, you should keep saving before making an investment. If the number is positive, that number is how much you can responsibly invest today.

> **#8**   **Investable assets** = Liquid assets − (3 × Monthly expenses)

Using this example, John can responsibly invest $12,200.

$$\text{Investable assets} = \underset{\text{(liquid assets)}}{\$24,200} - \underset{\substack{\text{(three months} \\ \text{of expenses)}}}{\$12,000} = \$12,200.$$

INVESTABLE ASSETS: John Robinson As of December 31, 2022	
Monthly Income	$4,000.00
Desired Reserve (months)	3
REQUIRED RESERVE ($)	**$12,000.00**
Liquid Assets	$24,200.00
Required Reserves	$(12,000.00)
INVESTABLE ASSETS	**$12,200.00**

Remember that this is just a rule of thumb, and everyone's situation is unique. This equation is just a simple way to help get you started budgeting for an investment.

Now that you know how to track your net worth, savings rate, and investable assets, it's time to move on and learn how to measure the financial health of your business (or future business). You'll notice in the next chapter that we'll be using many of the same concepts (assets, liabilities, income, expenses, etc.); we'll simply be applying them to a business, not an individual. Having learned these concepts already, you should find the next section a breeze.

HONE YOUR SKILLS: CHAPTER 1

- If you had $245,000 in assets and $218,000 in liabilities, what would your net worth be?
- Calculate the savings rate for someone who earns $4,200/month and has monthly expenses of $3,850.
- If your liquid assets total $72,000, your monthly expenses are $5,100, and you require three months of cash reserves, what are your investable assets?

CHAPTER 2
THE BALANCE SHEET

Chapter 2 will help answer the questions:
- What assets does my business have?
- What liabilities does my business have?
- How much is my business worth?

Measuring the financial position of a business is not much different than measuring your own personal financial position. With the Personal Financial Statement (PFS) in your tool belt, you're now in a great position to understand the first major financial statement used in the business and investing world—the balance sheet.

In this chapter, we're going to talk about what the balance sheet is, how you build one, and the reasons why you should create one for your business, regardless of how small or large that business might be. The balance sheet is very similar to a PFS in that it captures assets, liabilities, and net worth. However, it does this for a business, not a person.

#9
The **balance sheet** is a snapshot in time of everything your business owns, everything it owes, and the difference between those two numbers (which is the total value of the business).

In the last chapter, we built a PFS for a fictitious investor named John. You might remember that in John's asset list, John had an ownership interest in ABC Properties, LLC.

ABC Properties is a real estate business that John owns. For the sake of this discussion, let's assume:

- John is the sole owner of ABC Properties, LLC.
- The business holds one multifamily property that was purchased on January 1, 2018.
- The property is a seven-unit multifamily building purchased for $350,000, financed 80 percent with a bank loan ($280,000) and 20 percent with a cash down payment ($70,000).

We promised you in the last chapter we'd revisit this asset to determine how we arrived at its $65,000 value. We'll do that now by creating a balance sheet for this company. The balance sheet will not only tell us about the assets and liabilities of the company, but it will also give us an idea of the total value of the company. And if John's PFS is to be believed, the total value of the company should be about $65,000.

Let's see what the balance sheet for this business might look like:

BALANCE SHEET
For Year Ending December 31, 2022

ASSETS	
Investment in 123 Main Street	
Land	$75,462.00
Buildings/Improvements	$274,538.00
Furniture & Fixtures	$8,254.00
Accumulated Depreciation	$(20,094.00)
	$338,160.00
Other Assets	
Cash in Operating Account	$16,581.00
Replacement Reserves	$14,000.00
Rents Receivable	$2,220.00
	$32,801.00
TOTAL ASSETS	**$370,961.00**

LIABILITIES & OWNER EQUITY

Liabilities

Mortgage Principal Balance	$276,841.00
Accounts Payable	$16,875.00
Taxes Payable	$12,254.00
Tenant Security Deposits	$8,450.00
TOTAL LIABILITIES	**$314,420.00**
Owner Equity	
Initial Contributions	$40,000.00
Retained Earnings	$16,541.00
TOTAL OWNER EQUITY	**$56,541.00**
TOTAL LIABILITIES & OWNER EQUITY	**$370,961.00**

PFS AND BALANCE SHEET DIFFERENCES

At first glance, the balance sheet may look like the PFS, but there are also some glaring differences. Because the balance sheet is often used for very large companies (with assets and liabilities in the millions or billions of dollars), it's a bit more formal than the PFS and it arranges things differently to help us reconcile the numbers.

Here are the three main differences between a PFS and a balance sheet.

1. Equity Instead of Net Worth

Because businesses may have multiple owners with different percentages of ownership, we don't refer to the total value of the company using the term "net worth" like we do on the PFS. Instead, we replace net worth with the term "owner equity."

#10 **Owner equity** is the total value of the company to the owners.

Owner equity is basically the amount of cash that the owners of the company would walk away with if the company were to be liquidated (all assets turned to cash), with all liabilities paid off and the remaining cash distributed among the owners. You may hear owner equity also referred to as "shareholder equity" or "book value."

2. Rearranged Balance Sheet Equation

If you recall, the equation we used to relate Assets, Liabilities, and Net Worth on the PFS was:

Net Worth = Assets – Liabilities

For the balance sheet, we rearrange that equation. (Remember, we've changed net worth to owner equity.)

#11	The **balance sheet equation** is: Assets = Liabilities + Owner equity

This is the same relationship we used on the PFS, but it's rearranged so that we can better reconcile all the numbers. This will make sense in a bit, but for now, just notice that in the rearranged equation we are equating the total amount of the assets owned by the company to the total amount of liabilities plus the total amount of owner equity.

3. Modified Format

Finally, you'll notice that instead of assets and liabilities being listed side by side (like on a PFS), we'll often see a top-and-bottom format, with assets in a top section and liabilities and owner equity underneath. This is simply to make it easier to fit into typical media formats, where columns tend to be narrow.

You should also note that liabilities and owner equity are grouped together on the balance sheet. Because the balance sheet equation indicates that assets should be equal to liabilities plus owner equity, by grouping these two things together, we can more easily ensure that both sides of the equation reconcile (are equal).

ASSETS, LIABILITIES, AND OWNER EQUITY

Now that we have a basic understanding of how the balance sheet works and how the format is different than the PFS, let's dig into the details of the ABC Properties, LLC, balance sheet.

Assets

A balance sheet will contain many of the same types of assets that we saw on the PFS (cash, cash equivalents, property, and furniture), but will also include business-specific assets. For example, business assets include equipment, accounts receivable (money currently owed to the company by customers), tax-related items, product inventory, and intangible things like patents and trademarks that are worth money but have no physical presence.

Here is the assets section of the ABC Properties balance sheet:

BALANCE SHEET
For Year Ending December 31, 2022

ASSETS	
Investment in 123 Main Street	
Land	$75,462.00
Buildings/Improvements	$274,538.00
Furniture & Fixtures	$8,254.00
Accumulated Depreciation	$(20,094.00)
	$338,160.00
Other Assets	
Cash in Operating Account	$16,581.00
Replacement Reserves	$14,000.00
Rents Receivable	$2,220.00
	$32,801.00
TOTAL ASSETS	**$370,961.00**

First, you'll notice that we have a section specifically for the property investment at 123 Main Street. This is John's seven-unit multifamily property purchased several years back.

The property entry is broken down into pieces. We've separated the land value from the building value (also known as the "improvements") because the building value provides some specific tax benefits that we'll talk about later. Separating land and improvements will give John's tax adviser information they will need to better assess his future tax situation. Additionally, the furniture and fixtures (perhaps this is a furnished apartment or an office with furniture and equipment) provide a different tax benefit, so we call those out separately as well.

Finally, the accumulated depreciation is a tax item relating to the loss in building value over time. This is a tax deduction John has taken in the past and will have to pay back when he sells the property, so it's a negative number. Technically, it's a liability (keep reading if this doesn't make sense), but we include it on the asset side as a negative value so we can see the total value of the 123 Main Street property all in one place. We'll talk about depreciation in detail later in the book, but for now, know that it's a tax benefit while John owns the property, but it incurs a cost to him when he sells.

All these items together make up the total value of the property to John's business: $338,160. In other words, if he were to sell off the 123 Main Street property today, the total cash he'd expect to walk away with (not including selling fees and commissions) would be about $338,000.

The other assets in John's business include the cash he has on hand—both the cash in his operating account and the cash reserves he's saving for future replacement costs (expenses related to replacing or fixing up items on the property)—as well as the back rent owed to John from tenants (rents receivable).

The total assets in John's business are $370,961. This is the amount of cash that he'd have if he could liquidate everything in the business right now at face value.

Liabilities

On the bottom half of the balance sheet, we have liabilities and owner equity grouped together.

The liabilities are the things the business owes; this includes many of the same things as the PFS (the balance of any mortgages or loans, for example), as well as business-specific liabilities like money currently owed to vendors (accounts payable), the security deposits that are being held for tenants (remember, John owes these back to the tenants when they move out), wages owed to employees, and taxes on income that has been earned but not yet been paid.

Here is the liabilities section of the ABC Properties balance sheet:

LIABILITIES & OWNER EQUITY	
Liabilities	
Mortgage Principal Balance	$276,841.00
Accounts Payable	$16,875.00
Taxes Payable	$12,254.00
Tenant Security Deposits	$8,450.00
TOTAL LIABILITIES	**$314,420.00**

We see that the company has a mortgage on the property at 123 Main Street for $276,841. Note that the original loan amount was $280,000; the principal has now been paid down by a little more than $3,000.

The company also owes vendors $16,875 for work previously completed, owes estimated taxes of $12,254 for income previously earned, and is holding $8,450 in tenant security deposits.

Owner Equity

Beneath the liabilities, we have the owner equity section. This is the total value of the business to the owners, given the business's assets and assuming all liabilities are paid.

Here is the owner equity section of the ABC Properties balance sheet:

Owner Equity	
Initial Contributions	$40,000.00
Retained Earnings	$16,541.00
TOTAL OWNER EQUITY	**$56,541.00**

In the case of ABC Properties, the owner equity section is broken up into two separate line items. The initial contributions line reflects the amount of money John (the owner) invested into the business and has not yet repaid himself. This money is owed to John and is part of his equity. The other part of his equity is retained earnings, which is just a fancy name for profits that have been previously generated, but that haven't been taken out of the business and paid to John as of yet. In essence, John's owner equity is the sum of his total investment into the business and the earnings he has not yet paid himself.

When you put the liabilities and owner equity together, this is what we get:

LIABILITIES & OWNER EQUITY	
Liabilities	
Mortgage Principal Balance	$276,841.00
Accounts Payable	$16,875.00
Taxes Payable	$12,254.00
Tenant Security Deposits	$8,450.00
TOTAL LIABILITIES	**$314,420.00**
Owner Equity	
Initial Contributions	$40,000.00
Retained Earnings	$16,541.00
TOTAL OWNER EQUITY	**$56,541.00**
TOTAL LIABILITIES & OWNER EQUITY	**$370,961.00**

The total value of the business liabilities and owner equity is $370,961, which is equal to the business's assets, and what we expect. The reason we expect this is because the value of the business is simply the difference between its assets and liabilities; and this value is owned by the owners of the business. If that doesn't yet make complete sense, we can simply rearrange the balance sheet equation.

Assets = Liabilities + Owner Equity
is the same as
Owner Equity = Assets – Liabilities

Finally, notice that the owner equity in this business totals about $65,000; because John is sole owner of the business, that $65,000 is the value that John transfers to his PFS and can claim as his ownership value in the company.

So, now that we have our balance sheet for ABC Properties, what is it good for?

- First, it gives John an accurate view of what his investment in the company is worth. Businesses have a lot of moving parts. With money and assets constantly coming in and going out, it can be difficult to determine what a business is worth to the owners at a given point in time. The balance sheet gives us this information.
- When John applies for a new loan or a refinance on 123 Main Street, the lender will almost certainly ask for the company's balance sheet. This allows the lender to quickly determine what other assets the company owns and what other financial obligations the company might owe, giving the lender a quick overview of the business's (and owner's) ability to repay a new loan.
- As the business grows, the IRS may require John to submit the balance sheet as part of his annual business tax return.
- Much like a PFS, the balance sheet can quickly give John insight into the health of his business, the ratio of appreciating assets to depreciating assets, and the amount of good and bad debt the company is carrying.
- If John were to sell 123 Main Street to another investor, depending on how the sale was structured, the buyer may demand a copy of the balance sheet to get a quick overview of the assets and obligations they'd be purchasing.
- Finally, John's tax adviser and attorney can use the balance sheet to ensure that the company is structured in a way that provides the greatest tax and legal benefits.

If this seems like a lot of new information, don't worry. Remember, a balance sheet is just a business's slightly fancier version of a Personal Financial Statement, which you've already mastered.

Even if you're new to real estate investing and don't yet have a "business," it's still important to understand the concepts of a balance sheet. Real estate is a business, and as soon as you own your first piece of real estate, you're going to want to have the tools to track your financial well-being as a business owner who owns those assets. As you grow and gain experience as an investor, you will inevitably be dealing with balance sheets. Luckily, these concepts are the same as the PFS, and we have an Excel template for you to download when it comes time to make your first balance sheet.

In the next chapter, we're going to discuss the profit and loss statement, another financial statement that you'll likely find even more important when it comes to tracking your business's heath and success.

HONE YOUR SKILLS: CHAPTER 2

- What are the three main differences between a Personal Financial Statement and a Balance Sheet?
- Big Rents LLC is a business with two partners, each of whom own 50 percent of the business. The business has one holding, a small multifamily property. The business has $875,000 in assets and $631,000 in liabilities. How much owner equity does each partner have?
- True or false: A balance sheet tells you how your business is performing over time.

CHAPTER 3
THE PROFIT AND LOSS STATEMENT (P&L)

Chapter 3 will help answer the questions:
- How much money is my business making?
- What is my biggest income source?
- Which expenses cost me the most?
- How efficient is my business at making money?

If you were to ask people what the best measure of financial health and success is, most would likely say, "How much money you are making."

That's the purpose of the financial statement we'll be talking about in this chapter. The income statement is the second major financial statement that businesses use to track their financial performance.

You may recall from the previous section that the balance sheet is a business's equivalent of a Personal Financial Statement. Similarly, the income statement is a business's equivalent of a personal savings rate.

#12 The **income statement** (also known as the **profit and loss statement**) is a breakdown of revenue, expenses, and total profitability for a business or investment over a defined period of time.

Note that the income statement is often called the "profit and loss statement" or just the "P&L." But regardless of whether we refer to it as a profit and loss statement, P&L, or income statement, we're referring to the same thing. For the sake of less typing, we're going to refer to this financial statement as the P&L going forward.

Also, you might notice that the definition we provided indicates that a P&L can be used to track profitability for both a business and a single investment. While the example we use in this chapter will focus on creating a P&L for a business, we will be using the same concept throughout the book when we talk about analyzing individual deals and determining whether an income-producing property makes sense in our portfolio. As we'll discuss later, a single investment is just a mini business.

For now, we're going to look at how to build a P&L for a fictitious house-flipping company that we're going to call Great Flips, LLC. Because a P&L is always created for a specific period of time, we're going to assume that our P&L is for the 2022 calendar year.

INCOME STATEMENT FORMAT

At the highest level, the entire P&L is based upon the equation:

Income – Expenses = Profit

You may notice similarities here to how we calculated the savings rate earlier in the book. In both calculations we're simply examining how much we're left with when we subtract all our expenses from all our income.

Here is what the template for our Great Flips, LLC, P&L will look like:

PROFIT & LOSS STATEMENT - GREAT FLIPS, LLC
For the Fiscal Year 2022 (Jan. 1–Dec. 31, 2022)

INCOME	
Revenue Source #1	$-
Revenue Source #2	$-
...	
TOTAL INCOME:	$-
Cost of Goods Sold (COGS) #1	$-
Cost of Goods Sold (COGS) #2	$-
...	
TOTAL COGS:	$-
GROSS PROFIT:	$-

EXPENSES	
Expense Source #1	$-
Expense Source #2	$-
...	
TOTAL OPERATING EXPENSES:	$-
OPERATING INCOME:	**$-**

The top section is used to detail our income, and the bottom section is used to detail our expenses. If we subtract expenses from income, we get an indication of the profits the company has generated (which we call "operating income"). Again, this should look very similar to how we formatted and calculated our savings rate in Chapter 1.

The goal of the P&L is to allow us to analyze profitability, not just provide a single number. For this reason, we break income and expenses down into greater detail, which we'll discuss in the upcoming sections.

It's important to note that there will be some variation in how different types of businesses break down their information and format their P&L. For example, the P&L for a restaurant may vary in some respects from a P&L for a company that creates iPhone games, which will likely vary from this P&L that we're creating for our house-flipping business.

In other words, while we're building a perfectly reasonable P&L here in this chapter, don't be surprised if you see other P&Ls that look a little different or that name their line items differently.

Income

First, let's talk about the income section of the P&L.

#13   **Income** is a general term referring to the money flowing into a business or investment. Sometimes you will see income referred to as "revenue" or "sales" instead.

The income section of the P&L is typically broken down into two sections, Revenue and Cost of Goods Sold, as follows:

PROFIT & LOSS STATEMENT - GREAT FLIPS, LLC
For the Fiscal Year 2022 (Jan. 1–Dec. 31, 2022)

INCOME	
Revenue Source #1	$-
Revenue Source #2	$-
TOTAL INCOME:	$-
Cost of Goods Sold (COGS) #1	$-
Cost of Goods Sold (COGS) #2	$-
TOTAL COGS:	$-
GROSS PROFIT:	$-

The first part of the income section is used to list all our revenue sources. Given that Great Flips, LLC, is a house-flipping company, we should expect that the bulk of our income is going to come from selling our rehabbed properties. Let's also assume that we are licensed real estate agents under this business, and that we're collecting a commission from the seller each time we purchase a property—an additional revenue source.

Now, let's assume Great Flips, LLC, bought and sold three properties in 2022, with each property selling for $125,000 (Source #1). The company also collected a total of $25,000 in commissions (Source #2).

The first part of the income section might look like this:

PROFIT & LOSS STATEMENT - GREAT FLIPS, LLC
For the Fiscal Year 2022 (Jan. 1–Dec. 31, 2022)

INCOME	
Revenue from Sale of Properties	$375,000.00
Revenue from Commissions	$25,000.00
TOTAL INCOME	**$400,000.00**

Add it all up, and our total income for the company in 2022 was $400,000.

In the next part of the income section, we have something called "cost of goods sold" (COGS). Sometimes also called "cost of sales," this is the amount of money the company spends to create the products and services it sells.

#14   **Cost of goods sold (COGS)**, also called **cost of sales**, is the direct cost to produce the goods and services sold by a company.

When we talk about COGS, we are talking about the *direct* costs to produce products and services. For example, if a company produces metal widgets, COGS might include the metal and other materials that are used to create the widget, plus the labor costs of the employees who physically produce the widgets.

COGS doesn't include *indirect* costs, like the overhead cost of running the business. For example, rent, insurance, utilities, office supplies, and legal costs are not included in COGS. Also, salaries of those employees not directly involved in the manufacturing of the product are not included in COGS either.

For Great Flips, LLC, our product is the properties that we bought and sold. Therefore, any direct costs associated with buying, renovating, and reselling properties would be considered COGS.

Specifically, the 2022 COGS for Great Flips might look like this:

Property Purchase Costs	$120,000.00
Rehab Labor	$75,000.00
Rehab Materials	$30,000.00
Closing Costs	$6,000.00
TOTAL COGS	**$231,000.00**

The company spent $120,000 buying inventory (each of the three properties was purchased for an average of $40,000), $105,000 in labor and materials doing the renovations, and $6,000 in closing costs.

By subtracting the total COGS from the total income, we get our gross profit for the business.

PROFIT & LOSS STATEMENT - GREAT FLIPS, LLC
For the Fiscal Year 2022 (Jan. 1–Dec. 31, 2022)

INCOME	
Revenue from Sale of Properties	$375,000.00
Revenue from Commissions	$25,000.00
TOTAL INCOME	**$400,000.00**
Property Purchase Costs	$120,000.00
Rehab Labor	$75,000.00
Rehab Materials	$30,000.00
Closing Costs	$6,000.00
TOTAL COGS	**$231,000.00**
GROSS PROFIT	**$169,000.00**

In this case, the $400,000 in total income minus the $231,000 in COGS results in a gross profit of $169,000.

<table>
<tr><td>**#15**</td><td>**Gross profit** is the amount of income a company makes after subtracting the costs associated with making and selling its products and services from its total revenue.

Gross profit = Income – Cost of goods sold</td></tr>
</table>

That's all we need to complete the income part of our P&L. Next, let's focus on the expenses.

Expenses

In the expenses section of the P&L, we list all operating expenses associated with the running of the business.

<table>
<tr><td>**#16**</td><td>**Operating expenses** are the costs incurred in the normal operations of the business.</td></tr>
</table>

Operating expenses include our indirect business costs, like office rent, business insurance, employee salaries, office utilities, advertising, and office supplies. Keep in mind that these are generic business expenses—not expenses directly related to our products (the houses we sell). When we talk about insurance, this is the insurance for the *business*, not the specific properties.

If we assume Great Flips operates out of a rented office space and has one employee (the owner), the expenses for the business might look something like this:

EXPENSES	
Rent	$7,200.00
Owner Salary	$50,000.00
Insurance	$2,500.00
Office Supplies	$300.00
Tools	$2,200.00
Utilities	$1,800.00
TOTAL OPERATING EXPENSES:	**$64,000.00**

The total operating expenses for Great Flips in 2022 were $64,000.

On our operating expenses list, we include the owner's salary as one of the expenses. This is because the owner is also an employee of the business, and they should be compensated for the work they have done throughout the year. The income into the business should be separated from the owner's salary, as that reflects how much profit was generated after all costs, including cost of the owner's time and efforts.

Another reason it's important to break out the owner's salary is in the case where you one day decide to sell your business. Breaking out owner salary will provide information to the buyer that can be used to better understand how profitable the business really was. For example, the new buyer may decide that they don't want to work in the business; however, by knowing how much money you were paying yourself, the new owner can apply that amount to bring in someone else to run the business.

PROFITABILITY

Finally, we can determine the company's profitability by subtracting the total operating expenses for the company from the gross profit. This is called operating income, which is a basic measure of the profits generated by a business.

#17

Operating income is the amount of profit a company makes after subtracting both gross profit and operating expenses from revenue.

Operating income = Gross profit – Operating expenses

Operating income is the income generated in the normal course of business. It doesn't consider the costs associated with taxes or interest payments on loans/debt. For that reason, operating income is often referred to as Earnings Before Interest and Taxes (EBIT).

Here is what the basic P&L looks like for Great Flips, LLC, when we calculate operating income:

PROFIT & LOSS STATEMENT - GREAT FLIPS, LLC
For the Fiscal Year 2022 (Jan. 1–Dec. 31, 2022)

INCOME	
Revenue from Sale of Properties	$375,000.00
Revenue from Commissions	$25,000.00
TOTAL INCOME	**$400,000.00**
Property Purchase Costs	$120,000.00
Rehab Labor	$75,000.00
Rehab Materials	$30,000.00
Closing Costs	$6,000.00
TOTAL COGS	**$231,000.00**
GROSS PROFIT	**$169,000.00**
EXPENSES	
Rent	$7,200.00
Owner Salary	$50,000.00
Insurance	$2,500.00
Office Supplies	$300.00
Tools	$2,200.00
Utilities	$1,800.00
TOTAL OPERATING EXPENSES:	**$64,000.00**
OPERATING INCOME:	**$105,000.00**

As you can see, businesses have several measures of profitability. Gross profit is one measure (taking into account the cost to produce the company's goods and services). Operating income is another (taking into account the operating expenses for the company as well).

As we mentioned, operating income doesn't consider taxes and interest. If we were to deduct these costs as well, we would get a profitability measure we call net income.

#18

Net income is the amount of profit a company makes after subtracting cost of goods sold, operating expenses, taxes, and interest payments from the total revenue.

Net income = Operating income – Taxes – Interest

Let's assume that Great Flips, LLC, owes $21,000 in taxes at the end of 2022. Factoring that into our P&L, our net income would be as follows:

PROFIT & LOSS STATEMENT - GREAT FLIPS, LLC
For the Fiscal Year 2022 (Jan. 1–Dec. 31, 2022)

INCOME	
Revenue from Sale of Properties	$375,000.00
Revenue from Commissions	$25,000.00
TOTAL INCOME	**$400,000.00**
Property Purchase Costs	$120,000.00
Rehab Labor	$75,000.00
Rehab Materials	$30,000.00
Closing Costs	$6,000.00
TOTAL COGS	**$231,000.00**
GROSS PROFIT	**$169,000.00**
EXPENSES	
Rent	$7,200.00
Owner Salary	$50,000.00
Insurance	$2,500.00
Office Supplies	$300.00
Tools	$2,200.00
Utilities	$1,800.00
TOTAL OPERATING EXPENSES:	**$64,000.00**
OPERATING INCOME:	**$105,000.00**
2022 Taxes	$21,000.00
NET INCOME:	**$84,000.00**

Now that we've built our P&L for Great Flips, LLC, let's talk a little bit about how we can use this financial statement to glean information about the company's performance and determine what, if anything, we should be doing differently.

The most obvious benefit of the income statement is that it will tell you if a company is profitable—and, if so, to what degree. When the operating income (or net income) is positive, the company is profitable; when it's negative, the company has lost money for that time period.

However, just knowing whether a company is profitable or not—even when the operating income is a very large positive number—doesn't tell us a whole lot about the financial health of the company or whether it's performing well compared to its competitors or other companies in the same industry.

That's where profit margins come in.

Profit Margins

A company's profit margins are a measure of how much of a company's total income (which we also refer to as revenue) ends up as profit. Profit margins reflect how efficiently the company is run.

As an example, if a company generates revenue of $1 million, and if the company has no expenses, that $1 million in revenue is also $1 million in profit. That's an efficient business! On the other hand, if that same company spends $990,000 to generate their $1 million in revenue, it's safe to say that the business is much less efficient.

Profit margin is the ratio of the profit a business generates to the amount of revenue brought in. The more money a business keeps in profit, the higher its profit margins.

Profit margin = Profit ÷ Revenue

Again, when it comes to profit margins, there are several different metrics we can look at that give us a different perspective on the success of the business. They include:

1. Gross profit margin
2. Operating profit margin
3. Net profit margin

Let's look at each of these individually.

1. Gross Profit Margin

Gross profit margin measures the profitability of the product you are selling, without factoring in the overhead expenses of the business.

Gross profit margin is the ratio of the amount of gross profit a business generates to the amount of revenue brought in. This ratio indicates how efficiently the company is producing their products compared to their competitors.

Gross profit margin = Gross profit ÷ Revenue

The gross profit margin for Great Flips in 2022 was:

Gross profit margin = Gross profit ÷ Revenue
Gross profit margin = $169,000 ÷ $400,000
Gross profit margin = **42.25%**

Notice in our definition that gross profit margin can tell us how efficient we are, compared to our competitors, in producing our products. If our competitors have gross profit margins *greater* than 42.25 percent, that likely means they are *more* efficient in renovating their properties. Maybe they have lower labor costs. Maybe lower material costs. Maybe lower commissions and fees.

This doesn't mean that Great Flips is doing anything wrong, but it might mean that there is room for improvement in our ability to churn out renovated properties.

2. Operating Profit Margin

Operating profit margin measures the overall profitability of the business after all management and expenses are paid.

#21

Operating profit margin is the ratio of the amount of operating income a business generates to the amount of revenue brought in. This ratio indicates how efficiently the company is operating, including both product creation and management.

Operating profit margin = Operating income ÷ Revenue

The operating profit margin for Great Flips in 2022 was:

Operating profit margin = Operating income ÷ Revenue
Operating profit margin = $105,000 ÷ $400,000
Operating profit margin = **26.25%**

This number will tell us how efficient we are at running the business—the operations associated with both creating the product and managing business overhead. If the business is splurging on expensive offices and unnecessary employees, this number will be lower than if the business is careful with its expenses and not overspending on things that don't drive the profitability of the company.

The operating profit margin doesn't consider taxes or interest paid on business loans that the company might have. For that reason, the operating profit margin can tell us whether we can afford to take out loans that the business can repay. If the operating margin is very low, we should avoid business loans, as we may not have the ability to repay them and remain profitable.

3. Net Profit Margin

The net profit margin measures the *total profitability* of the company, including all expenses—even non-cash expenses like depreciation and amortization (we'll discuss those later in the book).

Net profit margin is the ratio of the amount of net income a business generates to the amount of revenue brought in. This ratio indicates how efficiently the company is operating overall.

Net profit margin = Net income ÷ Revenue

The net profit margin for Great Flips in 2022 was:

Net profit margin = Net income ÷ Revenue
Net profit margin = $84,000 ÷ $400,000
Net profit margin = **21%**

If your company has shareholders, this is going to be the profit margin ratio that is most important to them, as this indicates how efficiently the company converts its revenue into shareholder value.

PUTTING IT ALL TOGETHER

We now have our various profit margins. These numbers give us an idea of how efficiently our business is operating.

PROFIT & LOSS STATEMENT - GREAT FLIPS, LLC
For the Fiscal Year 2022 (Jan. 1–Dec. 31, 2022)

INCOME	
Revenue from Sale of Properties	$375,000.00
Revenue from Commissions	$25,000.00
TOTAL INCOME	**$400,000.00**

Property Purchase Costs		$120,000.00
Rehab Labor		$75,000.00
Rehab Materials		$30,000.00
Closing Costs		$6,000.00
	TOTAL COGS	**$231,000.00**
	GROSS PROFIT	**$169,000.00**
EXPENSES		
Rent		$7,200.00
Owner Salary		$50,000.00
Insurance		$2,500.00
Office Supplies		$300.00
Tools		$2,200.00
Utilities		$1,800.00
	TOTAL OPERATING EXPENSES:	**$64,000.00**
	OPERATING INCOME:	**$105,000.00**
2022 Taxes		$21,000.00
	NET INCOME:	**$84,000.00**
Gross Profit Margin		**42.3%**
Operating Profit Margin		**26.3%**
Net Profit Margin		**21.0%**

Are our numbers good? Are they bad? Do they mean we're operating efficiently or inefficiently?

By itself, these profit margins don't mean much. Some businesses will naturally have low profit margins. Businesses like Walmart and Target typically have profit margins at around 4–5 percent. Other businesses, like Google and Microsoft, will have higher profit margins, at around 25–35 percent. Purely service businesses, like accounting firms and law offices, can have even higher operating profit margins.

Typically, the more competition a business has—and the more the business is focused on competing purely on price (like a Walmart or Target)—the lower its profit margins will be. These companies rely on selling in large volumes to generate enough revenue to pay the bills, compensate their employees, and generate a profit.

On the other hand, service businesses generally have very little equipment and product costs, as well as a relatively small number of employees to whom they need to pay salaries. Much of their revenue turns into company profit.

Going back to our question, then: With all this variation in profit margins, how do we determine whether or not a particular business is being run efficiently?

The best way is to try to determine what the profit margins are for other businesses in your same industry. Whether it's the gross, operating, or net profit margins you're trying to improve, talking to others or gathering data on others who are operating similar businesses will give you an idea of how well you are doing, and where you can make operational improvements.

Successful businesses within an industry will have similar profit margins. For example, Apple, Microsoft, and Google should all have profit margins that are close to one another. If, next quarter, one of those companies sees a significant drop in profit margins, it would be reasonable to ask what is going on with management to cause the inefficiencies the company is seeing.

Likewise, in your business, it's worth talking to others who are running similar businesses and get an idea of what profit margins they are generating. If they're generating better margins than you, perhaps there's an opportunity for you to improve efficiency in creating your products or managing your company. Or perhaps there are tax strategies that you can use to improve your bottom line.

Also note that while all three profit margin numbers are important, the net profit margin is the one that will matter most to your shareholders (whether that's just you or others who have an investment in your company), because net profit margin ultimately indicates how efficiently you are converting revenue into owner value and profit.

INVESTOR STORY
Flipping Margins

When I (J) first started out flipping houses, I was very excited to see the large margins my business was generating. Sometimes close to 25 percent of the income we were generating was flowing to the "bottom line" (the profits). However, as I started to scale my flipping business, I noticed that my margins were starting to drop.

Over the first several years, my margins dropped from around 25 percent to 20 percent and then to 15 percent. I was making more money, but I was keeping a smaller percentage of it! What was going on?

It turns out that this is a natural consequence of scaling your business. As your volume increases, there's more overhead required to manage that additional volume. Flipping one house every three months is something I could do myself, but once I tried to flip three houses every month, I needed help. First, a project manager. Next, someone to help find and vet properties. Then a bookkeeper. Eventually, my business grew big enough that I needed someone to start managing the other people!

All of this overhead is necessary to scale a business, but it also has a cost. And that cost will impact your margins. As good business owners, part of our job is to ensure that we're managing our overhead costs well, so that scaling doesn't mean making less money. For example, earning $500,000 in revenue with 20 percent margins will generate the exact same amount of profit as earning $1 million with 10 percent margins. You'll spend a whole lot more time and energy, and endure significantly more headaches, generating that $1 million for the same profit.

When you see a situation like this, you need to ask yourself: Is there a way to improve margins while earning $1 million in revenue? And if not, perhaps it's time to consider falling back to the $500,000 in revenue, where you can make the same profit with a lot less time and risk.

HONE YOUR SKILLS: CHAPTER 3

- What are the three measurements of profit margin, and what does each metric measure?
- If a rental business collects $96,000 per year in gross profit and has $74,000 in operating expenses, what is the company's operating income?
- What is the difference between cost of goods sold (COGS) and operating expenses?

CHAPTER 4

EXAMINING A CASH-FLOWING PROPERTY

Chapter 4 will help answer the questions:
- What is the income potential of my property?
- What expenses should I expect?
- How much is my property cash-flowing?

The next step in preparing for the key metrics and concepts we'll be discussing throughout the book is to understand how cash-flowing real estate is analyzed. While we'll dig more into deal analysis in Part 5, in this chapter we're going to review how a typical cash-flowing property (whether a single-family property, a commercial property, or anything in between) is analyzed.

In the last chapter, we discussed the profit and loss statement (P&L). If you recall, the P&L is a financial statement used to measure the performance of a business. A cash-flowing property is itself a business. It's often a very small business, but a business nonetheless. And when we analyze a cash-flowing property, we can use the same methodology that we used when creating a P&L for a business.

That said, while the methodology is largely the same as what we covered earlier, some of the terms used will change when analyzing real estate deals in particular.

As with a business, the P&L for a cash-flowing asset is broken down by income and expenses.

GROSS OPERATING INCOME (GOI)

The first part of our analysis focuses on the income being generated by the property, known as the gross operating income (GOI). The GOI is the actual income the property expects to collect in a single year. In the previous chapter, when looking at a business P&L, we called this the gross profit; when analyzing a real estate deal, we call it GOI.

The GOI is calculated as follows:

#23	**Gross operating income (GOI)**
	GOI = Gross potential rent – Rent loss + Other income

INCOME	
Gross Potential Rent	-
Rent Loss	-
Other Income	-
GROSS OPERATING INCOME:	-

Gross Potential Rent

The gross potential rent is the total possible income the property can generate in a year, assuming every unit is leased and generating the full amount of projected rental income. To calculate gross potential rent, multiply the number of units by the market rent by 12.

#24	**Gross potential rent**
	Gross potential rent = Number of units × Market rent × 12

For example, if we were considering buying an eight-unit property with market rents of $1,250 per month, gross potential rent would be $120,000:

Gross potential rent = Number of units × Market rent × 12
Gross potential rent = 8 × $1,250 × 12 = $120,000

Rent Loss

Rent loss is the amount of gross potential rent not being collected, for one reason or another. There are five common reasons for rent loss.

1. **Vacancy:** Vacancy is the result of units physically not being occupied. For example, with a single-family rental property, you can expect that the average tenant will live in the property between one and two years. When that tenant moves out, you will spend time "turning over" the unit—performing routine maintenance, finding a new tenant, etc. During this turnover period, the property is not generating income, and the owner is losing money.

   For multifamily properties and commercial properties with multiple units, vacancy represents the fact that not every unit will always be occupied. For example, if a hundred-unit self-storage facility expects to only have ninety units rented at a given time, the vacancy rate can be said to be 10 percent.

2. **Concessions:** Concessions are the incentives that owners provide to tenants to entice them to move into or stay in their units. For example, in a competitive housing market, an apartment complex may need to provide a move-in special— say, $99 for the first month—to encourage new renters. If a complex offers a $99 first-month move-in special on a unit that rents for $1,000 per month, that's lost rent of $901 in the first month.

3. **Loss to lease:** Loss to lease is any amount of rent being collected that's less than the market rent. Two common situations lead to loss to lease. First, there is the case of an occupied unit where the rent is renewed at less than market rent to encourage a tenant not to leave. And second, a unit can be in a fast rent-growth market where the market rent increases during the lease period, leaving the tenant paying lower than market rent for the remainder of their lease term.

4. **Bad debt:** Bad debt is rent that isn't being collected due to a tenant's non-payment, often resulting in eviction.

5. **Model units:** For multifamily residential and commercial properties, it's not uncommon for one or more of the units to be used as an office, a storage facility, or as free housing for staff. These units could potentially be generating income, but aren't.

Other Income

Other income is the additional income that is collected for things other than rent. Common examples of other income include parking income (e.g., covered parking spaces tenants can rent), storage income (e.g., on-site storage lockers that tenants can rent), and laundry income (e.g., paid laundry machines on-site).

In addition, other income can result from common leasing practices and lease terms. For example, late fees due to late rent payments can contribute to other income, as can application fees paid by prospective tenants and pet fees charged to tenants with pets.

Gross Operating Income Example

To tie this all together, let's look at an example of how to calculate GOI using a fictitious investor, Catherine. Catherine is considering purchasing an eight-unit residential apartment building. Each unit is 800 square feet, with two bedrooms and two bathrooms. Speaking with a local property management company, Catherine is informed that market rents for such units in this area are $1,250 per month.

With that information, Catherine can calculate gross potential rent as:

Gross potential rent = Number of units × Market rent × 12
Gross potential rent = 8 × $1,250 × 12 = $120,000

Looking at the financial statements provided by the previous owner, Catherine sees that the total rent collected in the past twelve months is $108,000. Assuming she can expect the same collections for the foreseeable future, Catherine determines that the rent loss is the difference between the gross potential rent of $120,000 and the $108,000 in actual rent collected—for a total rent loss of $12,000. That's a 10 percent rent loss ($12,000 ÷ $120,000).

When Catherine talks to her local property management company, they confirm that rent loss for similar properties in the area is 9–11 percent, so she's comfortable with this assumption.

Finally, looking at the financial statements provided by the previous owner, Catherine sees that the building was generating an extra $250 per month in combined income from the laundry facility in the basement of the building and monthly pet fees.

That's other income of $3,000 per year ($250 × 12).

From here, Catherine can calculate her GOI as $111,000 per year.

GOI = Gross potential rent – Rent loss + Other income
GOI = $120,000 – $12,000 + $3,000 = $111,000

INCOME	
Gross Potential Rent	$120,000.00
Rent Loss	$(12,000.00)
Other Income	$3,000.00
GROSS OPERATING INCOME:	**$111,000.00**

OPERATING EXPENSES

Now that we have calculated the income portion of the P&L, it's time to jump into the expenses. We start with our operating expenses, which are those expenses incurred during the ordinary course of renting the property.

#25   **Operating expenses** (in real estate) are expenses associated with the basic functions and operations of the property, such as insurance, repairs and maintenance, and taxes.

Operating expenses for a rental complex could look like this:

EXPENSES	
Property Taxes	-
Insurance	-
Property Management	-
Turnover	-
Repairs & Maintenance	-
Utilities	-
Lawn Care	-
Snow Removal	-
Dumpster/Trash Removal	-
Grounds Cleanup	-
Office Costs	-
Legal	-
Accounting	-

Depending on the type of property and how you manage it, you may find that some of these expenses don't apply. But take care to account for all expenses that might reasonably be incurred during the normal course of managing the property. We've seen a lot of new property owners who have found themselves in a money-losing situation because they didn't adequately plan for all the expenses associated with running the property.

> ## *Quick Tip* | Property Management
> Many new owners plan to self-manage their rental properties, and as such, they don't include any cost for a property manager (PM). While there's nothing wrong with this, keep in mind that if you plan to hold the property long term, you may one day find yourself in the situation where you want or need to bring in a PM to help you.
>
> Perhaps you have to relocate out of town for work. Maybe you simply get sick of dealing with tenants yourself. If you include the cost of a good PM in your analysis of the deal up front, you'll know whether the deal will still be profitable should the day come when you want to stop managing the property yourself.

Returning to our example, here's what the operating expenses for Catherine's eight-unit building might look like:

EXPENSES	
Property Taxes	$5,250.00
Insurance	$2,810.00
Property Management	$8,640.00
Turnover	$4,800.00
Repairs & Maintenance	$10,000.00
Utilities	$400.00
Lawn Care	$3,600.00
Snow Removal	$-
Dumpster/Trash Removal	$-
Grounds Cleanup	$3,000.00
Office Costs	$-
Legal	$-
Accounting	$1,500.00
OPERATING EXPENSES:	**$40,000.00**

Each year, Catherine can expect that about $40,000 of income will go toward ordinary expenses associated with managing her property.

NET OPERATING INCOME (NOI)

Now that we have our GOI and our operating expenses, we can calculate our net operating income (NOI). This is an important number, as it will be used for many of the other calculations that we'll encounter throughout this book.

Net operating income (NOI) is the gross operating income of a property minus operating expenses.

NOI = Gross operating income – Operating expenses

Using Catherine's eight-unit example from above, we can determine the NOI for this property to be:

PROFIT & LOSS STATEMENT - CATHERINE CORP.
For the Fiscal Year 2022 (Jan. 1–Dec. 31, 2022)

INCOME	
Gross Potential Rent	$120,000.00
Rent Loss	$(12,000.00)
Other Income	$3,000.00
GROSS OPERATING INCOME:	**$111,000.00**
EXPENSES	
Property Taxes	$5,250.00
Insurance	$2,810.00
Property Management	$8,640.00
Turnover	$4,800.00
Repairs & Maintenance	$10,000.00
Utilities	$400.00
Lawn Care	$3,600.00
Snow Removal	$-
Dumpster/Trash Removal	$-
Grounds Cleanup	$3,000.00
Office Costs	$-
Legal	$-
Accounting	$1,500.00
OPERATING EXPENSES:	**$40,000.00**
NET OPERATING INCOME:	**$71,000.00**

Catherine's NOI for this property is $71,000.

 Quick Tip | **The Importance of NOI**

We mention a couple times in this chapter how important NOI is when analyzing real estate deals. We'll dig into this topic more in later chapters, but for now, it's important to point out that commercial real estate (everything other than one- to four-unit residential properties) are valued based on the income they generate. NOI is that income measure, and by knowing the NOI of a commercial property, we are halfway to being able to accurately determine the value of the property.

CASH FLOW

While NOI is an important number that we need to know for any property we're considering purchasing, it leaves out two very important expenses: debt service and capital expenses. We often refer to these expenses as "below the NOI line," as they are factored in after we calculate NOI and are not included in the NOI number.

Factoring in these two expenses allows us to calculate another important metric: cash flow. Cash flow is the amount of cash the property generates in a given time period, including all expenses other than taxes. In other words, it's an indication of how much your bank account has grown (or shrunk) thanks to you owning this property over the course of some period of time.

> **#27**
>
> **Cash flow** is the amount of pre-tax cash a property generates. It is equal to the net operating income minus debt service and capital expenses.
>
> Cash flow = NOI – Debt service – Capital expenses

Debt Service

Debt service is just a fancy term for a mortgage payment. When you take a loan against a piece of real estate, you will most likely be paying the lender back some combination of principal and interest (P&I) monthly. This regular P&I payment to the lender is referred to as your debt service.

We'll discuss this concept in depth in Part 4 of the book, but for now, just know that debt service is the same as mortgage payment.

Continuing our example from above, let's assume Catherine has a $750,000 loan against her property, and her monthly P&I payment to the lender is $3,350 per month, or $40,200 per year. This is her annual debt service.

Capital Expenses (CapEx)

Capital expenses (CapEx) are the big-ticket renovation items on your property necessary to keep it functioning and generating income. Some examples of CapEx items include replacing the roof, replacing an HVAC system, and upgrading the electrical or plumbing systems.

We account for CapEx items differently than regular maintenance items because they are treated differently by the IRS when it comes time to do our taxes. And, as we can see from our discussion here, they are technically not included as part of NOI. We dig into why that is later in the book.

Because CapEx *does* take money out of our pocket, we need to account for it in our analysis of a property.

DIG DEEP

CAPITAL EXPENSES

Capital expenses are the big-ticket items that pop up after five, ten, twenty, or more years. While we don't often think about these costs before they become necessary, we should. These expenses are generally the most expensive renovation costs we'll incur on our properties, and we don't want these costs to just sneak up on us.

Not considering CapEx costs poses two potential issues.

First, if the cost isn't planned for, it can put you in a bad financial situation. For example, if you suddenly find out that the roof on one of your properties is going to need to be replaced and it will cost $12,000, you now need to come up with that $12,000. Many smaller investors may not keep $12,000 lying around waiting for something to need repairing, so this surprise cost could require you to scramble to come up with the money.

Second, if you don't factor the cost of CapEx items into your budget, you will find that you are incorrectly calculating your returns. For example, let's say that you have earned an average of $2,000 per year on your rental property for the past twenty years, or $40,000 total. You can assume that your average annual profit from the property is $2,000, right? But if you have a $12,000 roof expense every twenty years that you haven't factored into your analysis, that means that your $40,000 assumed profit is just $28,000. And your average annual profit is really $1,400, not $2,000. If you're relying on your properties to support you with their profits long term, it's important that you have accurate profit numbers!

For these reasons, we typically recommend that investors determine what their average CapEx costs will be per year, even if those costs are years away. For example, if you believe you will spend $12,000 every twenty years for a new roof, that averages to $600 per year ($12,000 ÷ 20). Smart investors will assume a $600 per year (or $50 per month) cost in their analysis for the roof, even if that cost won't be incurred for another decade or more.

To continue our example, let's assume that Catherine has looked at her anticipated long-term CapEx costs, and has determined that she's likely to spend an average of $5,000 per year on CapEx items.

Based on these debt service and CapEx numbers, Catherine can calculate her cash flow:

PROFIT & LOSS STATEMENT - CATHERINE CORP.
For the Fiscal Year 2022 (Jan. 1–Dec. 31, 2022)

INCOME	
Gross Potential Rent	$120,000.00
Rent Loss	$(12,000.00)
Other Income	$3,000.00
GROSS OPERATING INCOME:	**$111,000.00**
EXPENSES	
Property Taxes	$5,250.00
Insurance	$2,810.00
Property Management	$8,640.00
Turnover	$4,800.00
Repairs & Maintenance	$10,000.00
Utilities	$400.00
Lawn Care	$3,600.00
Snow Removal	$-
Dumpster/Trash Removal	$-
Grounds Cleanup	$3,000.00
Office Costs	$-
Legal	$-
Accounting	$1,500.00
OPERATING EXPENSES:	**$40,000.00**
NET OPERATING INCOME:	**$71,000.00**
Debt Service	$(40,200.00)
Capital Expenses	$(5,000.00)
CASH FLOW BEFORE TAX	**$25,800.00**

Catherine's cash flow on this property is $25,800.

In other words, in an average year, Catherine should expect that her bank account will grow by about $25,800 (pre-tax) thanks to her owning this property. Of course, because those big CapEx costs won't show up every year, she'll likely see many years of higher cash flow than $25,800, with a few years of much lower cash flow when those big-ticket items need to be replaced.

As you can now see, building financial statements for rental properties is essentially the same as building a generic P&L, like we learned in Chapter 3. The concepts are easily translated—you just need to apply some industry-specific terminology and equations.

We'll have a whole lot more to say about NOI and cash flow later, in Part 3 of the book, and we'll revisit a lot of this methodology in Part 5 to determine the value of a particular deal. But, for now, all you need to do is learn the basic terms associated with cash-flowing rental properties.

HONE YOUR SKILLS: CHAPTER 4

- What are the five examples of rent loss?
- The net operating income (NOI) equation omits which two major expense categories (in addition to taxes)?
- If your rental property has an NOI of $84,000 annually, a monthly debt service of $2,100, and capital expenses of $25,000 per year, what is your annual pre-tax cash flow?

PART 1
CONCLUSION

A s we said in the introduction, our aim in this book is to help you identify the right questions to ask so you can grow and succeed as a real estate investor. In Part 1, we've identified some of the most important questions of all—the ones that, at the end of the day, really count.

Questions like "What is my net worth?" and "What is my business worth?" are the ultimate measurements of progress in investing. If you cannot answer those questions today and again in the future, you will never be able to judge your own progress.

Think of any goal you have and how to best achieve it. No matter the goal, the trick is to figure out the measurement of success, and then track that measurement over time. If you're trying to improve your golf game, the measurement you want to track is your score over time. If your goal is to lose weight, you need to know your weight on an ongoing basis. If you want to grow your social media presence, you need to know how many followers you have. Imagine trying to build a social media presence without knowing how many followers you had this week versus last! It's impossible.

Investing is the same thing. You need to be able to measure where you are today, and then compare that to where you are next month, year, or decade. You also need to be able to benchmark your performance against other investors and businesses. Financial statements give you the framework to do just that.

For your personal wealth, the ultimate measurement you need to track is your net worth. Tracking it over time by regularly completing a PFS is the key to knowing whether you're succeeding as an investor. Once you know your net worth, you can use metrics like your savings rate and investable assets to develop strategies to grow it. Remember, there are no wrong answers here. If your net worth and/or savings rate is not where you want it to be—welcome to the club! That is pretty much where everyone starts, and it's why most people get into investing in the first place. The key thing is that you're asking the right questions and can now answer those all-important questions. Armed with the answers, you're positioned to start making progress toward your investing goals.

Looking at a business is no different. You can use the same concepts of assets, liabilities, and profit that you learned in the PFS and apply them to a balance sheet to understand how valuable a business is. Likewise, you can then construct a P&L to see where your money is coming from and going to each month. This helps you evaluate where you are doing well, as well as where you can improve.

We started this book with financial statements because they are the ultimate measurement of success or failure. They are the scorecards that every investor needs to keep. Everything that follows in this book—all the concepts, metrics, and calculations—are ways to evaluate how a specific investment or deal is going to impact your financial situation. Ultimately, everything in investing rolls up to the value of your businesses, your personal income, and your own net worth. That's what you're here for, right?

So, as we continue through the rest of this book, keep these scorecards in mind. When you learn about compound interest in Part 2, you should be thinking, "How can this concept of compounding interest positively impact my net worth?" When you learn how to compare two types of loans against one another in Part 4, you should think, "Do I care more about growing my company's cash flow or owner equity right now? And which loan is best aligned with that goal?"

You now understand what the financial statements are, how to craft them, and why they are so vital to investing success. With that knowledge in mind, it's time to learn the key concepts, metrics, and calculations that will help you grow the value of your businesses and your net worth as effectively as possible.

PART 2
THE CONCEPTS

Now that we've learned how to assess our financial position and track our progress, it's time to learn how to put our money to work. Investing is all about using money to make more money, and in Part 2 we're going to help you learn to invest in a sophisticated and data-driven way.

To be a great investor, you first must understand some basic rules that money must follow. In fact, we like to think of finance/investing as its own little universe; just like our physical universe acts according to the laws of physics, the investing universe acts according to its own set of rules. If you understand those rules, you can begin to harness them and use them in your favor.

In this section, we will focus on some of those universal rules and laws that define how money works. Some of these concepts are simple; others are more complex. All of them are important. These concepts serve as the foundation for any great investing strategy. No matter what type of investor you are or strive to be—flipper, buy and hold, multifamily, or anything else—these concepts are universal. These rules about money and investing apply to every person, every deal, and every strategy.

Each chapter in this section is designed to stand alone, but even if you are already familiar with these ideas, pay careful attention to this section. The ideas presented here are crucial for investors to understand, and they serve as the foundation for everything else we'll discuss in this book.

Once you're comfortable with the financial concepts in Part 2, you'll be ready for Part 3, which will cover how to apply these concepts as a real estate investor. In Part 3, we'll dive into the key metrics needed to analyze a deal, compare investments against one another, and measure portfolio performance. But, for now, focus on understanding the concepts, not on how to apply them to your specific situation—we'll get to that in due time.

CHAPTER 5
INTEREST

Chapter 5 will help answer the questions:
- What is interest?
- Why is interest important to an investor?
- How much interest am I earning?

The first concept we're going to discuss is one of the most basic—but also one of the most important—when it comes to investing: interest.

Interest is everywhere. You see it when applying for a credit card, when checking your savings account, and, of course, when getting or making a loan. From these everyday applications of interest, you're likely already familiar with the concept. But we need more than a familiarity with interest if we're going to understand our investments on a deep level.

Interest is a simple concept. It is defined as the periodic payment against money that is borrowed or lent. When you borrow money, you pay interest as the primary benefit to the institution that lent the money to you (like a bank).

#28   **Interest** is the periodic payment against money that is borrowed or lent.

Why would a bank want to lend you money? What is their incentive?

Their incentive is the interest. The bank's profit for lending you money is the interest you pay on your loan.

Conversely, when you lend money, you receive interest as your primary benefit for the risk and opportunity cost you've taken by handing that money over to the borrower. The interest is the profit you are generating for lending out your money.

Let's look at an example.

If you were to borrow $10,000 from a bank and repay it over five years, you would have to pay the bank more than just the $10,000 that you borrowed. The bank would apply an interest rate—for example, let's say a 2 percent interest rate per year. This is the bank's fee for lending you that money.

Assuming *simple* interest was applied to the loan, the total cost of the loan would be $11,000 (more on this calculation in a moment). You borrowed $10,000, but you owe the bank $11,000. The $1,000 extra you're paying in interest is the profit earned by the bank for lending you money.

For the borrower (you, in this example), the $1,000 in interest is the cost you pay for the opportunity to borrow $10,000 for five years.

As you'll see when we get into more complex concepts in the following chapters, the formulas to calculate interest are foundational to evaluating all sorts of investments—not just loans.

There are three components to an interest calculation:

1. **Principal:** This is the amount of money lent or borrowed. In our example above, this would be $10,000.
2. **Interest rate:** This is the percentage return agreed upon by the lender and borrower. This amount is typically expressed as an annualized percentage (a percentage paid per year). In our example above, the interest rate was 2 percent per year.
3. **Time:** This is the amount of time the loan is outstanding. Our example used five years as the time frame.

Using just these three components, we can determine how much interest will be paid over the life of a loan.

DIG DEEP

PERCENTAGE-BASED CALCULATIONS

If you're comfortable with fractions, decimals, and basic percentages, you can skip ahead. However, for those of you who are math-phobic or more than a few years removed from high school math class, a little bit of knowledge now will make the rest of the book a whole lot easier to follow.

Most financial analyses, whether for real estate or any other type of investing, are going to deal with percentage-based calculations—in other words, multiplying and dividing using percentages, including converting them to decimals and fractions (and the other way around).

When doing a calculation using a percentage, it's often easier to first convert the percentage to a decimal value before doing the calculation. You do this by dividing the percentage value by 100.

For example, the percentage 5 percent would be the same as the decimal 0.05, as we can see here:

$$5\% = 5 \div 100 = 0.05$$

Conversely, when converting from a decimal value to a percentage value, we simply convert the decimal to a percentage by adding a percent sign and multiplying by 100. As an example, the decimal 0.2 would be the same as 20 percent:

$$0.2 = 0.2\% \times 100 = 20\%$$

In general, any percentage between 0 and 100 percent will be equivalent to a decimal between 0 and 1. Vice versa, any decimal between 0 and 1 will be equivalent to a percentage between 0 and 100.

We will be using both the decimal form (for example, 0.05) and the percentage form (5 percent) interchangeably in this book.

SIMPLE INTEREST

The basic form of interest is paid on a periodic basis without any consideration for whether and how much interest was paid in the past. The interest amount is consistent over time and any unpaid interest does not earn additional interest on itself. This is known as simple interest.

The formula for calculating simple interest is as follows:

#29	**Simple interest** Interest = Principal × Interest rate

Using our previous example:

Interest = Principal × Interest rate
Interest = $10,000 × 2% = $200

Remember, interest is typically expressed as an annual rate, so that $200 in interest is $200 *per year.*

As the borrower in this scenario, you would owe the bank $200 per year as a fee for borrowing $10,000. Because the length of the loan in our example was five years, the total interest you would pay over the life of the loan would be $200 per year multiplied by five years, which comes out to $1,000. Easy!

As another example, when you put your money into a bank savings account, you are essentially loaning money to the bank or institution providing that savings account. After all, the bank invests or lends your deposited money to other customers, so you should get paid for helping them earn a profit! The bank offers this payment to you in the form of interest on the money you keep in your account.

Let's say that a bank offers you a 5 percent interest rate on your savings account. (We know this isn't a realistic number these days—we're just trying to make the math a bit easier.) If you decided to keep $10,000 in that account, the simple interest you should expect to get paid would be:

Interest = Principal × Interest rate
Interest = $10,000 × 5% = $500

When lending your money to the bank by keeping it in their savings account, you are earning $500 every year that the money is in the account.

To see how much simple interest would be paid if we decided to keep our $10,000 in the savings account for a specific period of time, we use the total interest formula.

#30   **Total interest**
Total interest = Principal × Interest rate × Number of years

For example, if you were to keep the $10,000 in the savings account for five years, the total interest you'd receive would be:

Total interest = Principal × Interest rate × Number of years
Total interest = $10,000 × 0.05 × 5 = $2,500

At a 5 percent interest rate, you will have earned $2,500 in interest in your savings account after five years.

We can also easily modify the interest formula for partial years. In real life, you rarely keep an investment or a deposit at a bank for an exact number of years.

Let's say we left our money in the savings account we discussed above for two and a half years rather than five. In that case, the total interest generated would be:

Total interest = Principal × Interest rate × Number of years
Interest = $10,000 × 0.05 × 2.5 = $1,250

Pretty simple, right? Hence the name "simple interest."

DIG DEEP

OPPORTUNITY COST

We are going to refer to the idea of opportunity cost several times in this book, and it's an important concept to understand when dealing with investing and finance.

Opportunity cost is the risk of making a specific decision. Every time you make a decision, you risk the potential loss of a better outcome had you made a different decision.

Opportunity cost is all around us. Even going to a movie has an opportunity cost. When you go to a movie, the time you spent in the theater can't otherwise be put toward something that might have been more productive. Similarly, the money you spent on that movie now can't be used for something that might have had a more favorable impact on your life.

Given that most of us don't have unlimited amounts of cash (or time), it's especially important to think about opportunity cost when making investing decisions. If you decide to spend the hard-earned $20,000 that you've saved to fund a rental property, you now can't use that $20,000 if/when a more amazing investment opportunity comes along. Likewise, if you take 100 hours to renovate that rental property yourself, you've now lost 100 hours that could have otherwise been spent on other tasks that might have contributed to your investment success.

Luckily, there are a few mathematical tools that will help us better understand the opportunity cost of some of our investment decisions.

One last thing before we move on. We can also flip our interest formula around to determine an interest rate we're receiving on money lent or borrowed.

#31   **Interest rate**
Interest rate = Interest ÷ Principal

For example, let's assume that an investor friend offers you $350 if you will loan him $5,000 of your money for one year. In other words, you loan him $5,000, and he agrees to return the $5,000 in principal plus $350 in interest one year later.

The simple interest rate being offered by your friend is:

Interest rate = Interest ÷ Principal
Interest rate = $350 ÷ $5,000 = 0.07

And remember, the decimal (0.07) is equivalent to the percentage (7 percent). You will have received 7 percent simple interest on your $5,000 loan.

Applying Simple Interest to Real Estate

We've spent the bulk of this chapter talking about interest as it relates to lending or borrowing money, but it's important to note that these same concepts can be applied to the returns you'll make on other types of investments besides savings accounts and loans.

Imagine that you own a rental property that you purchased for $60,000 in cash.

Each month, you earn $250 in profit from that rental; at the end of the first year, you've earned a total of $3,000 in profit. While it wasn't interest that you received from your rental property, you can still calculate your returns in the same way that you would calculate interest.

In your first year, you earned $3,000 in profit on a $60,000 investment. Your return (using the same formula we used to calculate the simple interest rate) is:

Interest rate = Interest ÷ Principal
Interest rate = $3,000 ÷ $60,000 = 0.05

Using this example, you earned 5 percent on your investment. Just like when you deposit money in the bank and earn interest on your capital, you can deposit money into an investment and earn interest (profit) on your capital.

DIG DEEP

INTEREST VERSUS ROR

When applying interest concepts to situations outside of lending/borrowing, we often change the terminology from "interest rate" to "rate of return" (ROR). That allows us to differentiate between investments that are loans versus other types of investments.

This is important because the interest payments on loans are generally fixed and defined by a contract (often called a "promissory note"). They should never change.

On the other hand, other types of investments, like a rental property, may earn more in some months and less in others. Rate of return can often change month to month or year to year.

Keep in mind that interest rate and rate of return can be used interchangeably, but whenever possible, we like to use them to differentiate between loan returns and investment returns.

You have now earned $3,000 from your investment; you have two choices about what you can do with that $3,000 in profit:

1. You can spend it (remove it from your investing pool of money).
2. You can reinvest it.

If you go the first route and spend the money, the next year you will likely earn about $3,000 again on your $60,000 investment. This is equivalent to earning simple interest on your investment, year after year. The amount you've invested ($60,000) does not change, so assuming the investment doesn't change, the interest or profit you earn is likely not going to change very much either.

But what if you went with the second option? What if, rather than removing the $3,000 from the investment and spending it, you chose to reinvest that $3,000, either back into the same investment or into another investment?

As we'll see in the next chapter, this is where things really start to get interesting—and where investors can really start to grow their wealth.

HONE YOUR SKILLS: CHAPTER 5

- What are the three inputs for an interest calculation?
- How much total (simple) interest would be earned on an investment with a $50,000 principal, an interest rate of 10 percent, and a hold period of five years?
- If you pay a total of $15,000 in interest on a loan with $300,000 in principal, what interest rate did you pay?

CHAPTER 6
COMPOUNDING EFFECTS

Chapter 6 will help answer the questions:
- Why should I reinvest profits?
- What is the difference between simple and compound interest?
- How can I maximize the impacts of compounding?

In the last chapter, we looked at the example of an investment generating a return year after year. With simple interest, you assume that after each year, you pull your annual profit out of the deal to pay your bills or to spend on other things that aren't generating a return.

In this chapter, we'll look at another option. Rather than pulling your interest/profit out of the investment, what if you choose to reinvest that money instead—either back into the original investment or into another investment?

If you choose this option, you are increasing the total amount of money you have invested with each interest or profit payment; with a higher amount invested, you should expect future interest or profit payments to increase as well.

To illustrate this point, let's revisit our example from the last chapter, where you deposited $10,000 into a savings account that was paying you 5 percent simple interest. This is what five years in that investment would look like:

	YEAR-END BALANCE	INTEREST RATE	ANNUAL PROFIT
Year 1	$10,000.00	5%	$500.00
Year 2	$10,000.00	5%	$500.00
Year 3	$10,000.00	5%	$500.00
Year 4	$10,000.00	5%	$500.00
Year 5	$10,000.00	5%	$500.00

As shown above, if you do not reinvest your profits, you continue to make $500 per year.

But what if, instead of pulling out that $500 each year, you decide to put it back into the investment? You would earn interest not just on the principal, but also on the reinvested interest.

	YEAR-END BALANCE	INTEREST RATE	ANNUAL PROFIT
Year 1	$10,000.00	5%	$500.00
Year 2	$10,500.00	5%	$525.00
Year 3	$11,025.00	5%	$551.25
Year 4	$11,576.25	5%	$578.81
Year 5	$12,155.06	5%	$607.75

As you can see, you will still make $500 in interest in Year 1.

However, by reinvesting that $500 instead of taking it out, at the beginning of Year 2 you now have $10,500 in the account. In Year 2, at 5 percent interest rate, you can expect that $10,500 to generate $525.

Interest = Principal × Interest rate
Interest = $10,500 × 5% = $525

If you reinvest that $525 into the savings account, and continue reinvesting your profit every year, by the end of Year 5 you have $12,763 in your savings account (the $12,155 that you started Year 5 with, plus the $608 in interest you generated in Year 5). This is a $2,763 profit, compared to the $2,500 in profit generated in the first scenario.

By using your income to generate more income, you are creating a snowball effect that will allow you to grow your investment more quickly. Sure, that extra $263 in profit isn't life-changing, but as we get into larger numbers, higher rates of return, and, most importantly, longer time frames, this concept is often the primary driver of investment success.

As Benjamin Franklin famously said, "Money makes money. And the money that money makes makes more money." A bit of a tongue twister, but it's true!

This idea of reinvesting profits—and the snowball effect it creates—is called "compounding," and it's one of the most important and exciting concepts in investing. In fact, Albert Einstein once described compounding as "the eighth wonder of the world."

DIG DEEP

A PENNY DOUBLED

To put the power of compounding into perspective, consider a scenario where you're handed a penny on January 1. Let's say that penny doubles each day thereafter.

On January 2, you have two pennies.

On January 3, you have four pennies.

On January 4, you have eight pennies.

Skipping forward to January 15, you have $163.85.

By January 20, you have $5,242.88.

By the end of the month—on January 31—that single penny doubled every day would be worth over $10 million!

By February 8, you'd have over a billion dollars. And by Valentine's Day, you'd be the richest person on the planet (at least at the time of this writing) with nearly $400 billion.

All of that from a single penny doubled each day.

As an investor, or anyone looking to achieve financial freedom, compounding may be the single most important component of growing wealth. Now, we're not generally going to be able to achieve the kind of compounding we discussed in the penny-doubling scenario above—doubling your money every single day is unrealistic.

But we can do the same exercise with more reasonable numbers to give us an indication of the power of compounding. Let's say that you put $1,000 into an investment on your 25th birthday, and let's say that investment generates a 5 percent annual rate of return, with those returns paid out on your birthday each year.

In Year 1, the investment grows from $1,000 to $1,050. Perhaps you need that $50 for some expense, so at the end of the year, you take it and spend it. You still have $1,000 in the investment, so at the end of Year 2, you earn another $50 in profit. If you keep pulling the $50 in profit out of the investment each year, you'll continue to generate $50 per year as long as you have the investment (plus the $1,000 starting amount, of course). Simple interest in action.

But what if you decided you didn't need that $50 each year? Instead of taking it out of the investment, you instead decide to roll it back into the investment. After the first year, you still make your $50. When you put it back into the investment, by the second year, you're now generating a 5 percent profit on the $1,050. You roll that profit back into the investment and continue to do so, compounding your yearly returns.

- On your 35th birthday, you'd have about $1,628.
- On your 45th birthday, you'd have about $2,653.
- On your 55th birthday, you'd have about $4,321.
- And at retirement, on your 65th birthday, you'd have about $7,040.

That's the $1,000 you started with, plus over $6,000 in profit!

Without compounding (if you spent your profits each year rather than reinvesting), you would have only generated $2,000 by your 65th birthday ($50 per year for forty years). Compounding improved your forty-year return by 300 percent.

What if we increased those returns from 5 percent to 10 percent? What would doubling your rate of return do to your compounded results? Using the same scenario, here's what a 10 percent rate of return would achieve:

- On your 35th birthday, you'd have about $2,593.
- On your 45th birthday, you'd have about $6,727.
- On your 55th birthday, you'd have about $17,449.
- And at retirement, on your 65th birthday, you'd have about $45,259.

As you can see, simply doubling the return from 5 percent to 10 percent allows us to generate more than six times the total income over forty years. With compounding, even slightly higher returns can make a big difference in the outcome. This is why investors care so much about their rate of return.

Again, the difference between simple interest (spending your profits) and compound interest (reinvesting your profits) is dramatic. In this 10 percent annual return example, if you spent your profits instead of reinvesting, you would have generated $4,000 over forty years. But by reinvesting and compounding, you're able to generate $44,259 in that same period of time. In this example, failing to reinvest would decrease your overall return by almost 90 percent and lose out on over $40,000 for your retirement.

In other words, if you're investing for the long term, the strategy is simple: Continuously reinvest your profits at the highest possible rate of return.

It's important to note that the largest benefits of compounding are created by increasing the length of time in the investment. Looking at the following chart, you can see two scenarios for an investment of $10,000 with an 8 percent interest rate: one for simple interest and another for compounding interest.

Note that for the first several years of the investment, the difference in returns between the two scenarios is relatively small.

SIMPLE VS. COMPOUNDING INVESTMENTS

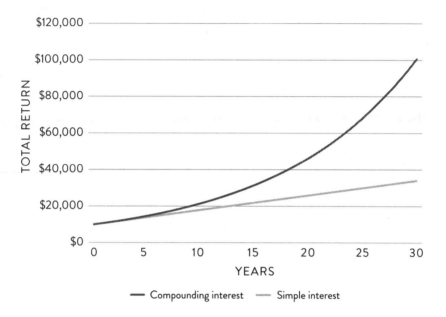

But as time goes on, the benefits of reinvesting get larger and larger as the total amount invested continues to grow.

The following chart illustrates the *increase in profits*, expressed as a percentage, generated by a compounding return versus a simple return at 8 percent interest over a given period of time.

SIMPLE VS. COMPOUNDING INVESTMENTS
(% DIFFERENCE)

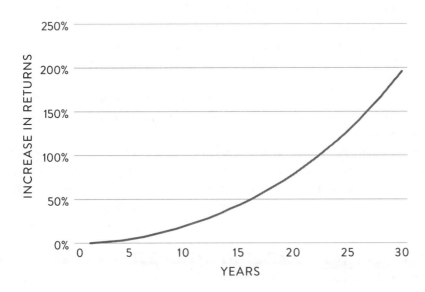

As you can see, at Year 10, the investment that compounds only outperforms the simple interest investment by 20 percent (Still, not bad!). But by Year 30, the compounding investment beats the simple interest investment by 196 percent. The longer your investment compounds, the greater the benefits become. This is why investors love the saying "It's not about timing the market; it's about time in the market." The longer you invest, the greater the benefit of compounding.

Before we move on, there's one more thing to consider when looking at the compounding effects of your investments: the compounding period.

COMPOUNDING PERIOD

The compounding period is the amount of time between payments back to the investment. In our previous example, you received the return on an annual basis—the full year's return was paid to you each year on your birthday.

But what if instead of paying out the full return once per year, the investment instead paid out smaller amounts monthly? This would put more money into the investment at earlier intervals, allowing you to compound sooner. In theory, you should be able to grow your money faster when you have shorter compounding periods.

Let's look at how your money would grow in the 10 percent return example. This time, though, let's assume that the investment is paying out one-twelfth of those returns each month instead of the entire return once per year.

Here is how $1,000 invested on your 25th birthday would grow:
- On your 35th birthday, instead of having $2,593, you'd have $2,707.
- On your 45th birthday, instead of having $6,727, you'd have $7,328.
- On your 55th birthday, instead of having $17,449, you'd have $19,837.
- And at retirement, on your 65th birthday, you'd have $53,700.

This scenario has you retiring with an investment balance of $53,700 rather than $45,259. Just compounding monthly versus once per year adds over 15 percent to your lifetime returns!

As investors, this is the reason why it's important to try to reinvest our returns as quickly as possible. Instead of taking the monthly rent your properties are generating and sticking it under the mattress until you have enough to buy another property, try to figure out how to invest the smaller sums more quickly to increase the compounding effects.

CALCULATING COMPOUND INTEREST

As you might expect, the formula for calculating the return of a compounded investment—in other words, an investment where the returns are automatically reinvested at the same rate of return—is a little more complicated than for simple interest.

Given the benefits of compounding, though, doing a little more math is well worth it!

#32   **Compound interest**
Compound interest = (Principal × (1 + Interest rate)^{Periods}) − Principal

Let's look at an example.

Imagine you loan $150,000 to an investor colleague for three years at a 9 percent annualized interest rate, with the agreement that the interest will compound once per year (in other words, interest is due at the end of each year, but instead of being paid back at that time, your colleague pays all of the interest owed at the end of the loan period). The total principal and interest is due at the end of the three-year time frame.

What is the total amount of interest you'll earn on that loan?

Compound interest = ($150,000 × (1 + 0.09)^3) − $150,000
Compound interest = ($150,000 × (1.09)^3) − $150,000
Compound interest = ($150,000 × 1.295029) − $150,000
Compound interest = $194,254.25 − $150,000
Compound interest = $44,254.35

At the end of three years, the borrower will repay you your $150,000, plus $44,254.35 in interest, for a total payoff of $194,254.35.

If you had lent your colleague the $150,000 at 9 percent but instead used simple interest, you would have earned:

Total interest = Principal × Interest rate × Number of years
Total interest = $150,000 × 0.09 × 3 = $40,500

In this example, by reinvesting the interest and compounding it, you increased your return by about $3,750 ($44,254.35 − $40,500 = $3,754.35) and increased your return on investment (ROI) from 27 percent to 29.5 percent. (We'll explain more about how to calculate ROI in Part 3.)

Quick Tip | The Rule of 72

We've discussed how to calculate the growth of a compounding investment using the compound interest formula. But there are a lot of situations where we'd like to estimate how quickly an investment will grow without having to use a formula.

Luckily, there is a mathematical trick that will help you estimate—in your head—how quickly you can grow your money through compounding. It's called the Rule of 72, and it will allow you to estimate how long it will take for an investment to double, assuming you're compounding at a specific rate of return.

The rule works as follows:

Number of years to double = 72 ÷ Rate of return

As an example, let's say that you are receiving an 8 percent return by investing in a diversified stock portfolio, and you are reinvesting your returns to compound your growth. An estimate for the time it would take to double your initial investment would be:

Number of years to double = 72 ÷ 8

Number of years to double = 9

Your investment would double about every nine years. In other words, someone who invests $10,000 in 2023 with an 8 percent return will have about $20,000 in 2032, $40,000 in 2041, and $80,000 in 2050.

Let's try the same thing with a 15 percent return:

Number of years to double = 72 ÷ 15 = 4.8

So, if the same investor were to invest $10,000 in 2023 with a 15 percent return, he would expect to have $20,000 in 2028, $40,000 in 2033, and $80,000 in 2038. That's a full twelve years sooner than if he were only able to get 8 percent! (A couple percents can make a big difference.) Remember, the Rule of 72 is a rough estimate of how long it will take your money to double at a given rate of return, not a precise measurement.

HONE YOUR SKILLS: CHAPTER 6

- What is the fundamental difference between simple interest and compound interest?
- How much total (compound) interest would be earned on an investment with a $50,000 principal, an interest rate of 10 percent, and a hold period of five years?
- For an investment of $10,000 that has an interest rate of 5 percent over the course of ten years, what is the difference in total return for simple versus compound interest?

CHAPTER 7
EXPECTED VALUE

Chapter 7 will help answer the questions:
- What tools can I use to make better decisions?
- How can I best choose between two investments with several potential outcomes?

Making big financial decisions is hard. But it's also the backbone of good investing. Successful investors have an array of decision-making tools at their disposal, and they know how and when to use them.

Certain types of decisions require complex analysis and are often influenced by more than just a formula or equation. This especially applies to those types of decisions that don't come along very often and can result in a catastrophic outcome should the wrong decision be made—for example, whether to marry someone, whether to start a business, or whether to a commit to a "once in a lifetime" deal.

Then, there are those decisions that you will face over and over, dozens or even hundreds of times. For example, whether to split a pair of eights in blackjack or whether to play the Powerball next Saturday night.

For those decisions that you'll find yourself making over and over, and where you will judge the likelihood—and financial result—of each potential outcome, there is a great decision-making tool called expected value (EV). Expected value is simply the long-term average result you should expect when you make the same financial decision over and over.

AN EV EXAMPLE

As a very simple example, let's say that we were to offer you a betting game that you can play as many times as you'd like.

We roll a six-sided die, and you guess which number it will land on. If you guess correctly, you win $10. If you guess incorrectly, you lose nothing. However, it will cost you $2 each time you play the game.

Should you play this game?

We know that if you don't play the game, you have no financial gain or loss. The question is, if you *do* play the game, can you expect to win more than $0? We can use EV to answer this question.

The EV formula considers each possible outcome from the game and multiplies the likelihood of each outcome by the financial gain or loss.

#33

Expected value

$$EV = (E_1 \times P_1) + (E_2 \times P_2) + ... + (E_N \times P_N)$$

Where

E = The expected financial result of the outcome, and

P = The probability of the outcome.

In our game example, there are two possible outcomes:

1. You pay $2 to play the game, you guess the correct number, and you win $10. Your total financial gain in this scenario is $8 ($10 in winnings minus $2 to play the game).

2. You pay $2 to play the game, you guess the incorrect number, and you win nothing. Your total financial loss in this scenario is $2 (the $2 to play the game).

In addition to determining all the possible outcomes, we also need to determine the probability of each occurring.

In this case, the likelihood of Scenario No. 1 occurring is 1 out of 6 (there are six sides to the die, and each has an equal chance of being rolled). That's about 16.7 percent. The likelihood of Scenario No. 2 occurring is 5 out of 6, or about 83.3 percent.

We can summarize this game as follows:

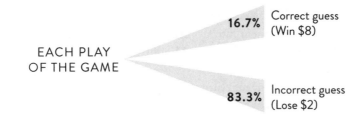

EACH PLAY
OF THE GAME

16.7% Correct guess (Win $8)

83.3% Incorrect guess (Lose $2)

To determine the EV of each play of the game, we multiply the financial result of each potential outcome by the likelihood of that result occurring, and then add them all up.

EV = ($8 × 16.7%) + (-$2 × 83.3%)
EV = $1.34 – $1.67
EV = -$0.33

The expected value of this game is negative $0.33. That means for each time you play this game, you can—on average—expect to lose $0.33.

Now, that doesn't mean you'll lose $0.33 each time you play. In fact, you never will. Each time you play, you'll either earn $8 or lose $2. But, if you play this game enough times, your average result will be a $0.33 loss. If you play 1,000 times, you can expect to lose about $330 (1,000 × $0.33).

The logical decision is that your best financial interest is *not* to play this game.

As you can see, EV is great tool because it takes a decision that can feel like a simple matter of opinion (whether to play the game) and turns it into a quantifiable decision (you will lose money if you repeatedly play this game).

SELECTING BETWEEN MULTIPLE INVESTMENTS

A common use for EV in the business and investing world is when choosing between multiple potential investments where each has several potential outcomes. You can use EV to estimate the probability of each outcome occurring.

Let's assume you have the option of investing $10,000 in two companies. Since you only have $10,000, you must choose between the two.

Company A is a startup—it's a high-risk investment with a potentially high return should the company do well. You estimate that there's a 70 percent chance Company A won't succeed and you'll lose your $10,000 completely. There's also a 20 percent chance the company will stall out early and your investment will break even (you'll get your money back but not generate a profit), and there's a 10 percent chance the company will get bought by a big competitor, in which case you expect you'll earn about $250,000 in profit on the investment.

Company B is a much bigger company, with less potential upside, but also less risk. You estimate that an investment into Company B has a 10 percent chance of losing everything, a 60 percent chance of earning $10,000 in profit, and a 30 percent chance of earning a $30,000 profit.

Which investment is likely to return the largest profit?

Here's what this decision would look like:

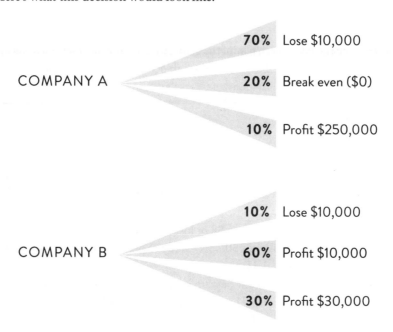

COMPANY A	**70%**	Lose $10,000
	20%	Break even ($0)
	10%	Profit $250,000

COMPANY B	**10%**	Lose $10,000
	60%	Profit $10,000
	30%	Profit $30,000

And here's what the expected value of each investment is:

Company A

EV = (-$10,000 × 70%) + ($0 × 20%) + ($250,000 × 10%)

EV = -$7,000 + $0 + $25,000

EV = $18,000

Company B

EV = (-$10,000 × 10%) + ($10,000 × 60%) + ($30,000 × 30%)

EV = -$1,000 + $6,000 + $9,000

EV = $14,000

While there are certainly other factors that need to be considered here—for example, the risk of losing all your money with Company A—the EV of investing in Company A is higher than the EV of investing in Company B.

In other words, assuming your estimates are correct, if you could make this same investment over and over, an investment in Company A will generate more profit in the long run than an investment in Company B.

Several years ago, after doing about 200 flips, I (J) realized that I was spending a lot of money on insurance policies for my flips, despite having very few insurance claims (and no large claims). It made me wonder whether I was throwing money away by purchasing insurance policies for my flips, and whether it would be more cost-effective to "self-insure" my properties.

Instead of purchasing insurance, by self-insuring, I would assume the cost and risk of any loss myself. While I would obviously incur a cost every time something happened where I would otherwise make an insurance claim, there would be a lot of saved money by not making insurance payments.

I decided to run an expected value analysis to help make my decision.

Here were the assumptions I used, based on the information I had collected from my previous flips and from talking to other investors. (Note that these assumptions might vary between investors, and costs could be higher these days.)

A typical insurance policy for a flip will cost about $1,000.

On about 1 out of 50 flips (2 percent), I'd have a small ($10,000) claim.

On about 1 out of 200 flips (0.5 percent), I'd have a big ($100,000) claim.

On the rest of the flips (97.5 percent), I'd have no insurance claim.

If I were to self-insure, I wouldn't have a claim about 97.5 percent of the time, and I'd simply be saving $1,000 on an insurance policy. But, about 2 percent of the time, I'd have to cover a $10,000 claim, and about 0.5 percent of the time, I'd have to cover about $100,000 for a big claim.

This is what the decision tree looked like for this decision:

PAY FOR INSURANCE	100%	Spend $1,000
	97.5%	No cost ($0)
SELF INSURE	2%	Cost of $10,000
	.5%	Cost of $100,000

The EV for paying for insurance is very simple:

EV = $1,000 × 100%

EV = $1,000

The EV for self-insuring would be:

EV = ($0 × 97.5%) + ($10,000 × 2%) + ($100,000 × 0.5%)

EV = $0 + $200 + $500

EV = $700

The EV on self-insuring each flip is $700, versus $1,000 by purchasing an insurance policy for each project. That means, on average, by not spending the $1,000, I'd spend $700 per project paying for things that would have otherwise been covered by insurance.

In other words, on average, I'm saving $300 per flip by self-insuring!

Of course, if you were looking to make a similar decision, you'd want to use the numbers that make sense for your flips (both insurance costs and likely claims), but you can see why a lot of house flippers who are doing large volumes of flips choose to self-insure.

There are thousands of scenarios you'll run into—both with your investments and in your daily life—where EV allows you to make much better decisions than just "going with your gut."

Of course, the key to accurate decision-making using expected value is assigning accurate probabilities to use in your calculations. If you use inaccurate probabilities, your EV calculations can be skewed and lead to a misinformed decision. However, assuming you are confident in the probabilities you assign to your potential outcomes, EV can be one of the most useful decision-making tools at your disposal.

HONE YOUR SKILLS: CHAPTER 7

- What three pieces of information are needed in order to do an expected value calculation?
- What is the key to making good decisions using expected value?
- You're investing $10,000 in a deal that has three potential outcomes: 20 percent chance of tripling your money, 45 percent chance of breaking even, 35 percent chance of losing all your money. What is your expected value for this investment?

CHAPTER 8
TIME VALUE OF MONEY

Chapter 8 will help answer the questions:
- What is some amount of money today likely to be worth in the future? (Future value)
- What should I be willing to pay today for some amount of money in the future? (Present value)

One of the most important concepts in all of investing is the idea of "time value of money."

Even if you don't know exactly what it means, you've probably heard the term. It is the basis for many of the decision-making processes we use when evaluating potential investments, and it's also factored into many of the metrics we use to evaluate the performance of existing investments.

Time value of money (TVM) is a concept that builds on our previous discussion of compounding effects; if you haven't already read Chapter 6, it might be worth starting there, at least as a refresher. Because TVM plays such a big role in analyzing investments, we're going to devote several chapters to the topic, with each chapter covering a different way that TVM can help us with our deal analysis.

For those of you who are stronger with math or who are familiar with the concept of TVM specifically, you may find that we are redundant in much of our discussion, reinforcing a few key points over and over. This is done intentionally. We've read many different tutorials on TVM over the years, and most of them are geared toward those with some background in finance and financial analysis. We wanted our discussion of the topic to be graspable by anyone, so we've done our best to simplify these topics, build the foundation slowly, and reiterate key points throughout the text.

Let's start with the basic concept of TVM.

#34 **Time value of money (TVM)** is the concept that money in hand today is worth more than money in hand at some future time.

The idea behind the time value of money is simple: Money in hand today has earning potential, and we can turn money today into more money tomorrow by investing it. Therefore, getting that same amount of money tomorrow is less valuable to us than getting it today. And it's even less valuable getting it the day after tomorrow, and even less the day after that. Every day you have money in hand, you have the potential to grow it.

Long story short, the sooner you receive money, the more valuable it is.

DETERMINING FUTURE VALUE

As a simple example, let's say we offered you $1,000 today or $1,000 one year from now. Which would you rather have? If you were to take that $1,000 today and invest it for the next year, you would have more than $1,000 come next year. Not to mention, simply due to inflation, that $1,000 is going to have less purchasing power in a year than it does today.

Either way you look at it, that $1,000 is more valuable if you receive it today than it would be if you received it next year (or at any point in the future).

As investors, we tend to spend all our time thinking about making more money. But the best investors don't just think about making more money; they also think about making money sooner. That's because, thanks to the time value of money, sooner ultimately leads to more.

It's such a simple concept, but the implications to us as investors are enormous!

Let's dig into this a bit more.

Let's say you take that $1,000 offered to you today and put it into an investment that pays you a guaranteed 12 percent annual return, compounding monthly. (Okay, perhaps this is not the most realistic example these days with interest rates near zero, but it makes the math a lot easier for explanation purposes!)

If you remember from Chapter 6, "compounded monthly" means that profits are paid monthly and immediately reinvested at the same rate of return.

If your annual rate of return is 12 percent and you're receiving your returns monthly, then your monthly rate of return would be 12% ÷ 12 = 1%. You are getting 1 percent of your investment back each month.

This is what the first year of that investment would look like:

MONTH	PRINCIPAL	ROR	RETURN
January	$1,000.00	1%	$10.00
February	$1,010.00	1%	$10.10
March	$1,020.10	1%	$10.20
April	$1,030.30	1%	$10.30
May	$1,040.60	1%	$10.41
June	$1,051.01	1%	$10.51
July	$1,061.52	1%	$10.62
August	$1,072.14	1%	$10.72
September	$1,082.86	1%	$10.83
October	$1,093.69	1%	$10.94
November	$1,104.62	1%	$11.05
December	$1,115.67	1%	$11.16
End of Year	**$1,126.83**		

As you can see, after the first month, you would have generated $10 in return. You then compound your return by putting that $10 back into the investment, bringing your total investment to $1,010. In February, you earn $10.10 and reinvest that too. If you do this for a full year and add the final distribution to the total, you will see that you ended up with $1,126.83 after one year.

This example makes clear two important points:

1. Receiving that $1,000 today is clearly more beneficial than receiving that $1,000 a year from now (or at any point in the future).
2. Assuming you would invest the money at 1 percent per month, $1,000 received today is worth exactly the same as $1,126.83 received one year from now.

To that second point: That means if you had the ability to generate 12 percent annual returns, compounded monthly, and we asked you, "Would you rather have $1,000 now or $1,126.83 a year from now?" your answer would be "It's exactly the same to me!"

And that's the basis of TVM.

PRESENT VALUE, FUTURE VALUE, AND INTEREST RATE

When applying TVM to investment analysis, we like to use some common terminology.

This allows us to talk to other people without confusion, and it also lets us build some mathematical equations that can make tables like the previous one a little less complicated.

There are four terms we need to define:

1. **Present value (PV):** The PV is today's value of the investment.
2. **Future value (FV):** The FV is the value of the investment at some point in the future.
3. **Interest rate (i):** The interest rate is the rate of return we could expect to earn on our money if we were to receive it today and invest it immediately. Remember to adjust the interest rate based on the compounding period—for example, if your investment will compound monthly, be sure to divide the annual rate of return by 12 to get your interest rate.
4. **Number of compounding periods (n):** The number of compounding periods between PV and FV for the investment.

In our previous example, the $1,000 you started with would be your present value (PV). The $1,126.83 that you ended with after a year would be your future value (FV). The interest rate would be the monthly rate of 1 percent. And the number of compounding periods would be the number of months you compounded, which was twelve.

The FV formula (often just called the TVM formula) ties all four of these values together into a single concise equation.

#35	Future value formula $FV = PV \times (1 + i)^n$

This may seem like a complicated formula, but it's not that complex. Let's plug in our numbers and demonstrate.

$$FV = PV \times (1 + i)^n$$
$$FV = \$1,000 \times (1 + 0.01)^{12}$$
$$FV = \$1,000 \times (1.01)^{12}$$
$$FV = \$1,000 \times 1.126825$$
$$FV = \$1,126.83$$

As we might have expected, the future value of your $1,000 compounded monthly at 12 percent annual rate of return is the same as what we calculated above using the larger table—the formula is just a lot easier to use.

INVESTOR STORY
Future Value of J's Money

A few years ago, I (J) was selling a property that I owned free and clear (no mortgage). It was listed for $120,000 and I was getting a reasonable amount of interest from a nice couple to buy the property for around full price. They were planning to make the house their primary residence.

I also received an inquiry from an investor. He told me that he really wanted to buy the house, but that he wasn't going to have the money for about seven more months, as he was waiting for a seasoning period to end on another property he owned that he was planning to refinance. The investor offered to purchase the property now, assuming I agreed to hold off on receiving the cash for another seven months.

Luckily, I was familiar with TVM, and I knew that getting the $120,000 now would be more valuable than getting it in seven months. I also knew that I could use the FV formula to determine how much that $120,000 would be worth to me seven months from now.

At the time, I was doing a good number of private loans, and I was lending money at about 13 percent annual interest (1.0833 percent monthly interest). So, if I plugged the PV ($120,000), the periodic rate of return (1.0833 percent, or 0.010833), and the number of periods (seven months) into the TVM formula, I could get a good approximation of what that $120,000 would be worth if I were to have it now and could loan it out for the next half year.

This is what I got:

$$FV = PV \times (1 + i)^n$$
$$FV = \$120,000 \times (1 + 0.010833)^7$$
$$FV = \$129,401.15$$

In other words, if I were to get that $120,000 today and loan it out at 13 percent annualized interest for seven months, I should expect to have $129,401.15 at the end of that time.

If the investor offering on my property were willing to pay me more than that $129,401.15 in seven months, I'd be making more money than if I were to sell the property for full list price today.

I told the investor that if he would purchase the property for $130,000 in the next couple of weeks (to ensure that he actually went through with it), I'd be happy to wait seven months to accept payment. He agreed, and not only did he pay me the $130,000, but his refi also went through faster—so he paid after about five months, increasing my return even more!

DETERMINING PRESENT VALUE

In our TVM examples, we started with the premise that we knew the present value of our money—we had the money in hand—and we wanted to determine how much that money would be worth at a particular point in the future.

But TVM allows us to look at this from the other side of the coin as well. In other words, TVM lets us look at a future sum of money and determine what that money would be worth if we had it in hand today.

Another way of saying this is to ask the question, "How much would I be willing to pay today for some guaranteed amount of money in the future?"

Let's say we told you that if you gave us $1 today, we'd give you $100,000 back next year. You wouldn't have to do any math to determine that this was probably a great deal (assuming you trusted us, of course). Likewise, if we told you by giving us $1 today, we'd give you back $1.25 in ten years, your gut could confirm that this wasn't much of an opportunity.

But what about when the situation is a little more even? For example, what if we asked you how much you'd be willing to pay today for $1,000 a year from now? Would you pay $500 to get $1,000 in a year? Would you pay $800? Would you pay $950?

Answering this question is very important to real estate investors. If you are considering purchasing a rental property that will be delivering you cash flow well into the future, you need to understand how much that future cash flow is worth to you in today's dollars. This concept is foundational to determine how much to pay today for a return sometime in the future.

To demonstrate the theory behind this concept, we're going to take the brute-force approach to answer that question. (In math, "brute force" simply means to do things the long, tedious way.) Don't worry, we'll show you the simple way to do this a little later.

First, we need to start by asking ourselves the question, "What rate of return would we have gotten on the money we'd be handing over today?" And let's say that it's the same as in our earlier example: We believe we could get a 12 percent annualized return, compounded monthly (1 percent monthly return).

Next, we can build a chart that works backward; it assumes that we are getting our $1,000 a year from now and *discounts* that final value by the amount we could have been earning each month between now and then.

MONTH	FV	DISCOUNT RATE	PV
December	$1,000.00	1%	$990.10
November	$990.10	1%	$980.30
October	$980.30	1%	$970.59
September	$970.59	1%	$960.98
August	$960.98	1%	$951.47
July	$951.47	1%	$942.05
June	$942.05	1%	$932.72
May	$932.72	1%	$923.48
April	$923.48	1%	$914.34
March	$914.34	1%	$905.29
February	$905.29	1%	$896.32
January	$896.32	1%	$887.45
		Present Value = $887.45	

(Yes, we introduced a new term, "discount rate." We'll talk about that more soon.)

As you can see, to get to our $1,000 next December, with an investment generating 1 percent per month, we'd need to start with an amount in November that would grow 1 percent in that month; that amount is $990.10. (Note that 1 percent of 990.10 is $9.90, and adding them together gets us to $1,000.) To get to $990.10 in November, we'd have to start with $980.30 in October. And so forth, all the back to today—January.

In other words, if we wanted to have $1,000 one year from now at our current expected rate of return, we would need to start with $887.45 today.

To return to the question: If someone asked us how much we'd be willing to pay for $1,000 a year from now, we now know that the break-even amount is $887.45.

$887.45 today is worth $1,000 a year from now, assuming a 12 percent annual return that compounds monthly. If you pay more than $887.45 for $1,000 a year from now, you're paying too much. You would be better off investing your money at the 12 percent rate. If you paid less than $887.45, you're getting a great deal and exceeding your expected 12 percent annualized rate of return.

To put this in TVM terms, we can say that, assuming a 1 percent monthly rate of return, the present value of $1,000 one year from now (the future value) is $887.45.

We introduced the term "discount rate" in the chart, and you may have noticed it works exactly like "interest rate" did in our earlier examples. When talking about TVM, interest rate and discount rate are often used interchangeably. We like to use the term interest rate when building a model that is *growing* money (like going from

PV to FV) and discount rate when building a model that is *discounting* money (like going from FV to PV).

<table>
<tr><td>**#36**</td><td>**Discount rate** is the rate of return used to discount future value (or future cash flows) back to their present value.</td></tr>
</table>

As we mentioned, we used the brute-force way of doing things in this example by drawing up every month's present value. Luckily, our future value formula can answer this question for us much more simply. By flipping around the FV formula, we can take a future monetary value and determine what it would be worth today (which would also tell us what we should be willing to pay for it today).

We call this the present value formula.

<table>
<tr><td>**#37**</td><td>**Present value formula**
$PV = FV \div (1 + i)^n$</td></tr>
</table>

Let's look at the example we just went through, using the PV formula this time:

$PV = FV \div (1 + i)^n$
$PV = \$1,000 \div (1 + 0.01)^{12}$
$PV = \$1,000 \div (1.01)^{12}$
$PV = \$1,000 \div 1.126825$
$PV = \$887.45$

As we hoped, the answer is the same. $887.45 today is the same as $1,000 a year from now, assuming our investment strategy generates 1 percent monthly returns.

INVESTOR STORY
Present Value of J's Money

This isn't a real story, but I (J) wanted to take the example from our last investor story and use it to illustrate how the PV formula may have been helpful in the situation I discussed.

Let's say I went back to the investor with my counteroffer of $130,000 in seven months. And let's say that instead of accepting my offer, he counteroffered at $125,000 and indicated that this was his final offer—he wasn't willing to pay a penny more. Let's also say that the homeowners I was negotiating with ultimately decided to offer $115,000 and refused to go any higher.

What's a better financial decision on my part—the $115,000 cash now or the $125,000 in seven months?

We know what the $115,000 is worth today ($115,000, of course). But if I accepted the $125,000 in seven months, how much of my list price *today* does that correspond to?

Let's use our PV formula:

$$PV = FV \div (1 + i)^n$$
$$PV = \$125,000 \div (1 + 0.010833)^7$$
$$PV = \$115,918.60$$

In other words, accepting $125,000 in seven months would have been the equivalent to accepting about $115,918.60 today, which would still be over $900 more than what I was getting from the other buyers, who offered $115,000. All other things being equal, I now know that the investor's offer was better (at least from a financial perspective).

HONE YOUR SKILLS: CHAPTER 8

- What is the basic premise of the time value of money?
- What is the future value of a $5,000 investment invested at an 8 percent interest rate over seven years?
- What would a $25,000 payout in five years be worth in today's dollars, assuming a 10 percent discount rate?

CHAPTER 9
DISCOUNTED CASH FLOW (DCF) ANALYSIS

Chapter 9 will help answer the questions:
- What is a stream of future income worth today?
- How much should I be willing to pay for this future stream of income?
- Which investment is more profitable in today's dollars?

In the previous chapter, we learned how to determine the future value of an investment given an interest rate and today's value. We also learned how to determine present value (today's value) given a future amount and a discount rate. These are both important tools when trying to determine the value of a lump sum at different points in time.

In real estate, however, we are rarely dealing with lump sums. Real estate often deals with *streams* of income, meaning recurring income of cash over periods of time. When we buy a rental property, for example, we are going to receive income every month (hopefully) for as long as we own the property. Then we'll receive a large lump sum of income when we eventually sell the property.

Because each of these future monthly income payments happen at different points in time, the value of each payment will be different in today's dollars. A rent payment we collect next month is going to be worth more to us than a rent payment collected next year (remember, money received sooner is worth more).

Let's look at a concrete example to give you a better idea of what we mean. Assume we purchase two properties today. And assume we hold each property for three years—collecting rent each month—and then sell both properties in the fourth year. The difference between the properties is that they generate a different amount of rent each year, and then sell for different amounts, as follows:

YEAR	PROPERTY #1	PROPERTY #2
1	$5,000	$15,000
2	$8,000	$15,000
3	$12,000	$15,000
4	$125,000	$105,000
Totals:	$150,000	$150,000

(Note that we're assuming the *sales proceeds* after all selling costs in Year 4 were $125,000 and $105,000 respectively. The sale price of the properties likely would have been higher. Always remember that we need to subtract out selling costs and commissions from our numbers to get an accurate result when doing an analysis like this.)

At the end of Year 4, we look back and it appears that over the course of four years, we earned $150,000 in income on each deal. But did we really earn the same amount on each deal?

In absolute dollars we did. However, as we learned in the previous chapter, absolute dollars are less important than the timing of when we spend or receive those dollars. When we get money sooner, we can *reinvest* it sooner, *earning* us more money sooner, and allowing us to *compound* that money faster.

Quick Tip | Absolute (Nominal) Dollars

The concept of "absolute" dollars (sometimes also referred to as "nominal" dollars) is a way of looking at money that does not consider the time value of money. It simply looks at the amount of money present—not how or when it appeared. In the example above, the two investments are equal in absolute terms because they both generated a total of $150,000 in four years, even though the cash flows were very different. As we'll show below, this is an overly simplistic way to look at an investment. Factoring in the TVM is vital to any investment analysis.

When considering the time value of money, which of these two properties was a better investment?

The answer is: the one that would be worth the most money *today*.

In other words, the property with the highest present value. But how do we determine the present value of an investment with many years of incomes and profits? The method is similar to what we did in the previous chapter, but we now need to discount not just one value, but the entire income stream.

DISCOUNTING INCOME STREAMS

Discounting a stream of income is very similar to discounting a single future value. By discounting each income in the stream, and then adding them all up, we can determine the total value—in today's dollars—of the entire stream of income.

This is important because—like we saw in the previous section—we often must evaluate two or more investments to determine which one is more profitable. And as we've already learned, we can't rely on the total amount of money we end up with in the future to tell us how good of an investment something is. We need to know the present value of the entire investment.

To do this, we need to apply a discount rate to each of the income values generated over the life of the investment. Remember, a discount rate is often just the rate of return we could get if we took our cash right now and invested it in something else (our opportunity cost of having it tied up for some future amount of time).

This analysis is called a discounted cash flow (DCF) analysis, and again, it simply involves adding up the present value of a stream of future cash flows to determine a PV for that stream of income.

#38

Discounted cash flow (DCF) gives you the present value of an entire stream of income.

$$DCF = (CF_1 \div (1 + i)^1) + (CF_2 \div (1 + i)^2) + ... + (CF_x \div (1 + i)^x)$$

where
    CF is each of the future cash flows, and
    i is the discount rate.

We know this looks like a crazy equation, but notice that each element of the DCF formula is a PV calculation. The first part of the equation above, $(CF_1 \div (1 + i)^1)$, is just a single PV calculation—like we saw in the previous chapter—applied to the first cash flow. We then add that to the PV calculation for the second cash flow, $(CF_2 \div (1 + i)^2)$, then add the third calculation, and so on for as many cash flows as we have. By adding up all PV calculations for all future income payments, we can determine a present value of that entire stream of income.

Let's look at what the discounted streams of income from our two properties from the example earlier would look like. Further, let's assume that if we didn't buy these properties, we'd instead be investing in the stock market, where we believe we could earn a consistent 8 percent. In other words, we'll use 8 percent as our discount rate.

Here's what the discounted income stream looks like for the first property:

Property 1
Discount Rate: 8.00%

YEAR	CASH FLOW	PRESENT VALUE
1	$5,000	$4,630
2	$8,000	$6,859
3	$12,000	$9,526
4	$125,000	$91,879
TOTALS:	$150,000	$112,893

Let's explain what we're seeing in the chart. The $5,000 in cash flow we're generating by the end of Year 1 is equivalent to about $4,630 at the beginning of Year 1. This is because at an 8 percent interest rate, $4,630 at the beginning of the year would increase in value to $5,000 by the end of the year. If someone offered us cash today to give up $5,000 a year from now, we'd need them to give us $4,630 for it to be a fair trade.

We can apply that same logic to the income earned in each year of the investment. The $8,000 earned in Year 2 is worth about $6,859 if we were to receive it today. (Remember, we have to discount it for two years, not just one!) And so forth for the other two cash flows.

As you can see, in absolute dollars, we earned $150,000 over the course of the investment. But the present value (the value in today's dollars) is only $112,893, because all of the income was earned in the future—some of it far into the future. If someone offered us cash today instead of this four-year investment, they'd have to give us $112,893 today for it to be a fair exchange.

Now let's look at the discounted income stream from the second property:

Property 2
Discount Rate: 8.00%

YEAR	CASH FLOW	PRESENT VALUE
1	$15,000	$13,889
2	$15,000	$12,860
3	$15,000	$11,907
4	$105,000	$77,178
TOTALS:	$150,000	$115,835

While we earned the same in absolute dollars over four years, when considering the timing of the incomes received, the present value of the investment is $115,835. So, while Property 2 sold for considerably less than Property 1, the value of the income stream for Property 2 was about $3,000 more.

Someone would have to give us $115,835 today for this investment to be a fair trade. In other words, the four-year profit from the first investment is equivalent to having $112,893 in our pocket today; the four-year profit from the second investment is equivalent to having $115,835 in our pocket today.

All other things being equal, the second property outperformed the first. If we only had the money to invest into Property 1 or Property 2, we should highly consider Property 2 because the present value of the income it generates is higher. The beauty of this exercise is that it has allowed us to look at two properties with varying cash flows and sales prices, and easily compare them against one another by calculating what each of them are worth in today's dollars.

Quick Tip | Monthly Income

Note that in our examples above, we assume that all the cash flow from each year is discounted back a full year. In reality, we're receiving income on a monthly basis, so some of that income in Year 1 should only be discounted one month, while other income should be discounted more.

For a more accurate representation of the PV of each income stream, we could do a DCF analysis on a monthly basis as opposed to an annual basis—though that would obviously involve more work.

Before we move on, it's important to note that adding up all the present values of income within a stream, like we did above, is going to represent the value of the investment specifically for the given discount rate (8 percent, in our example).

In other words, the cash value of Property 1 to someone looking to earn 8 percent returns is exactly $112,893. If an investor pays more in cash than $112,893, they would be receiving less than 8 percent returns on their investment. If they pay less than $112,893, they'd receive a greater return than $112,893. And if they were to pay exactly $112,893, that investment of cash would earn them exactly an 8 percent return. If you used a different discount rate—say, 9 percent—the values would change entirely.

WOULD YOU RATHER?

DCF analysis can be a confusing topic, but there's a great "Would you rather?" question we often see posted on social media that drives home this concept tremendously well.

The question is typically a variation of:

Would you rather have $2 million in cash right now or $200,000 per year for the rest of your life?

It never fails that the comments section of such posts is filled with strong opinions about the answer, without any substantiation for why one opinion or the other might be best. And invariably, the opinions are split between the two answers!

You probably recognize this as a classic example of a time value of money situation—choosing between a large lump sum available to be invested immediately and a smaller stream that will last far into the future. While most of us probably won't be lucky enough to be offered either of these options, it's a fun thought experiment about which is the better financial decision.

Let's dig into the example above and see which option is likely the better choice.

As you're probably thinking, the goal of this exercise is to determine the present value of each option, with the assumption that the option with the higher PV is likely the best.

The PV of the $2 million option is straightforward: We are given the $2 million today, so the PV of that option is—you guessed it!—$2 million.

But what about the PV of the $200,000 per year for life? You may recognize that the best way to determine the present value of a stream of income is a discounted cash flow (DCF) analysis. Let's look at that equation again:

$$DCF = (CF_1 \div (1 + i)^1) + (CF_2 \div (1 + i)2) + \ldots + (CF_x \div (1 + i)^x)$$
where
  CF is each of the future cash flows, and
  i is the discount rate.

Remember, each piece of that equation is just a present value for each cash flow. By discounting each of the cash flows individually back to today and adding them up, we can determine the PV of the entire stream of income.

To do that, we need to know three things:
1. The amount of each of the future cash flows
2. The discount rate
3. The number of future cash flows that we will receive

No. 1 is clear; the amount of each of the future cash flows is $200,000 (the annual amount we're receiving).

No. 2 is a bit less clear. We know that the discount rate represents the rate of return we could expect if we were to have that income now, theoretically investing it over the period until we actually receive it. The first question we would then need to ask ourselves is, "If we had this money today, what would we be investing it in, and what would our return be?"

While that answer will be different for each of us, for the sake of this discussion, I'm going to assume that we would take that money and invest it either in the stock market or in a conservative real estate fund. In either of these, we could expect about an 8 percent annualized return. In other words, our discount rate (i) will be 8 percent.

Finally, No. 3 is the hardest question to answer. We're receiving $200,000 per year for life, but how long do we plan to live? If we knew we'd die next year, we probably wouldn't have to do this exercise—we'd just take the $2 million option. But assuming we're going to live for another twenty, thirty, or fifty years, the question becomes more interesting.

For the sake of this example, let's assume we plan to live another twenty-five years. For someone in their forties, this is a pretty conservative assumption based on average life expectancy. But, since we lose our income stream when we die, and since many of us will want to pass our net worth to others, it's probably better to be too conservative versus being too aggressive.

Obviously, for both discount rate and years to live, you're welcome to plug in whatever number makes sense for you; for this example, we'll be using 8 percent and twenty-five years.

Okay, let's take a look at our DCF analysis:

Discount Rate: 8.00%

YEAR	CASH FLOW	PRESENT VALUE	EQUATION
1	$200,000	$185,185	$\$200{,}000 \div ((1 + 0.08)^{\wedge}1)$
2	$200,000	$171,468	$\$200{,}000 \div ((1 + 0.08)^{\wedge}2)$
3	$200,000	$158,766	$\$200{,}000 \div ((1 + 0.08)^{\wedge}3)$
4	$200,000	$147,006	$\$200{,}000 \div ((1 + 0.08)^{\wedge}4)$
5	$200,000	$136,117	$\$200{,}000 \div ((1 + 0.08)^{\wedge}5)$
6	$200,000	$126,034	$\$200{,}000 \div ((1 + 0.08)^{\wedge}6)$
7	$200,000	$116,698	$\$200{,}000 \div ((1 + 0.08)^{\wedge}7)$
8	$200,000	$108,054	$\$200{,}000 \div ((1 + 0.08)^{\wedge}8)$
9	$200,000	$100,050	$\$200{,}000 \div ((1 + 0.08)^{\wedge}9)$
10	$200,000	$92,639	$\$200{,}000 \div ((1 + 0.08)^{\wedge}10)$
11	$200,000	$85,777	$\$200{,}000 \div ((1 + 0.08)^{\wedge}11)$
12	$200,000	$79,423	$\$200{,}000 \div ((1 + 0.08)^{\wedge}12)$
13	$200,000	$73,540	$\$200{,}000 \div ((1 + 0.08)^{\wedge}13)$

14	$200,000	$68,092	$200,000 ÷ ((1 + 0.08) ^ 14)
15	$200,000	$63,048	$200,000 ÷ ((1 + 0.08) ^ 15)
16	$200,000	$58,378	$200,000 ÷ ((1 + 0.08) ^ 16)
17	$200,000	$54,054	$200,000 ÷ ((1 + 0.08) ^ 17)
18	$200,000	$50,050	$200,000 ÷ ((1 + 0.08) ^ 18)
19	$200,000	$46,342	$200,000 ÷ ((1 + 0.08) ^ 19)
20	$200,000	$42,910	$200,000 ÷ ((1 + 0.08) ^ 20)
21	$200,000	$39,731	$200,000 ÷ ((1 + 0.08) ^ 21)
22	$200,000	$36,788	$200,000 ÷ ((1 + 0.08) ^ 22)
23	$200,000	$34,063	$200,000 ÷ ((1 + 0.08) ^ 23)
24	$200,000	$31,540	$200,000 ÷ ((1 + 0.08) ^ 24)
25	$200,000	$29,204	$200,000 ÷ ((1 + 0.08) ^ 25)
TOTALS:		**$2,134,955**	

As you can see, the discounted value of that stream of payments over twenty-five years is more than $2.1 million. While the $2 million today is obviously worth $2 million today, the $200,000 for twenty-five years is worth *the equivalent* of more than $2.1 million today!

Long story short, if someone were to offer you $2 million today or $200,000 per year for the next twenty-five years, the optimal financial decision—assuming earning the most money is our primary objective—is to take the $200,000 per year, as it's worth more than $2 million in today's dollars.

By the way, the decision is a close one. And if we were to be off by just a little bit on either the discount rate assumption (what we could earn on this money) or on our life expectancy, the correct answer could easily flip.

Regardless, unless those on social media believe that they could earn significantly more (or less) on their investments, or unless they believed that they would live significantly longer (or shorter), it's hardly obvious which decision is financially optimal without actually doing the math.

Next time you encounter this question, make sure you take the time to educate those who seem to be so sure of themselves!

REVISITING $2 MILLION VERSUS $200,000 PER YEAR

It can be difficult to get your head around the concept of time value of money and discounted cash flow analysis. And while it may take you more thought than just reading this part of the book, we find that one of the best ways to understand the results of our TVM problems is verifying our results using methods that rely more on common sense.

Here's how we might do that for the example of whether we'd rather have $2 million today or $200,000 for the next twenty-five years. Our DCF analysis says that $200,000 per year for the next twenty-five years is the better option, assuming an 8 percent discount rate. Let's verify this.

In the case where we were handed $2 million today, we know (based on our discount rate) that we could invest that money for an 8 percent compounded return. If we plug the numbers into a compound interest calculator (starting with $2 million, compounding annually at 8 percent for twenty-five years), we see that this bucket of money would grow to nearly $13.7 million over that twenty-five years.

Now, let's plug the $200,000 per year into that same compound interest calculator. Assuming we start with $0, then add $200,000 per year and compound annually for twenty-five years, this stream of income will grow to nearly $15.9 million over that time—$2.2 million more than if you took the $2 million today.

Turns out our DCF analysis was correct, and the $200,000 per year over twenty-five years is more profitable than just taking the $2 million in one lump sum.

HONE YOUR SKILLS: CHAPTER 9

- Why is a discounted cash flow analysis helpful for real estate investors?
- What is the discounted cash flow of an income stream that pays you $5,000 per year, for the next three years? Use an 8 percent discount rate.

CHAPTER 10
NET PRESENT VALUE (NPV)

Chapter 10 will help answer the questions:
- Is this deal profitable?
- Will the money I earn later justify a specific investment today?

The discounted cash flow analysis techniques we discussed in the previous chapter give us powerful insights into the present value of future cash flows. But DCF has a major limitation: It doesn't account for the initial investment. For real estate investors, this is the equivalent of looking at the present value of your future rent income, but without considering the purchase price of the property, closings costs, and other expenses that went into acquiring the property.

This is where the concept of net present value (NPV) comes in.

#39   **Net present value (NPV)** looks at the present value of all future cash flows generated by a project while considering the initial capital investment, in order to determine whether the investment will be profitable.

NPV allows us to look at the whole picture of an investment by factoring in these key inputs:
- How much money are you putting into an investment?
- How much money are you generating in return?
- When are your returns realized?
- What could you earn on your money if you invested it elsewhere (discount rate)?

By taking all of those inputs into account, NPV produces a single metric that tells us whether a deal will make us more or less money than our alternative investment (given that investment's discount rate).

Remember, NPV tells us the value of the investment in *today's* dollars, so we can compare it to *today's* cost of doing the investment. By now it should be clear that an investment can generate more money than it costs but still not be profitable, when considering TVM. For example, after reading Chapter 8, you wouldn't necessarily trade $1,000 now for $1,100 next year, right?

AN NPV EXAMPLE

To help demonstrate the power and importance of NPV, here's a real-life situation that I (J) encountered a few years back.

I had purchased a property with the intent of doing some minor repairs and planned to resell the property to another investor. The price of acquiring the property, closing costs, and completing the rehab totaled $77,000.

I put the property on the market and received an offer for $96,000. The offer was contingent on owner financing. Specifically, the prospective buyer was proposing that instead of giving me $96,000 all at once, he would instead pay me $800 per month for the next 120 months, putting nothing down.

Was this a good offer? A bad offer? Without NPV, it's difficult to say for sure.

INTEREST-FREE?

In the example we're currently discussing, some of you might be thinking, "He's offering you $96,000, but he wants an interest-free loan for ten years!" That is true. But in this instance, we shouldn't get hung up on interest rates and time frames.

Here's why.

Had this buyer offered me $300,000 for the property, with 120 payments of $2,500 per month, that would also be an interest-free loan—but I think we all agree it would be a much better deal.

Also keep in mind that if he had offered me a $70,000 purchase price with an interest rate of about 6.65 percent, that would also come out to 120 payments of $800 per month to pay off the loan (you can plug the numbers into an online mortgage calculator to verify). In this case, I'm getting a good interest rate, but I'm still making the exact same amount of money in the exact same amount of time.

For this reason, we shouldn't get caught up in the interest rate being offered with the payment. That doesn't tell us anything by itself. The key to understanding this deal lies in the time value of money.

As we know from the previous chapters—and specifically from our DCF examples—the fact that this buyer was offering me $96,000 over the next ten years means that the value of that $96,000 is *less* than if we were getting it all at once, today.

But exactly how much less?

If that $96,000 over ten years is equivalent to us getting $90,000 today, and we would be happy getting a $90,000 cash offer today, then that's not too bad. But, if that $96,000 over ten years is equivalent to getting $50,000 today, then we would essentially be losing money making this deal (remember, we are all in on this property for $77,000).

This is where the DCF analysis from the last chapter comes in. The DCF analysis can tell us exactly how much that stream of income over the next ten years is worth to us *today*. And NPV allows us to take that one step further, comparing the value of the entire income stream to the initial investment.

NPV is the sum of the present values of many future cash flows, including our initial investment(s). Let's run the NPV analysis on our $96,000 offer over ten years so we can see exactly how it works:

Discount Rate: 12%
Initial Cost: $77,000

	YEAR	CASH FLOW	PRESENT VALUE	FORMULA
1/1/20	0	$(77,000)	$(77,000)	
1/1/21	1	$9,600	$8,571	$PV = (9,600 \div (1+.12)^1$
1/1/22	2	$9,600	$7,653	$PV = (9,600 \div (1+.12)^2$
1/1/23	3	$9,600	$6,833	$PV = (9,600 \div (1+.12)^3$
1/1/24	4	$9,600	$6,101	$PV = (9,600 \div (1+.12)^4$
1/1/25	5	$9,600	$5,447	$PV = (9,600 \div (1+.12)^5$
1/1/26	6	$9,600	$4,864	$PV = (9,600 \div (1+.12)^6$
1/1/27	7	$9,600	$4,343	$PV = (9,600 \div (1+.12)^7$
1/1/28	8	$9,600	$3,877	$PV = (9,600 \div (1+.12)^8$
1/1/29	9	$9,600	$3,462	$PV = (9,600 \div (1+.12)^9$
1/1/30	10	$9,600	$3,091	$PV = (9,600 \div (1+.12)^{10}$
	NET PRESENT VALUE		**$(22,758)**	

Let's break down what we're looking at in this chart.

We start with our discount rate, which we set to 12 percent—this is what we believed we could earn on our money back then if we had received it all at once and invested it into a different property.

Next, we see our initial investment was $77,000, which is noted as a negative number (since it's money going out) in the row for Year 0. There are two things to note here:

1. Because NPV measures cash flow, any money you invest into your deal is treated as negative cash flow; and
2. We typically refer to the initial investment as happening in Year 0 instead of Year 1. The reason for that is that the initial investment is happening today—in today's dollars—and therefore doesn't get discounted.

To calculate NPV, all we need to do is calculate the present value for every year of cash flow—including the initial investment—and add them all together.

To make things a bit simpler in this example, we assumed that instead of getting monthly payments, we would receive all twelve payments at the end of each year. In Year 1, we collect $9,600 at the end of the year; applying our PV formula, we can calculate the PV of that $9,600 (the value if we received it today) to be $8,571. We can then do that same PV calculation for each subsequent year.

Quick Tip | **DCF versus NPV**

This NPV analysis is looking exactly like our DCF analysis, right? It's pretty much the same, with the exception that for NPV, we include the initial investment amount as part of our total. NPV is simply an application of DCF to provide additional valuable information on our deal.

When we add together all the PVs for each year (making sure to include the -$77,000 in Year 0), the net present value returns -$22,757.86.

The fact that the NPV result is a negative number tells us that if we were to make this investment (if we were to accept this deal), the value of all the payments over the next ten years in today's dollars would be worth less than our $77,000 investment. In other words, we would be losing money by accepting this deal.

Exactly how much would we be losing by accepting this offer?

Well, if we add up the PV sums for Years 1 through 10, we see that the present value (today's value) of all payments over the next ten years would be $54,242.14. In other words, accepting this offer of $9,600 per year for 10 years (total of $96,000 in payments) would be equivalent to accepting about $54,242 in cash right now. Would we accept $54,242 in cash right now on this deal? Given that we paid $77,000 for this property, accepting $54,242 right now would likely be a big mistake! And because $9,600 per year for ten years is the same as $54,242 right now (from a TVM standpoint), accepting that would be just as much of a mistake.

Note that the difference between our initial investment of $77,000 and the PV of the offer ($54,242.14) is $22,757.86—which is exactly the number our NPV formula spit out. Running the NPV calculation showed us that we'd be losing $22,575.86 in today's dollars by accepting this deal.

DISCOUNT RATE

The discount rate that we choose is a vital part of all TVM calculations. But this value can be tremendously difficult to approximate accurately, especially if we're not sure what we're comparing our investment to.

In some cases, discount rate will relate to opportunity cost—it will be the rate that we believe we can earn if we had the money now and were to invest it in another opportunity. In our example above, this is how we chose 12 percent. We believed we could earn that rate of return if we had the money in hand and invested in another opportunity available to us.

But, depending on the situation, discount rate could also represent something else.

For example, discount rate could be the rate at which we originally borrowed the funds for this project, and at which we are currently repaying the loan (we'll talk more about this later in the chapter). Or the discount rate could simply be the rate of return that we want to achieve to make the deal worthwhile to us.

Perhaps we did some retirement planning and determined that we needed to earn a 12 percent rate of return between now and retirement to hit our goals, so we use a 12 percent discount rate in our model. For this reason, discount rate is often referred to as the "hurdle" or "hurdle rate." It's the hurdle we have to surpass to achieve our required or desired rate of return.

INTERPRETING NPV RESULTS

One of the nice things about NPV is that the results are simple to interpret. If NPV is negative, you would lose money on the deal (taking the time value of the money into account). If NPV is positive, you would gain money on the deal.

Isn't that cool? This seemingly complex decision of whether to accept a set of future payments is made very simple by using NPV to determine what the equivalent value of those future payments would be if we were to receive a lump sum payment today.

A good rule of thumb is that if NPV is positive, it's an opportunity you should consider pursuing. If the NPV is negative, it's an opportunity that should be ruled out (or renegotiated).

This type of computation is not just useful for calculating the viability of owner-financed deals—it should also be used for BRRRR (buy, rehab, rent, refinance, repeat) investments, traditional rentals, short-term rentals, and many others. Any deal where you have multiple inflows and outflows of cash over an extended period of time (pretty much all real estate deals!) can warrant an NPV analysis.

NPV: CHECKING OUR WORK

Before moving on, let's look at one more thing that might bring this whole concept of NPV into better focus.

Knowing that the NPV of our potential deal was -$22,758 tells us that the total value of the sum of all the future payments in today's dollars is about ($77,000 − $22,758) = $54,242. In other words, the value of all those future payments would be about $54,242 in today's dollars.

That means if we happened to have been all in to our deal for $54,242 (instead of $77,000) and were offered the same seller financing deal, we'd essentially be breaking even by taking it.

And, to verify that, we can plug the numbers back into our Excel spreadsheet, using the initial cost of $54,242.14 rather than $77,000.

Discount Rate: 12%
Initial Cost: $54,242

	YEAR	CASH FLOW	PRESENT VALUE
1/1/20	0	$(54,242)	$(54,242)
1/1/21	1	$9,600	$8,571
1/1/22	2	$9,600	$7,653
1/1/23	3	$9,600	$6,833
1/1/24	4	$9,600	$6,101
1/1/25	5	$9,600	$5,447
1/1/26	6	$9,600	$4,864
1/1/27	7	$9,600	$4,343
1/1/28	8	$9,600	$3,877
1/1/29	9	$9,600	$3,462
1/1/30	10	$9,600	$3,091
	NET PRESENT VALUE	$0.00	$0.00

As we had suspected would happen in this scenario, the NPV goes to 0.

We have confirmed that, with an initial investment of $54,242, we would have broken even had we accepted the offer provided.

USING NPV TO ANALYZE A FINANCED DEAL

In our NPV example, we chose a discount rate that was equivalent to the rate of return that we believed we could generate from an alternative investment. But in the investing and finance world, we're often dealing with projects that are financed through debt. When financing a deal, the question often isn't "Do the returns on this investment beat out the returns on an alternative investment?" Instead, the question is often "Are the returns on this investment enough to surpass our cost of debt?"

Let's look at a quick example.

Let's say that we have the opportunity to invest $100,000 in a deal that would return $2,000 per year for four years, and then $130,000 in Year 5.

Further, let's say that we didn't currently have the cash to make this investment, but we knew that we could take out a home equity line of credit (HELOC) on our personal residence to acquire the $100,000 to invest. (If you're unfamiliar with a HELOC, for now all you need to know is that it's a common type of loan. We'll discuss this in detail in Part 4.) The interest rate on the HELOC in this example would be 5 percent.

Does it make sense to borrow money against our personal residence at 5 percent interest for this investment? NPV can give us that answer:

Discount Rate: 5%
Initial Cost: $100,000

	YEAR	CASH FLOW	PRESENT VALUE
1/1/20	0	($100,000)	($100,000)
1/1/21	1	$2,000	$1,905
1/1/22	2	$2,000	$1,814
1/1/23	3	$2,000	$1,728
1/1/24	4	$2,000	$1,645
1/1/25	5	$130,000	$101,858
		NET PRESENT VALUE	$8,950.30

Our NPV in this scenario is positive. In other words, we would make money—in today's dollars—by borrowing $100,000 at 5 percent interest for five years to do this deal. Specifically, the return on this deal would surpass our hurdle (discount rate) of 5 percent interest on the loan we took out to fund the deal.

From a purely financial perspective, we should be willing to do this deal.

NET PRESENT VALUE RULE

In business, there is a concept called the "net present value rule." In essence, this is the idea that a company should only invest in and undertake projects with a positive NPV. Further, they should always avoid investing in projects that have a negative NPV.

At this point, it should be clear why NPV can be a great tool for companies to make investment decisions. But companies that abide by the NPV rule take it to the next level, using NPV for every investment decision and following the math provided by the analysis.

When I (J) worked at eBay several years ago, the NPV rule was in full effect at the company. Every project—whether a small user interface change to the website or a multi-year company initiative, and everything in between—would go through an NPV analysis that would drive the decision of whether the project should be pursued or not.

HONE YOUR SKILLS: CHAPTER 10

- What input does net present value consider that discounted cash flow does not?
- What does a positive NPV indicate about an investment? What does a negative NPV indicate?
- Consider an investment that costs $50,000 up front, earns you $1,500 per year for four years, and then generates $60,000 at sale. With a 7 percent discount rate, what is the NPV of this investment? Should you consider this deal?

INTERNAL RATE OF RETURN (IRR)

Chapter 11 will help answer the questions:
- How profitable will the deal be when taking TVM into account?
- What is my time-weighted compound annual growth rate?

In the last chapter, we discussed using net present value (NPV) to determine whether an investment made sense to pursue. Remember, if NPV is positive, it's an investment that will make us money. If NPV is negative, it's an investment that's going to lose us money (in today's dollars).

Whether an investment opportunity will make us money is obviously a tremendously important question to answer. But once we know that an investment is good, we start to ask ourselves an equally important question: How good is it?

This is where internal rate of return (IRR) comes in. To start, IRR can tell us how profitable an investment is. And just as importantly, IRR can help us evaluate investments with variable inflows and outflows of capital over time. Specifically, IRR is a value that indicates the compounded return of the investment over time, given the different timing of money going in and money coming out of the project.

As you might be able to guess from that description, IRR is reliant on TVM concepts, and—as we'll see in a bit—is deeply entangled with NPV.

To explain, let's go back to the last example in the previous chapter, where we asked whether it would make sense to borrow $100,000 against our personal residence at 5 percent interest to invest in an opportunity that would pay us $2,000 per year for four years, and then $130,000 in year five.

This was our NPV analysis, which calculated a positive NPV—indicating the investment was worth pursuing and our return would surpass the 5 percent hurdle (discount rate) of the loan:

Discount Rate: 5%
Initial Cost: $100,000

	YEAR	CASH FLOW	PRESENT VALUE
1/1/20	0	($100,000)	($100,000)
1/1/21	1	$2,000	$1,905
1/1/22	2	$2,000	$1,814
1/1/23	3	$2,000	$1,728
1/1/24	4	$2,000	$1,645
1/1/25	5	$130,000	$101,858
		NET PRESENT VALUE	$8,950.30

NPV indicated that this deal is worth pursuing, but it doesn't answer the question of how worth pursuing it is. It tells us that our return would beat 5 percent, but it doesn't tell us exactly how much it would beat 5 percent or what the actual rate of return would be.

Except that it can!

By identifying the discount rate where the NPV = 0, we can isolate the exact compounded rate of return we should expect on this investment.

In this example, the discount rate that would get NPV = 0 is 6.87 percent. Yes, we're cheating a bit here by just telling you the discount rate is 6.87 percent, but this will us help explain the concept of IRR.

We'll return to how we got that 6.87 percent in just a minute, but first, let's rerun the NPV analysis just to verify that number is accurate.

Discount Rate: 6.87%
Initial Cost: $100,000

	YEAR	CASH FLOW	PRESENT VALUE
1/1/20	0	$(100,000)	$(100,000)
1/1/21	1	$2,000	$1,871
1/1/22	2	$2,000	$1,751
1/1/23	3	$2,000	$1,638
1/1/24	4	$2,000	$1,533
1/1/25	5	$130,000	$93,241
		NET PRESENT VALUE	$0

Knowing the discount rate that makes the NPV = 0 tells us the compounded rate of return for this particular investment. And that compounded rate of return equals the discount rate.

In other words, if we were to invest in this specific deal, we should expect a compounded annual return of exactly 6.87 percent. We already knew it was higher than 5 percent because the NPV for this deal was positive, but now we know exactly what it is—which is essential when comparing investments against one another.

The name of the specific discount rate that makes NPV = 0 is the IRR.

The IRR on this deal is 6.87 percent.

#40   **Internal rate of return (IRR)** is the discount rate that makes NPV = 0 for an investment; IRR is the compounded return of that investment.

IRR is both a discount rate and a rate of return metric. Here we talk about how it's a discount rate; in the next section of the book, we'll talk about IRR as a return metric. In other words, we'll discuss how we can use IRR to analyze deals to determine whether they might be worth pursuing. IRR is one of the most common return metrics used in commercial real estate (and even some residential real estate) analysis, so it's important to understand both where it comes from and how it's used.

For now, the key takeaways are where IRR comes from (again, the discount rate that makes an NPV analysis equal to zero) and how it relates to the concept of TVM.

CALCULATING IRR

Much like NPV, it's possible to use brute force to calculate an IRR. You can start with the NPV analysis for the investment, and then keep tweaking the discount rate until the NPV = 0. This is horribly tedious, though, and is probably more work than most of us want to do for every deal we analyze.

In addition, the math required to do an IRR analysis by hand is not for the faint of heart. Luckily, we have spreadsheets these days, and any decent spreadsheet is going to have a set of functions that will calculate IRR for you at the touch of a button.

Going back to our previous example, once we have the list of cash flows and the dates associated with them, we can use the XIRR( ) function in Excel to easily calculate the IRR of this investment.

	YEAR	CASH FLOW
1/1/2020	0	($100,000)
1/1/2021	1	$2,000
1/1/2022	2	$2,000
1/1/2023	3	$2,000
1/1/2024	4	$2,000
1/1/2025	5	$130,000
	IRR	6.88%

Remember when we cheated before and told you the discount rate that got NPV to equal zero in our example? This is how we figured it out. We used the XIRR( ) function in Excel. We recommend doing it this way, rather than attempting it by hand. If you're unfamiliar with Excel or you want to master the use of this function, there are many great tutorials online that will show you how to properly use this function. And if you jump into the bonus Excel file that comes with the book (www.biggerpockets.com/numbersbonus), you can play with the numbers yourself!

Quick Tip | **XIRR()**

In Microsoft Excel, there are several IRR functions. The one we use most commonly is the XIRR() function, as it's very simple. The syntax is =XIRR(values, dates, [guess]), where values = cash flow values, and dates = the dates you will receive those cash flows. The guess is optional, and we're not going to get into that here. For our example, the cash flows were in cells c2:c7, and the dates were in cells a2:a7; therefore, the formula in Excel would look like =XIRR(c2:c7, a2:a7).

C8	▲▼	✕ ✓	*fx*	=XIRR(C2:C7, A2:A7)
	A	**B**		**C**
1		Year		Cashflow
2	1/1/20	0		($100,000)
3	1/1/21	1		$2,000
4	1/1/22	2		$2,000
5	1/1/23	3		$2,000
6	1/1/24	4		$2,000
7	1/1/25	5		$130,000
8		**IRR**		**6.87%**

We're now at the end of our explanation of the time value of money and the many calculations and concepts that help us understand TVM. We recognize these concepts can be difficult to understand, and you should applaud yourself for taking the time to thoroughly learn about TVM. We promise it will be worth it. You cannot be a great investor without these tools, and in Part 3 we're going to show you how to apply these theories to your own investing.

Before we do that, we need to shift gears quickly and talk about a different set of concepts that are important for investors to understand: taxes. In Chapters 12 and 13, we'll give you an overview of real estate investing tax concepts to ensure you have a firm grasp of all the fundamentals of investing before moving into Part 3.

HONE YOUR SKILLS: CHAPTER 11

- What is a simple way to describe what IRR measures?
- What is the relationship between IRR and NPV?
- What is the IRR of an investment that costs $75,000 up front, earns you $22,000 per year for four years, and then generates $115,000 at sale?

CHAPTER 12
INTRODUCTION TO REAL ESTATE TAXES

Chapter 12 will help answer the questions:
- What types of real estate deals are tax advantaged?
- How are taxes calculated for a rental property?

With the complexities and nuances of the U.S. tax code, along with ever-changing tax laws, it can be difficult to write about taxes and their implications without risking that information being outdated at some point. That said, a book on real estate math just wouldn't be complete without discussing this topic and providing an overview of how investors are impacted by taxes.

The truth is, taxes tend to be a blind spot for many investors—even the most seasoned ones. As we were developing the outline for this book, we were talking about taxes and realized we share a common regret about our respective investing careers: We both waited too long to understand how taxes impact our returns.

We want to make sure other investors don't make the same mistake. Even if you're just starting out, understanding the relationship between real estate and taxes is vital and will make you a more successful investor.

While we will do our best to give an overview of the important aspects of tax law as it relates to us as investors, keep in mind that any or all of what we write below could be out of date at any point, including at the time this book is published. So, we do recommend that you consult with a qualified tax professional when trying to determine the specific impact the tax law will have on you and your business.

It's worth mentioning as well that BiggerPockets Publishing has two books on this subject—*The Book on Tax Strategies for the Savvy Real Estate Investor* and *The Book on Advanced Tax Strategies*—by tax experts Amanda Han and Matthew MacFarland. If you really want to use the U.S. tax system to your benefit, these books are an excellent resource to help you be a top-notch, money-saving investor.

TAX FOR FLIP PROPERTIES VERSUS RENTAL PROPERTIES

First, we want to clear up what may be the most prevailing myth of real estate investing and taxes—that any time you are doing real estate deals, you are getting tax benefits. While certain forms of real estate investing are tremendously tax advantaged, other forms are not. In fact, some types of real estate income are likely to be taxed even higher than your salary or other non–real estate income!

Specifically, properties that are bought and sold for profit (for example, fix-and-flip deals or wholesale deals) are treated much differently from a tax perspective than properties that are bought for investment purposes (for example, buy-and-hold rentals). And while buy-and-hold investing provides several tax benefits, buying with the intent to resell for a profit is typically not a very good way to reduce your tax burden.

There are some exceptions, but the IRS typically considers buying and reselling property to be an active investment strategy that generates *ordinary* income. Conversely, the IRS typically considers the buying and holding of capital assets (assets that are expected to appreciate and provide value over a long period of time) to be a non-active investment strategy that generates *passive* income.

Ordinary income is taxed similarly to salaried job income, consulting income, or business income—the earner will pay income taxes on their profits at their marginal tax rate. The more ordinary income you earn, the higher the tax bracket you'll find yourself in, and the more tax you'll pay on that top level of income.

In other words, if you're in the business of flipping houses or wholesaling properties, you should expect to pay taxes at whatever rate that corresponds to the tax bracket you are in, no different than if you were working a 9-to-5 job. On top of that, since this income will typically be considered business income, you may also be subject to self-employment taxes (Social Security and Medicare) as well, which could be up to another 15 percent of that income in owed taxes!

Long story short, flipping houses is not going to provide tax benefits. When you hear about the tax advantages of investing in real estate, these aren't advantages that house flippers are enjoying. In fact, house flippers often pay *more* in taxes than they would if they were simply earning money as employees.

On the other hand, passive income generated by buying and holding capital investments provides several tax benefits, and the long-term profits earned on the eventual sale of those investments is typically going to be taxed at a rate lower than your marginal tax rate.

WHAT IS YOUR INTENT?

One of the big questions we get asked when it comes to taxation of real estate income is whether it's possible to get around the high taxes incurred by flipping houses by spending a longer amount of time on the flip (for example, spending more than one year on the project, making it appear to be a buy-and-hold capital investment).

When determining whether income earned from a real estate investment is likely to be considered active or passive, the IRS will often look at the original *intent* for that purchase—meaning they will attempt to determine whether the purchaser originally planned to buy the property to resell for a profit or planned to hold the property as a long-term investment. If the intent of the purchaser was to buy and resell, then it doesn't matter if the property was held for one month, one year, or ten years—it will still likely be subject to active income tax rates (ordinary taxes at the investor's marginal tax rate).

How does the IRS determine intent, and how do you prove intent?

It's a great question, and one you should discuss with your tax adviser. In general, the IRS is going to look at several things.

What is your track record, both overall and within the entity the property is held? Did you flip ten properties last year and hold no rentals? If so, the IRS is going to be more likely to assume your next property is a flip and not a rental, as there is no evidence to the contrary. Do you have an LLC with five rental properties in it and have never flipped a house? If so, the IRS is more likely to determine that a property you purchased in that entity is a rental, assuming there is no evidence to the contrary.

The IRS will also look at things like:
- How long was the property held?
- Was there ever a tenant in the property?
- Did you market the property as a rental?
- Did you engage a property management company at any point?
- Did you advertise to sell the property prior to completing renovation?

Long story short, it's important to know your intent for a property up front, and—especially if the plan is to buy and hold—document and accumulate evidence of your intent. If you are ever audited, having documentation and other evidence of your intent may be helpful.

And again, please consult with a qualified tax professional before undertaking any investment strategy.

By the way, just because flipping isn't a great way to directly shelter or reduce taxes doesn't mean that there aren't financial (and tax) benefits associated with a flipping business. For example, as an "active" business, a house-flipping business can create and fund retirement accounts, and those retirement accounts can be used to reduce and/or defer taxes. This is an advantage that rental property investors can't benefit from.

TWO TYPES OF TAXES ON RENTAL PROPERTY

As an investor holding rental property or other capital assets, you should expect to pay taxes both annually (on the net income generated by the property) and at the sale of the property (on the profit generated over the life of the project).

 | **Property Taxes**

In this section, we're talking about the taxes that you—the investor—pay on profits earned from rental property investing. That said, as a rental property investor, you will also pay property tax on any properties you own. Property taxes are an unavoidable operating expense for your business, and there are no important concepts or advantages to discuss regarding property tax.

We're not avoiding the concept of property taxes; they are a completely different discussion, and one that is better suited for a different part of the book. In this chapter, we'll focus on how profits are taxed, and we'll revisit property tax again in Part 5 during our discussion of deal analysis.

Let's look at how each of these taxable amounts is determined.

Annual Taxable Income

Let's start with the general formula for calculating what the annual taxable income will be for a capital investment, like a rental property.

#41	**Taxable income**
	Taxable income = NOI – Mortgage interest – Depreciation – Amortization

You probably recognize all those words from previous discussions in this book, but it's worth digging in a bit more to understand exactly what they mean in the context of calculating our taxable income.

Net Operating Income (NOI)

We talked back in Part 1 about net operating income (NOI). As a reminder, this is the cash generated after subtracting all operating expenses from the income received. NOI is a great starting point for determining taxable income; from that, we need to subtract three other amounts: mortgage interest, depreciation, and amortization.

Mortgage Interest

When you make a mortgage payment, some portion of the payment is made up of principal and some is made up of interest. We'll talk about this in great detail in Chapter 30 ("The Anatomy of a Loan"), but for now, just know that for a capital investment, the interest portion of each mortgage payment is deductible from your NOI before determining taxable income. Note that the entire mortgage payment is not deductible—just the interest portion of the payment. You benefit from the principal part of the mortgage payment in another way. Specifically, when you sell or refinance the property, the amount you spend to pay off the loan is reduced by the principal payments you had previously made.

Luckily, you don't have to figure out the allocation of principal and interest yourself. Your lender(s) should send you an IRS Form 1098 at the end of each year indicating the amount of interest paid for the year, and this number will be used for your mortgage interest deduction. If you have multiple loans against a property, you will receive multiple Form 1098s, and each interest amount will be deductible in that year.

Depreciation

As a real estate investor buying and holding rental property, you are likely going to hear the term *depreciation* a lot. That's because depreciation is one of the most advantageous ways real estate helps reduce and defer taxes. In fact, when you read about big-time real estate investors who make tons of money, but pay little in taxes, depreciation is likely playing a big role in that accomplishment.

Even as a small-time investor, you can use this amazing tax benefit to pay less tax now, allowing you to use the savings to reinvest and grow your portfolio.

So, what is depreciation and how does it work?

Depreciation is the term we use in the financial world to describe the decline in the condition and value of an asset over time. In real estate, the physical structure(s) sitting on a piece of land will decline in condition over the years, and the government gives us a tax deduction (depreciation) that we can use to account for this decline.

Specifically, this tax deduction only applies to the cost of the physical structure, and the tax benefit is divided equally over a set period—27.5 years for residential property and 39 years for commercial property.

As an example, if you own a single-family rental property where the physical structure costs $200,000, the IRS allows you to depreciate (take a tax deduction for) that $200,000 value over 27.5 years. The annual depreciation deduction amount would be $200,000 ÷ 27.5 = $7,272.73.

In other words, for each year you hold that property in service as a rental, the government is going to allow you to deduct $7,272.73 from your NOI when determining your taxable income. Because this deduction doesn't come out of your bank account—there's no actual cost to you—we often refer to depreciation as a "paper" deduction.

There are two important things to note about depreciation:

1. Depreciation isn't a way to eliminate your tax burden; it's just a way to push it off until the time you sell the property. You will have to "recapture" any depreciation you were entitled to at the time you sell. We'll talk about how this is done in the next section.

2. Even if you don't claim your depreciation deduction each year, the IRS will assume you did, and you will be responsible for recapturing that deduction at sale. So, make sure you take your maximum depreciation each year!

#42 **Depreciation** is a tax deduction or write-off that accounts for the declining condition of a physical property. It allows real estate investors to delay a portion of their income taxes for a given property until that property is sold.

Amortization

In this case, amortization doesn't refer to the principal portion of your loan that you're paying down each month. Here, amortization refers to certain expenses associated with a loan you take out on your property that must be deducted over a period of time, as opposed to all at once in the year they were incurred.

#43 **Amortization** refers to tax deductions for loan costs that are taken over a period of time, as opposed to all at once.

A good example is the refinance of a mortgage loan. When you refinance a loan against a property, you will often pay a fee for the loan—sometimes called "points" or "discount points." These fees typically represent interest that is paid up front to originate the loan, and as such, these fees are deductible (as are all interest payments!). However, any points paid up front are often not deductible all at once in the year the loan was received. Instead, these fees are typically deducted (amortized) across the entire term of the loan.

As an example, say you refinanced a loan for one of your rentals, and the total points paid on the refinance was $5,000. If the new loan term is twenty years, you will likely be able to deduct $5,000 ÷ 20 = $250 per year, every year, over the twenty-year period.

This deduction reduces your taxable income for that rental property each year for the life of the loan.

Taxable Income Example

Let's look at an example of how to determine taxable income on a rental property.

Assume you purchase a five-unit building for $1 million that you plan to hold long term as a rental property. In Year 1, let's assume the NOI on this property is $61,428.

Looking at the Form 1098 your lender sent you, you see that the total amount of interest paid on your loan in Year 1 was $32,817.

Examining the county tax assessment, you estimate the structure value is about 73 percent of the total property value. You purchased the property for $1 million, so you assume that the cost of the structure is $1,000,000 × 73% = $730,000.

Because this is a residential property, you can depreciate that $730,000 over 27.5 years, which is an annual depreciation of $730,000 ÷ 27.5 = $26,545.

Finally, you paid $13,000 in points on your twenty-five-year loan. Your accountant says that you can amortize those points at $13,000 ÷ 25 = $520 per year.

To determine your taxable income, use the taxable income formula:

$$\text{Taxable income} = \text{NOI} - \frac{\text{Mortgage}}{\text{interest}} - \text{Depreciation} - \frac{\text{Points}}{\text{amortization}}$$

Taxable income = $61,428 − $32,817 − $26,545 − $520
Taxable income = $1,546

Looking at your total income for the year (including all other sources), you determine that you are in the 24 percent marginal income tax bracket, so you can expect to pay about $1,546 × 24% = $371 in taxes on your property income for this year. Not bad given that your NOI was over $60,000!

NOI	**$61,428**
Interest Paid	**$32,817**
Purchase Price	$1,000,000
Structure Value (%)	73%
Structure Cost ($)	$730,000
Depreciation Period (Years)	27.5
Depreciation ($)	**$26,545**
Mortgage "Points"	$13,000
Amortization Period (Years)	25
Amortization ($)	**$520**
Taxable Income	**$1,546**
Tax Rate	24%
Taxes Owed	$370.93

CAPITAL GAINS AT SALE

In addition to paying taxes annually on the income generated by the property, you will incur a tax burden on any gain (profits) generated by the property between the time of purchase and the time of sale.

For those inexperienced with the U.S. tax code, this may seem simple: Just subtract the purchase price from the sale price to determine your profit, right?

Unfortunately, nothing is that simple when it comes to the tax code.

When determining your profit on the sale of a property, you must start by determining the cost basis for the property. The cost basis (or just "basis") is generally the purchase price of the property, plus the legal costs (e.g., title fees, recording fees, survey) and any transfer taxes associated with the purchase.

 #44 Basis (or "cost basis") is the starting point for the tax liability associated with selling a property. It is generally defined as the purchase price plus any closing costs.

As an example, if you purchase a single-family house for $250,000 and pay $5,000 in legal fees, closing costs, and transfer taxes, your cost basis for that property is going to be $255,000.

Purchase Price	$250,000
Closing Costs	$5,000
Basis	**$255,000**

Next, your cost basis will increase based on the capital improvements you make to the property over the years. Operating expenses, including maintenance costs, are deductible in the year they are incurred. But capital expenses (large renovation items that extend the life of the property, like replacing a roof or HVAC system, performing a full cosmetic renovation between tenants, and so on) are not deductible. Instead, those costs will increase your basis.

On your hypothetical property above, let's assume that you spend $45,000 on capital expenses throughout the hold period of the property. Your basis has now increased from $255,000 to $300,000.

This basis is going to change over time, based on several costs and credits. We refer to this running total of the basis as the *adjusted basis*.

 #45 Adjusted basis is the end point for the tax liability associated with selling a property. It adjusts the "basis" by accounting for capital expenditures, sales costs, and depreciation.

For example, we mentioned earlier that depreciation—the paper loss you get each year to account for the deterioration of your property—must be *recaptured* at sale. This is done by subtracting the depreciation you were entitled to from your adjusted basis, thereby lowering your adjusted basis, and increasing your potential future gain at sale.

Going back to our example property, if you owned the property for five years and were entitled to $30,000 in depreciation over those five years, your adjusted basis would decrease from $300,000 to $270,000.

Finally, when you sell the property, all legal costs, title fees, commissions, and transfer taxes will be added to your adjusted basis. Assuming you sell the example property for $400,000 and pay $35,000 in selling costs, your adjusted basis would increase from $270,000 to $305,000.

To put it all together, your adjusted basis is defined as purchase price + purchase costs + capital expenditures + selling costs − depreciation.

#46 **Adjusted basis formula**
Adjusted basis = Purchase price + Purchase costs + Capital expenditures + Selling costs − Depreciation

Purchase Price	$250,000
Purchase Costs	$5,000
Capital Expenditures	$45,000
Sellings Costs	$35,000
Depreciation ($)	($30,000)
Adjusted Basis	**$305,000**

To determine your taxable gain/loss (the amount on which you will be required to pay capital gains tax), you subtract your adjusted basis from your sale price.

#47 **Taxable gain/Loss at sale**
Taxable gain/Loss at sale = Sale price − Adjusted basis

In this example, our sale price was $400,000 and our adjusted basis was $305,000, so our taxable gain/loss at sale is calculated as follows:

Taxable Gain/Loss at Sale = $400,000 − $305,000
Taxable Gain/Loss at Sale = $95,000

This example shows a taxable gain of $95,000. If our adjusted basis had been greater than the sales price, we would then have a loss at sale. Barring any other deductions that you may be entitled to (for example, if you didn't fully amortize your points, you are entitled to deduct the remaining balance), this taxable gain will determine your tax liability.

Specifically, this taxable gain will be broken into two parts:
1. The depreciation taken
2. The balance of the taxable gain

In this case, the depreciation taken was $30,000, so $30,000 of our gain is treated as depreciation recapture. The balance of the gain, $65,000, is treated as a capital gain.

The depreciation is generally recaptured (taxed) at your marginal tax rate or at 25 percent—whichever is lower. The remainder of the taxable gain is taxed at your capital gains rate, which is usually 15 percent (assuming you earn below ~$460,000 per year, or below ~$517,000 per year if you're married, filing jointly).

In our example, you are in the 24 percent tax bracket, so you would owe $30,000 × 24% = $7,200 in tax on the recaptured depreciation, and $65,000 × 15% = $9,750 in capital gains tax on the remainder of the gain. This is a total federal tax burden of $7,200 + $9,750 = $16,950. (Note that you may incur state and/or municipal taxes as well.)

Sale Price	$400,000
Adjusted Basis	$305,000
Taxable Gain	**$95,000**
Depreciation Recapture	$30,000
Depreciation Recapture Rate	24%
Depreciation Recapture Owed	**$7,200**
Capital Gains	$65,000
Capital Gains Tax Rate	15%
Capital Gains Tax Owed	$9,750
Total Tax Owed	**$16,950**

HONE YOUR SKILLS: CHAPTER 12

- True or false: All types of real estate investments are tax-advantaged.
- What is the annual depreciation for a residential property with a cost of $385,000?
- What would your adjusted basis be for a property that cost $400,000 and had $25,000 in purchase costs, $40,000 in capital expenses, $30,000 in sales costs, and $45,000 of depreciation?

CHAPTER 13
TAX BENEFITS OF REAL ESTATE

Chapter 13 will help answer the questions:
- Why should I try to defer taxes?
- How can I delay or reduce my taxes?

One of the biggest benefits of real estate investment is the potential tax benefits. We've already talked about the ability to generate paper losses year after year without any hit to your actual income (through depreciation). And we also discussed the tax advantage of buying and holding—the ability to pay capital gains, which is often taxed at a lower rate than ordinary income.

There are several other ways that we can either reduce and/or defer (put off) our tax burden using strategies offered to us through real estate investing. We will examine a few of those below.

FOUR REASONS TO ATTEMPT TO REDUCE/DEFER TAXES

Before we go into some of the strategies that we can use to reduce or defer taxes, it's important to understand why doing so is helpful in the first place. Most of us talk about the importance of reducing and deferring taxes, but having spoken with a lot of investors over the years, we've found that the majority of them never really consider why it's valuable.

Worse yet, many of the investors we have spoken with—and admittedly, this sometimes applies to us as well—don't prioritize the tax reduction and deferment nearly as much as they might if they understood how that reduction and deferment could help them achieve their long-term financial goals.

Let's quickly look at the four big reasons why we should care about lowering our tax burden, and the specific benefits doing so can provide us.

1. Boost compounded returns

Remember our discussion from earlier in the book: Money today is worth more than money tomorrow. Pushing off paying taxes until tomorrow (or, better yet, twenty years from now) allows us to reinvest those dollars today to boost our returns over the long term.

2. Pay taxes in inflated dollars

Again, thanks to inflation, a dollar tomorrow is worth less than a dollar today. Paying your taxes later means paying less in today's dollars. Assuming a rate of inflation of 2.5 percent per year, a dollar today is going to be worth less than 50 cents in the time it takes to pay off a thirty-year mortgage. Deferring your taxes for thirty years can cut the total hit to your net worth in half!

3. Wait for more favorable tax laws

Tax laws are always changing, and there's a chance that putting off paying may allow you to take advantage of future tax benefits that don't exist today. Don't get us wrong, taxes at the time of this writing (2022) are at historical lows, but real estate investors have been fortunate to receive some amazing tax breaks over the years, and we are hoping that future tax advantages are even better. (Of course, the flip side is always a risk—tax laws can get less favorable!

4. Perhaps put it off completely

While we may not like to think about it, one day we will die. If we can defer taxes long enough, we may never have to pay those taxes ourselves. And depending on other changes to the tax code and our ability to structure our asset holdings in the best possible way, we may be able to reduce, defer, or even eliminate the payment of taxes on our gains long after we're gone.

WAYS TO REDUCE/DEFER TAXES

There are many strategies for reducing and deferring taxes, and while we don't intend the following to be an exhaustive list, it will hopefully give you some ideas on how you can reduce and/or defer taxes on your real estate holdings as much and as long as possible. (Note that our tax code can—and will—change. Before undertaking any of the strategies we discuss below, ensure that you consult a qualified tax professional.)

1031 Exchange

Under Section 1031 of the United States Internal Revenue Code, we have the legal ability to *exchange* a piece of real property for another, similar piece of property, putting off having to pay any taxes we would otherwise incur for selling that first property. Think of this as real-life Monopoly, where we can trade smaller assets (four house pieces) for a larger asset (one hotel piece), without having to pay taxes until we sell that larger asset. If we're smart, we can trade that larger asset at some point in the future, pushing off taxes even further. There are some very specific rules around how 1031 exchanges must be completed, so be sure to consult a qualified tax adviser before attempting this strategy.

INVESTOR STORY
1031 in Practice

I (Dave) sold a multi-unit building a few years ago and embarked on my first 1031 exchange. One of the key rules about 1031s is that the time between selling a property and identifying a new property is fixed. At the time of this writing, you have just forty-five days to find a new investment in which to put the proceeds of your sale. I found a deal that I liked in a close-by neighborhood and confidently proceeded through my due diligence and closing process, excited about the tax savings I was going to get on this new great deal.

That is, until my real estate agent figured out that the seller had not disclosed some crucial information about the property, and I had to pull out of the deal—with only ten days until the 1031 deadline.

I started to panic; I didn't want to lose out on this incredible tax advantage. Luckily, I go to open houses and look at listings for fun, and I knew of a property with good return prospects that I could still try to get under contract. When I ran the numbers, though, the return was a bit lower than I would normally accept. I didn't know what to do. I didn't want to lower my standards for a deal, but I also didn't want to lose my ability to defer taxes by using a 1031 exchange.

Thankfully, before the deadline to identify a new property passed, I realized that I was thinking about this problem all wrong. I was seeing the tax deferment and the deal analysis as separate when, in reality, they should be looked at together. When I finally looked at the long-term impact of doing this deal with a 1031 exchange, my opinion of the deal changed completely. Doing a deal with "good" cash flow and a 1031 was far superior to waiting for a deal with "excellent" cash flow and no 1031. I was still earning a good return, and because I was deferring a large amount of taxes, I was able to put more money to work. It was a no-brainer, and I did the deal.

This experience taught me a valuable lesson about real estate investing and taxes—one I wish I had learned earlier in my investing career. Taxes cannot be an afterthought for investors; they should be a key component of your deal analysis and your larger investing strategy. It's not just about how much return you can *generate*. It's about how much return you can *keep* and *reinvest*.

Of course, I wish my first deal hadn't fallen through, but I have no complaints with how this deal has worked out.

Personal Residence Exclusion

One of the simplest ways to benefit from real estate tax advantages is by using your personal residence exemption, also known as the Section 121 exclusion. (That's the section of the tax code that addresses this benefit.) The personal residence exemption allows you to sell your personal residence and avoid having to pay taxes on the first $250,000 in gain ($500,000 if you're married), so long as you have owned and lived in the property for at least two of the previous five years. There are many investors who take advantage of this exemption by selling their personal residence every two years. We're not saying you have to do this, but it's something to consider.

Hold for a Minimum of One Year (and a Day!)

Remember, when selling a capital investment, you will pay capital gains tax. But not all capital gains taxes are created equal. If you have held the property for *less* than a year and a day, you will pay taxes at the short-term capital gains rate, which is substantially higher than if you have held for *at least* a year and a day, where long-term capital gains kicks in.

Invest from a Self-Directed IRA

There are lots of rules and regulations that you need to understand to avoid penalties and prohibited transactions when investing out of your retirement account. However, when done correctly, investing out of a tax-advantaged account, like a self-directed IRA, can provide substantial tax benefits. Make sure to consult a good tax professional before doing so, as certain types of IRA investments can still trigger a tax burden. But this may be a great way to put your old 401k or IRA to work for you.

Sell When Your Income Is Low

Remember, part of your depreciation recapture will be taxed at 25 percent or your current marginal tax bracket rate, whichever is lower. But by timing the sale of a capital investment for when your total income is low (and your marginal tax rate is lower than 25 percent), you can reduce the amount of depreciation recapture you might pay when selling a property.

Installment Sales
An installment sale is the sale of an asset where at least one of the payments for the purchase is received in a tax year following the sale. By not receiving the entire purchase price in the year of the sale, you may have the ability to defer part of your tax burden to future years. This can allow you to reduce your income in any one year to reduce your total tax owed, or perhaps to move some portion of your tax burden to a year where your total income is lower, and you can reduce your depreciation recapture burden.

Qualified Opportunity Zones
A qualified opportunity zone (QOZ) is an economically distressed community where investments may be eligible for preferential tax treatment. Specifically, when taking the proceeds from the sale of a capital investment and reinvesting in a QOZ, you may be able to defer paying the capital gains for several years that otherwise would have been owed upon the sale of the original investment. If you're interested in a QOZ opportunity, we would recommend talking to a qualified tax professional who specializes in these types of investments.

There are lots of nuances to how real estate can provide tax advantages to investors, and this section was by no means intended to be comprehensive. But hopefully this gives you a good overview of what you can expect from a tax perspective when buying and selling real estate investments, and hopefully it encourages you to dig into these strategies that allow you to reduce, defer, and possibly even eliminate your tax burden.

HONE YOUR SKILLS: CHAPTER 13
- What are four reasons you should consider deferring taxes?
- What is a 1031 exchange?
- Why should you hold property for at least one year and a day?

PART 2
CONCLUSION

I n Part 2, we began a discussion about how to put your money to work effectively; this discussion will continue through the end of this book. Of all the ways we could start with the broad topic of investing, we chose to begin with the high-level concepts and rules that govern the financial world. We did this because, no matter what type of investor you are or aspire to be, and no matter what strategies or deal types you are considering, these concepts are universal.

Whether you're a newbie looking for your first rental property or a deal sponsor on a major syndication, these concepts should be foundational to your strategy.

In Part 2, we explained these concepts at their highest level, and we delved into the details of the math and execution to ensure you have a firm grasp of the ideas. We know there was a lot to learn here. If you need to refer back to the previous chapters to remember how to calculate future value, or how to interpret a net present value calculation, please do. We intended and expected that when we wrote this book. This book is meant to be both a continuous text and a reference guide for the future. You're not expected to remember every formula as you read through the first time.

That said, try to keep the core concepts top of mind. They will help you with every decision you make as an investor. They are the universal ideas that work across strategies and experience levels. To review, these concepts are:

1. **Put as much money to work as possible.** The more money you have invested, the more opportunity you have to earn interest/returns on that money. That doesn't mean you should be reckless—use the formulas you learned in Part 1 to determine your investable assets, and then strive to put as much money as you

can to work. Even if your investable assets are small right now, invest as much as you can as soon as possible.

2. **Earn the highest rate of return possible.** In Part 3 we'll discuss the various ways to measure your rate of return, but for now, keep in mind that a small difference in your rate of return will make a big difference in your long-term earnings when considering the concept of compounding. Even a 1 percent difference in return matters greatly over a long time horizon.

3. **Reinvest your profits as often as possible.** Compounding is perhaps the single most important concept an investor must understand and utilize. By continually reinvesting your profits, your returns will grow exponentially over time. Remember, the longer you allow your money to compound, the greater the benefit.

4. **The sooner you receive money, the more valuable it is.** The time value of money teaches that the sooner you receive money, the sooner you can reinvest it and add to your continuous compounding machine. Investing isn't just about making a lot of money—it's about making a lot of money quickly.

5. **Keep as much money invested as possible by utilizing tax advantages.** As we've learned, keeping money in the market and allowing it to compound are the fundamentals of successful investing. Take advantage of tax strategies that will help you put more money to work for a longer amount of time.

If you keep these five concepts at the core of your investing strategy, it's very likely that you'll start to see the values on your Personal Financial Statement moving in the right direction, and in a very exciting way.

Now, it's time to move on to Part 3, where we'll discuss the array of metrics available to real estate investors, as well as how to use them. Part 3 is designed to build on what you've already learned. In Part 1 of this book, you learned how to measure success as an investor by crafting financial statements. In Part 2, you read about the universal concepts that should govern your overall investing strategy. In Part 3, you'll learn to assess individual investments to identify opportunities that fit with your investing strategy and will help you meet your personal financial goals.

PART 3
THE KEY RETURN METRICS

W e often get asked—from new and experienced investors alike—what the best metrics are for analyzing investment deals and returns. On the surface, it's a reasonable question; as investors, we always want to ensure that we're implementing the best tools to maximize our returns.

When you dig into this question, however, you start to realize that financial metrics are a lot like transportation: They come in a variety of forms and functions, but there is no "best." There's only what's best for the situation at hand.

For example, what's better: a car or an airplane? Without knowing the specific need of the traveler, it's impossible to say. If you're trying to get from home to your office five miles away, a car is obviously superior. But if you're trying to get to a meeting 2,000 miles away, a plane has tremendous benefits over driving. You can argue all day that a Lamborghini is superior to a Nissan Pathfinder, but if you're trying to haul a couch across town, I think most of us would agree that we'd rather have a Pathfinder.

When it comes to the alphabet soup of financial metrics (ROI, AAR, CAGR, IRR, etc.), the debate is similar. Each of these is a way of measuring the success or failure of an investment, but there is no "best" metric—only a best metric for the specific task.

Now that we have a good grasp of the concepts that make these metrics meaningful, we're ready to jump in and look at them individually—to see what they can provide, when they apply, how they differ, and how they can be used in conjunction with one another.

CHAPTER 14
ASKING THE RIGHT QUESTIONS

Chapter 14 will help answer the questions:
- What are the different ways to think about investing returns?
- When should I use one metric versus another?

A metric is simply a way to measure things. Pounds and kilograms are weight metrics—ways to measure weight. Inches and meters are length metrics—ways to measure distance. In the investing world, we often want to measure the magnitude of return that an investment can provide or has provided. We refer to this group of metrics as "return metrics."

There are lots of different return metrics; some are very simple and some very complex. Some can be calculated in our heads, and some require computers. Some give us a general approximation of how an investment might perform, and some give us nitty-gritty details. Some return metrics can be combined to provide even more insight than an individual metric on its own.

The thing that all return metrics have in common is they make us better investors. By understanding them, we can stop making decisions—and evaluating past decisions—based on instinct or intuition. Instead, we can start making decisions based on math and logic.

We're not saying that instinct and intuition don't have a role in investing. There's a reason we say, "Trust your gut!" But, at the end of the day, your gut and the math should go hand in hand, working together to help you make good decisions.

GETTING TO THE RIGHT QUESTION

As we said at the beginning of this book, so much of investing is about asking the right questions. Thinking about return metrics—or any metrics, for that matter—is no different. Let's start with the most basic question that we as investors like to ask:

How much money will I make from this investment?
In other words, are you going to make $1,000 or $5,000 if you choose to pursue a particular investment? Obviously, $5,000 is a better outcome than $1,000, right? More money is always better than less money! Or is it?

What if you have to invest $2,500 to make that $5,000, but you only have to invest $100 to make that $1,000? That certainly changes things, doesn't it? With the $2,500 investment, you make 2X your initial investment in profit; with the $100 investment, you make 10X your initial investment.

Clearly, if you must put in a disproportionately large amount of money to generate a relatively small return, it likely isn't worth it. While knowing how much money you will make from an investment is good information, it's often just as important—or even more important—to be able to answer the question:

What percentage of my initial investment will this investment return?
If one investment will generate a 2X return and another investment will generate a 10X return, and if you can only choose one of them, you should pursue the 10X return, right?

But wait. What if turning the $100 into $1,000 would take twenty years, but turning the $2,500 into $5,000 would only take one year? A 10X return is great, but is it worth waiting twenty years when you could get a 2X return much, much faster?

Clearly, the time horizon of the investment (the amount of time the investment would last, from start to finish) plays a role here. The longer the investment, the higher-percentage return you'll likely need to compete with a shorter investment.

Instead of just knowing what percentage return you should expect from your investment, you are also going to want to answer the question:

What percentage of my initial investment will this investment return per year?
If one investment will return 10X over twenty years (or about 0.5X per year), that doesn't sound nearly as good as the investment that will return 2X over one year (obviously, 2X per year).

Think back to the time value of money (TVM) concepts that we discussed in the last section of the book. The amount of money we earn, or even the time horizon of the investment, can be much less important than when exactly we realize that money. Money earned sooner is more valuable to us than money earned later.

For example, on the $100 investment, if you were going to get 95 percent of your return on Day 2 and the last 5 percent after twenty years, that's going to be a much better investment than if you got the entire return at the twenty-year mark. In fact, given the TVM and your ability to compound your returns, it might even make it a better investment than turning the $2,500 into $5,000 after one year, depending on the timing of the returns for that investment.

The timing of the returns matters because timing directly impacts our ability to compound our profits. So, instead of simply knowing the percentage return relative to the time horizon, you're also going to want to answer this question:

What is the compounded return of this investment over time?
Whew! We started by looking for the answer to a basic question ("How much money will I make from this investment?"), and we eventually realized that, at least in some cases, the question we really needed to answer was much more complicated.

And that's why we have so many different return metrics. They each answer a different question, and by knowing what question we want to answer at any given point in time, we can determine which return metric(s) are best to use, depending on the situation.

DIFFERENT RETURN METRICS ANSWER DIFFERENT QUESTIONS

Running through our scenarios above, we came across four different questions, each a little bit deeper than the last.

Q1. How much money will I make from this investment?

Q2. What percentage of my initial investment will this investment return?

Q3. What percentage of my initial investment will this investment return per year?

Q4. What is the compounded return of this investment over time?

Each of the metrics we will discuss in this section will aim to answer one of those questions. As you go through the remainder of Part 3, or if you want a refresher in the future, you can always come back to our Metric Matrix below as a good reminder of what metrics are used to answer what questions.

	ANSWERS			
RETURN METRIC	Q1	Q2	Q3	Q4
Profit	X			
Net Operating Income (NOI)	X			
Cash Flow (CF)	X			
Return on Investment (ROI)		X		
Equity Multiplier (EM)		X		
Capitalization Rate (Cap Rate)			X	
Cash-on-Cash Return (COC)			X	
Average Annual Return (AAR)			X	
Compound Annual Growth Rate (CAGR)				X
Internal Rate of Return (IRR)				X

At the end of Part 3, you will understand what each of these metrics measures, how to calculate each one, and the scenarios in which to apply each of them.

CHAPTER 15
MEASUREMENTS OF PROFIT

Chapter 15 will help answer the questions:
- What are the different types of measurement of profit?
- What can each measurement of profit tell me?

"Profit" is a catchall term that can mean a lot of different things to different people in different situations. At its most basic, profit is simply a measure of how much more money we have now than at some point in the past.

For example, if we were to tell you that we bought a house last year for $100,000 and sold it today for $150,000, we could say that we made a $50,000 profit. However, in real estate, things are rarely that simple.

What if we earned $10,000 in cash flow during that period? Do we treat cash flow as part of the profit or treat it separately?

What if we sold the property using seller financing? Do we count the interest payments on the loan as part of the profit or count it separately?

How about taxes? Do we refer to the profit as pre-tax or post-tax earnings?

And do tax benefits factor into the profit or not?

For lots of reasons, "profit" is a term so generic that most people who are serious about investment analysis often hesitate to use it without more context.

Additionally, the term has no time reference. As we discussed earlier, without some understanding of the amount of time it took to earn the profit, we have no idea whether $50,000 in profit is better or worse than $100,000 in profit. If it took 10X as long to earn the $100,000, I think most of us would agree that this was an inferior investment to the one that returned $50,000 in 10 percent of the time. Therefore, in real estate investing, we rarely use the word "profit" by itself. It simply doesn't have a clear enough definition.

Knowing all of that, we still need metrics to answer Question 1 from our Metric Matrix, "How much money will I make from this investment?" As real estate investors, we'll often focus on two real estate–specific metrics to answer that question: net operating income (NOI) and cash flow.

NET OPERATING INCOME

We introduced the concept of net operating income (NOI) toward the end of Part 1, but it's an important measurement, so let's review it here. NOI represents the annual property income after we subtract rent loss (due to vacancy, concessions, etc.) and our operating expenses. NOI doesn't take into consideration debt service or income taxes paid, so we think of NOI as the pre-tax income a property generates.

NOI is calculated as:

NOI = Gross operating income – Operating expenses

As a refresher, let's go back to our example in Chapter 4:

PROFIT & LOSS STATEMENT - CATHERINE CORP.
For the Fiscal Year 2022 (Jan. 1–Dec. 31, 2022)

INCOME	
Gross Potential Rent	$120,000.00
Rent Loss	$(12,000.00)
Other Income	$3,000.00
GROSS OPERATING INCOME:	**$111,000.00**
EXPENSES	
Property Taxes	$5,250.00
Insurance	$2,810.00
Property Management	$8,640.00
Turnover	$4,800.00
Repairs & Maintenance	$10,000.00
Utilities	$400.00

Lawn Care	$3,600.00
Snow Removal	$-
Dumpster/Trash Removal	$-
Grounds Cleanup	$3,000.00
Office Costs	$-
Legal	$-
Accounting	$1,500.00
OPERATING EXPENSES:	**$40,000.00**
NET OPERATING INCOME:	**$71,000.00**

NOI is an important concept because it's used in so many other real estate valuation and return metrics. We'll be revisiting NOI throughout this book.

DIG DEEP

NOI AND CAPITAL EXPENSES

We discussed earlier that capital expenses (CapEx) are technically not included as part of the NOI. From an accounting perspective, this is accurate. If you were to provide your property data to an accountant or CPA to prepare your key financial statements, you would almost certainly find CapEx listed *below* the NOI line.

In the real world, however, this isn't always how it's done. For several reasons, you may sometimes find CapEx listed as part of the operating expenses. Let's discuss when and why that might be.

First, many investors will include CapEx as part of operating expenses because, in reality, CapEx is an out-of-pocket expense. While the IRS treats it differently than other operating expenses, from the perspective of an investor's bank account, CapEx is no less an expense than insurance or maintenance.

In some cases, investors won't put CapEx above the NOI line, but they will create a new category of expense called "Capital Reserves" or "Replacement Reserves." This is just a fancy name for expected capital expenses and is a placeholder for the amount of CapEx expected to be spent in a given year on the property. When you see either of these terms on a P&L statement, know that it is likely just the investor's way of incorporating the real cost of CapEx into their determination of income.

Finally, later in this part of the book, we're going to discuss how to determine the worth of a property. Spoiler alert: One of the key valuation metrics we'll discuss is based on NOI. All other things being equal, the higher the NOI of a property, the more that property is likely to be worth.

For any real estate transaction, there is going to be a buyer and a seller. The buyer is looking to prove a value as low as possible when negotiating a purchase. The seller is looking to prove a value as high as possible when negotiating that same deal. For this reason, we'll often find that *buyers* will include CapEx *above* the NOI line (to reduce NOI and the perceived value), while sellers will include CapEx *below* the NOI line (to increase NOI and the perceived value).

Long story short, it's important to recognize that CapEx will appear in different places when you're evaluating deals, and it's important that you take this into consideration to ensure you're doing an apples-to-apples comparison between properties.

CASH FLOW

Cash flow, like NOI, is a metric for measuring profit for cash-flowing investments, like a rental property. If you recall, NOI measures profit after all operating expenses are subtracted from your income. Cash flow takes that one step further and measures the profitability of the investment after all expenses have been accounted for (not just operating expenses). In other words, cash flow measures the amount of actual dollars that flow into or out of your bank account each year.

Unfortunately, "all expenses" is a loaded term, and not everyone agrees on whether it includes the payment of income taxes. For this reason, we generally break cash flow down into two separate calculations: (1) cash flow before taxes and (2) cash flow after taxes.

Cash Flow Before Taxes

"Cash flow before taxes" measures your total gain or loss for the year, before the application of any tax payments or refunds. Cash flow before taxes starts with NOI, and then factors in three additional cash expenditures (debt service, CapEx, and loan additions).

#48 | **Cash flow before taxes**
Cash flow before taxes = NOI – Debt service – Capital expenses + Loan additions

We've already discussed what NOI is, and we know that debt service is simply our total mortgage payments throughout the year and capital expenditures are big-ticket renovation costs. Finally, we have a new category called "loan additions."

Loan additions is a term we made up, but it accounts for all other cash proceeds you may accumulate throughout the year (generally from loan transactions). The two most common types of loan additions would be any interest you may have earned throughout the year and any cash generated through a refinance.

Remember, cash flow aims to capture the real amount of profit that you received, so all cash inflows and outflows must be accounted for in a cash flow calculation.

Continuing our example P&L, here is what cash flow before taxes might look like:

PROFIT & LOSS STATEMENT - CATHERINE CORP.
For the Fiscal Year 2022 (Jan. 1–Dec. 31, 2022)

INCOME	
Gross Potential Rent	$120,000.00
Rent Loss	$(12,000.00)
Other Income	$3,000.00
GROSS OPERATING INCOME:	**$111,000.00**
EXPENSES	
Property Taxes	$5,250.00
Insurance	$2,810.00
Property Management	$8,640.00
Turnover	$4,800.00
Repairs & Maintenance	$10,000.00
Utilities	$400.00
Lawn Care	$3,600.00
Snow Removal	$-
Dumpster/Trash Removal	$-
Grounds Cleanup	$3,000.00
Office Costs	$-
Legal	$-
Accounting	$1,500.00
OPERATING EXPENSES:	**$40,000.00**
NET OPERATING INCOME:	**$71,000.00**
Debt Service	$(40,200.00)
Capital Expenses	$(5,000.00)
CASH FLOW BEFORE TAXES	**$25,800.00**

Cash Flow After Taxes

As you can probably guess, "cash flow after taxes" starts with the cash flow before taxes and simply deducts any income tax payments made or received throughout the year (that's federal, state, and local taxes).

#49   **Cash flow after taxes**
Cash flow after taxes = Cash flow before taxes − Income tax

Building on the previous example, all we need to do is calculate the taxes owed and subtract that from our cash flow before taxes. We'll use a tax rate of 35 percent. When we multiply 0.35 by the cash flow before taxes, we get $9,100 in taxes.

PROFIT & LOSS STATEMENT - CATHERINE CORP.
For the Fiscal Year 2022 (Jan. 1–Dec. 31, 2022)

INCOME	
Gross Potential Rent	$120,000.00
Rent Loss	$(12,000.00)
Other Income	$3,000.00
GROSS OPERATING INCOME:	**$111,000.00**
EXPENSES	
Property Taxes	$5,250.00
Insurance	$2,810.00
Property Management	$8,640.00
Turnover	$4,800.00
Repairs & Maintenance	$10,000.00
Utilities	$400.00
Lawn Care	$3,600.00
Snow Removal	$-
Dumpster/Trash Removal	$-
Grounds Cleanup	$3,000.00
Office Costs	$-
Legal	$-
Accounting	$1,500.00
OPERATING EXPENSES:	**$40,000.00**
NET OPERATING INCOME:	**$71,000.00**
Debt Service	$(40,200.00)
Capital Expenses	$(5,000.00)
CASH FLOW BEFORE TAXES	**$25,800.00**
Tax Rate	35%
Taxes Owed	$(9,100.00)
CASH FLOW AFTER TAXES	**$16,900.00**

When the $9,100 in taxes is subtracted from our pre-tax cash flow of $26,000, we wind up with a cash flow after taxes of $16,900.

Remember, cash flow after taxes represents the actual amount of cash increase or decrease attained by the investment throughout the year. We mentioned earlier that we don't like to use the term "profit," as it's too generic. You could say, however, that cash flow after taxes may reasonably be considered your bottom-line profit for the year on an investment.

HONE YOUR SKILLS: CHAPTER 15

- What are the two most common measurements of profit for real estate investors?
- What is the cash flow before taxes of a property with an NOI of $41,000, annual debt service of $28,000, capital expenses of $4,000, and loan addition of $1,000?
- What is the cash flow after taxes for the property above, assuming a 30 percent tax bracket?

CHAPTER 16
RETURN ON INVESTMENT (ROI)

Chapter 16 will help answer the questions:
- How much return has my investment generated?
- What is the average ROI of my investment per year?

Even those of you who haven't done much investing are probably familiar with the term "return on investment" (ROI). This is a catchall term that provides an idea of how successful an investment is or might be.

Like profit, ROI is a very basic and generalized term. There is often a better metric to use. But, like profit, it's a good starting point for several other return metrics. While ROI doesn't take all aspects of an investment into account, it is often the simplest way to measure the percentage return on a basic investment.

Unlike the measurements of profit from the previous chapter, ROI is not represented as a dollar value. ROI is a ratio, typically displayed as a percentage. Instead of just measuring the total amount of cash gained or lost, ROI compares that gain or loss to the amount of the original investment. As we pointed out earlier, two investments that return the same profit aren't necessarily equivalent—the one that requires less cash up front (relative to the return) is often the better investment.

Unlike profit, ROI takes that initial cash outlay into account.

RETURN ON INVESTMENT (ROI)

#50	**Return on investment (ROI)** ROI = (Ending value − Starting value) ÷ (Starting value)

The "starting value" is the value of the investment at the time the investment is made. For example, if you deposited $1,000 into a high-yield savings account, your starting value would be $1,000.

The "ending value" is the value of the investment at the end of the investment. If you withdrew your money from the savings account after it had grown to $1,100 over the course of a year, your ending value would be $1,100.

Because ROI is a measurement of an investment's success, the higher the percentage, the greater the relative overall return on the investment.

Let's calculate ROI for that hypothetical savings account.

On January 1, you put $1,000 into a bank account (starting value). On the following January 1, you cash out the account for a total of $1,100 (ending value).

Using the ROI formula, we can see that your ROI on the investment is:

ROI = (Ending value − Starting value) ÷ (Starting value)
ROI = ($1,100 − $1,000) ÷ ($1,000) = 0.10

You started with $1,000 and ended up with $1,100 after a year, for a return on investment of 10 percent.

Quick Tip | Positive and Negative ROI

The ROI calculation might return a positive value or it might return a negative value. A positive ROI indicates that the investment *earned* money during the investment period; a negative ROI indicates that the investment *lost* money during the investment period.

It's important to note here that ROI doesn't factor time into the equation. Because we know from our earlier discussion of TVM that time is an essential component in evaluating investments, we must recognize that two investments with the same ROI aren't necessarily equally good investments. We've mentioned this a couple of times, but it bears repeating.

If you have an investment that earns a 20 percent ROI after one year, and if you have a second investment that also earns a 20 percent ROI but after three years, TVM tells us that the shorter investment is likely the preferred investment (even though ROI alone would measure those investments as equal).

ROI VERSUS INTEREST RATE

You may have noticed that the ROI formula is just the simple interest formula from earlier in the book flipped around. This is a key concept to understand.

ROI and interest rate are essentially the same thing. When we talk about investing $10,000 in a rental property and earning $1,000, we call that our return. When we talk about investing that same $10,000 in a savings account and earning $1,000, we call that interest. The only difference between ROI and interest rate is the vehicle being used to generate the return.

We generally reserve the term "interest rate" for investments relating to debt, but these two terms are often used interchangeably within the finance world.

ANNUALIZED ROI

As we just mentioned, the ROI calculation by itself doesn't take time into account. In other words, holding an investment for ten minutes or ten years will not impact the ROI of the deal, given our basic ROI metric. This makes it very difficult to compare even simple investments in an apples-to-apples fashion.

However, there *is* a way to compare investments of different durations using ROI. We do that by annualizing the ROI for each investment.

Annualizing ROI means that regardless of the actual length of the investment, we calculate what the average ROI would be for each year of the investment. All you must do is divide the total ROI for the investment by the number of years the investment was held.

#51	**Annualized ROI**
	Annualized ROI = ROI ÷ Years held

For example, if you had an investment that earned a 200 percent ROI over two years, the annualized ROI would be:

Annualized ROI = ROI ÷ Years held
Annualized ROI = 200% ÷ 2 = 100%

Similarly, if you had an investment that earned a 50 percent return over six months, you could easily determine this investment also returned a 100 percent annualized ROI.

Annualized ROI = ROI ÷ Years held
Annualized ROI = 50% ÷ 0.5 = 100%

Now, this doesn't mean that just because you can earn a 50 percent return in six months, that same investment will return 100 percent in a year. Perhaps it's only a six-month investment and then it goes away. Perhaps it was simply an amazing six months that can't be replicated. Or perhaps the investment is structured such that it returns 50 percent in the first six months and then a lesser amount in the next six months. Annualizing a return isn't indicative of future returns (or past returns). It's simply a way to average a return over a common period of time so that it can be compared against other investment returns in a somewhat apples-to-apples way.

To further demonstrate how to use an annualized ROI, let's return to our example from earlier, where we started with $1,000 and ended up with $1,100 from our investment. We should expect that our annualized ROI should increase if we earn that $100 profit faster. Let's look at three scenarios to prove this out.

Scenario 1: Our investment goes from $1,000 to $1,100 (ROI of 10 percent) in two years:

Annualized ROI = ROI ÷ Years held
Annualized ROI = 10% ÷ 2 = **5%**

Scenario 2: Our investment goes from $1,000 to $1,100 (ROI of 10 percent) in one year:

Annualized ROI = ROI ÷ Years held
Annualized ROI = 10% ÷ 1 = **10%**

Scenario 3: Our investment goes from $1,000 to $1,100 (ROI of 10 percent) in six months:

Annualized ROI = ROI ÷ Years held
Annualized ROI = 10% ÷ 0.5 = **20%**

As we expected, our annualized ROI *increases* as the time it takes to generate the return *decreases*.

Annualizing ROI does make ROI a much more useful metric. With an annualized rate of return, you can compare two relatively simple investments against one another. But these metrics should only be used for a broad, simplistic analysis. We wouldn't recommend making any real estate investment decisions based on ROI or annualized ROI alone. To properly analyze a real estate investment, we need to add metrics to our arsenal that take into account compounding and the time value of money—which is exactly what we'll do in the coming chapters.

- What is the major limitation of the ROI equation?
- What is the ROI of an investment with a starting value of $6,000 and an ending value of $21,000?
- What is the annualized ROI of the above question if the investment was held for five years?

CHAPTER 17
EQUITY MULTIPLIER (EM)

Chapter 17 will help answer the question:
- How many times has my initial investment increased over the course of the investment?

We don't see the equity multiplier (EM) used nearly as often as some of the other return metrics that we're discussing, but it does pop up on occasion. It tends to be more commonly used among investors/operators who are investing in passive deals. But EM can be a handy tool in the right situation, as it gives you a quick glimpse into how hard your money is working for you over the course of an investment's life.

FINDING YOUR EQUITY MULTIPLIER

#52	**Equity multiplier (EM)**
	EM = Ending value ÷ Starting value

In short, EM gives us an indication of how many times our investment has increased, inclusive of all cash flow and profits generated throughout the hold period.

The "hold period" of an investment is simply how long you own or operate the investment. Many real estate investors go into an investment unsure of how long they intend to hold on to the property, and that's okay. But operators who raise outside capital from other investors, like in a syndication, will need to define the hold period up front to give investors an idea of when they can expect their money back. (This is because the investors understand the time value of money!)

Although the actual hold period can vary from what was defined in the business model, defining a hold period allows you to forecast the total returns generated from an investment. From there, you can calculate useful metrics like the equity multiplier (and many other metrics we'll discuss shortly) and share them with prospective investors.

An EM of 1 indicates that you didn't make or lose any money—your ending value is the same as your starting value. An EM of 2 indicates that you doubled your money over the course of the hold period. An EM of 3 indicates that you tripled your money from start to finish. And so on.

For example, let's say you were to invest $100,000 into a passive investment that returns $5,000 in cash flow in Year 1, $8,000 in cash flow in Year 2, $12,000 in cash flow in Year 3, and, in Year 4, returns you $200,000—consisting of your original $100,000 investment plus $100,000 in profit that year.

YEAR	CASH FLOW
Year 1	$5,000
Year 2	$8,000
Year 3	$12,000
Year 4	$200,000
ENDING VALUE	**$225,000**

Your EM would be:

EM = Ending value ÷ Starting value
EM = $225,000 ÷ $100,000 = 2.25

In other words, your initial investment grew 2.25 times over the course of the investment.

Much like ROI, EM doesn't factor in the length of time the investment was held. So, an EM of 3 isn't necessarily better than an EM of 2 without having more information about the length of the investment. Given our earlier discussion of the time value of money, it should be clear that a much faster doubling of your money could be better than a longer tripling of that same investment. For this reason, EM is best used as a very easy way to see how much your money has grown over time; however, it should be combined with more time-sensitive metrics as part of a holistic deal analysis.

A good rule of thumb is that when you see an equity multiplier advertised as part of an investment, ask more questions. While the investment may be perfectly reasonable, we've seen situations where investment offerings advertise an equity multiplier without other important information (like the hold period) to give a false sense of the returns. To put it in more blunt terms, hearing that you may triple your investment (an equity multiplier of 3) sounds great, but without knowing how long that will take, you can't say whether that deal is really very profitable.

HONE YOUR SKILLS: CHAPTER 17

- What does an equity multiplier of 1 mean?
- What is the equity multiplier for an investment with a starting value of $65,000 and an ending value of $173,000?

CAPITALIZATION RATE (AS A METRIC)

Chapter 18 will help answer the questions:
- **What does cap rate actually measure?**
- **When and how should I apply the cap rate formula?**

Of all the real estate metrics, capitalization rate (cap rate) is one of the most useful and important. Unfortunately, there is also a lot of confusion around how it can and should be used. To see where this confusion comes from—and how to use this important metric properly—we need to start with the mathematical definition of cap rate, which is rather simple.

#53	**Capitalization rate (cap rate)** Cap rate = NOI ÷ Value

WHAT DOES CAP RATE TELL US?

As you can see from the formula above, cap rate is directly related to NOI (the amount of income a property produces) and value (how much a property is worth). These are three key pieces of information about any investment property, and depending on how we rearrange the formula above, we can glean different information about our investment.

In fact, it wouldn't be difficult to argue that the cap rate formula is the most versatile, and important, in real estate deal analysis.

For the rest of this chapter, we're going to talk about one use for this formula and how cap rate can measure the rate of return on an investment property. But please keep in mind that this is by far the least important use for cap rate—and for the formula above. Much more important is how the idea of cap rate, and the cap rate formula, can provide insight into a property's NOI and/or value. In fact, these applications of cap rate are not only much more common when analyzing deals but also much more important to us as investors.

We'll talk about those applications of cap rate in Chapter 24, when we dig into the question of how to determine the value of an investment property.

In the meantime, let's talk about using cap rate as metric, while keeping in mind that most investors won't actually use cap rate in this way, for reasons we'll dive into during our discussion.

CAP RATE AS A RETURN METRIC

When used as a metric, cap rate can tell us the annual return of a property purchased for all cash, without considering any debt on the property, capital costs, or tax implications. For example, if a property is purchased all cash for $1,000,000 and generates $50,000 in NOI in the first year, the cap rate of that property is said to be:

Cap rate = NOI ÷ Value
Cap rate = $50,000 ÷ $1,000,000 = 0.05, or 5%

Cap rate deliberately omits debt service, capital expenses, and taxes from the equation—because each of can vary from investor to investor. Even for the same property, each individual investor is likely to make different choices about the amount and type of debt they use, have a different renovation strategy affecting their capital budget, and have a unique tax situation. Omitting the personal decisions of any individual investor allows us to make an apples-to-apples comparison of properties.

In other words, the theoretical return we should expect to receive if we purchase the property should be the same as the return you should expect to receive if you purchased it, regardless of whether we finance the deal differently, what capital renovations we perform, or how much we might be paying in taxes. Because only the theoretical return will be the same—the actual return will depend on three factors unique to each investor—many investors don't like to use cap rate to measure investment returns.

But there's another reason why most investors shy away from using cap rates as a return metric. As you might guess, it's natural to assume that, given two similar properties, the one with the higher cap rate will be the better investment. That would seem to make sense—if one property is generating a 5 percent return (5 percent cap rate) and another is generating a 7 percent return (7 percent cap rate), it should be reasonable to assume that the property returning 7 percent is a better investment than the one returning 5 percent. Right?

Unfortunately, it's not that simple. (Are you tired of hearing us say that?)

Cap rate is typically applied to commercial property, and when dealing with commercial properties, markets tend to be "efficient." This means investors within that market tend to be particularly knowledgeable and sophisticated, and there is enough demand for those properties that they will sell for very close to what they are worth. (We will discuss how to determine what a property is worth in a bit.) In other words, in efficient markets, it's often difficult to get a smoking-hot deal, simply because you are competing with a lot of other smart investors for the same assets.

For that reason, if you find two similar properties in the same market, and if one is listed for a price that indicates a considerably higher cap rate than the other, it's unlikely that the property with the higher cap rate is wholly a better deal. More likely, the one with a higher cap rate has additional risk associated with it.

Perhaps the property has a lot of deferred maintenance (needed repairs), which poses a risk to a new owner. Perhaps it's in a pocket of town where there tends to be more crime. Perhaps it's just a little farther from public transportation, making it less desirable for tenants.

Whatever the reason, a higher cap rate property is less likely to be a better deal than it is to simply be a greater risk and more headache to the new buyer.

Long story short, similar properties within a location will have similar cap rates. If you find a property that appears to be selling with a cap rate significantly higher than the cap rate for similar properties in that market, instead of assuming it's a great deal, you should instead be asking yourself what is wrong with the property.

CAP RATE EXAMPLE

To clarify this concept, let's look at an example. At the time of this writing, I (J) am buying large multifamily properties in the Houston, Texas, metro area. I'm looking for properties that are at least 150 units, built after 1980, class B properties, and close to downtown Houston. The going cap rate (often called "market cap rate") for these types of properties in this specific area is currently about 4.75 percent.

Earlier this week, I received three potential deals from a local broker.

Deal #1 was a 187-unit property that, for the previous twelve months, had an NOI of $1,058,000. The seller was asking $22,000,000.

Deal #2 was a 304-unit property that, for the previous twelve months, had an NOI of $2,157,000. The seller was asking $36,000,000.

Deal #3 was a 252-unit property that, for the previous 12 months, had an NOI of $1,165,000. The seller was asking $30,000,000.

Calculating the cap rates for each of these properties, we see:

	DEAL #1	DEAL #2	DEAL #3
NOI	$1,058,000	2,157,000	$1,165,000
Value (Asking Price)	$22,000,000	$36,000,000	$30,000,000
Cap Rate (NOI ÷ Value)	4.80%	6.00%	3.90%

For Deal #1, the cap rate is pretty much what we would expect for this particular property in this area. It's likely priced reasonably well at $22,000,000.

For Deal #2, the cap rate is a good bit higher than the market cap rate for the type of property we expect to see. This leads us to the question: Why? Is the property not really a class B (instead, could it be a class C property, which tends to have cap rates more along these lines)? Is there a lot of deferred maintenance? Is the property situated in a flood zone or in some less-desirable location? Regardless, the high cap rate is a red flag that this property likely comes with more risk than Deal #1.

For Deal #3, we see just the opposite. The cap rate at the listed price is well below the market cap rate, indicating that this property is likely overpriced for the market. Perhaps the property is in above-average condition, or maybe it's in a more desirable part of town. But when a selling cap rate is significantly below the market cap rate, it's safe to assume that the property is overpriced as a turnkey investment.

While we'll end our discussion of cap rate as a return metric here, we're far from done with cap rate overall. We mentioned above that a much better use of the cap rate formula is to determine NOI and value—we'll discuss that later in the book.

HONE YOUR SKILLS: CHAPTER 18

- Why is cap rate so useful for comparing properties?
- What is the cap rate of a property with an NOI of $75,000 and a value of $950,000?

CASH-ON-CASH RETURN (COC)

Chapter 19 will help answer the question:
- How much cash flow will each dollar of my investment generate?

Cash-on-cash return (COC) is one of the simplest, yet perhaps the most ubiquitous, of all real estate investing metrics. It provides a concise measurement of how much annual cash flow an investor can expect for each dollar invested into a deal. For investors whose primary focus is generating cash flow, COC is a critical metric.

#54 **Cash-on-cash return (COC)**
COC = Annual cash flow ÷ Cash invested

We discussed back in Chapter 4 how to calculate annual cash flow for a rental property. As a brief reminder, you take your gross rental income and subtract all your expenses, including your debt service and capital expenditure. What you have left over is your cash flow. (Note that COC is generally calculated on pre-tax cash flow.)

To determine how much cash was invested into the deal, you need to add up all your out-of-pocket expenses incurred to purchase the property and put it into service. This will typically include the down payment, closing costs, and any rehab or capital costs you pay for out of pocket.

As an example, let's say we generate cash flow of $7,000 per year on a property that required a $100,000 investment ($80,000 for a down payment, $7,500 in closing costs, and $12,500 in improvements to the property).

In this scenario, our COC would be:

COC = Annual cash flow ÷ Cash invested
COC = $7,000 ÷ $100,000 = 0.07 (7%)

The higher the COC, the more efficient the investment is at generating cash flow. In other words, the higher the COC, the more income we're generating for each dollar we put into the deal.

Kevin O'Leary—one of the sharks on Shark Tank—likes to say that his dollars are like little soldiers. We love this analogy. Investing your dollars is like sending them into battle to conquer and bring back more dollars; the best soldiers bring back the most dollars. Cash-on-cash return is a great way to measure just how good your soldiers are at the specific task of generating cash.

COC is also a handy tool because it's so easy to calculate, but it does have its limitations. Most notably, COC is best used at the time of purchase—not afterward. COC does not account for multiple inflows or outflows of capital, changes to income or expenses, or the time value of money. It also doesn't consider how our equity grows over time through loan paydown or appreciation.

Make sure to use COC for the time period it's intended to be used—at the time of purchase and shortly thereafter. We like to tell investors that COC is a great metric for forecasting the success of the first year of an investment, but to determine the long-term performance of an investment, we're better off using other metrics, which we will discuss in the coming chapters.

INVESTOR STORY
Every Rental Property is a Time-Share

When I (J) started investing in real estate, I remember hearing other investors say they would buy rental properties to afford their splurges. I didn't fully grasp the concept until after purchasing my first rental property, which cost me a $25,000 down payment and generated about $3,000 per year in income.

My wife and I had just come back from a trip to the Caribbean, and on our trip, the resort tried to sell us a time-share with an up-front, one-time fee of between $20,000 and $25,000. We obviously didn't seriously consider the time-share, but after purchasing the rental, I half-joked to my wife, "The rental cost us the same as the time-share and is generating enough income to get us just as nice of a vacation every year. Plus, we got a house out of the deal as well!"

That's when it hit me—every rental property is potentially a way to finance those things in our lives that we might not otherwise consider buying.

Want a Tesla that's going to cost you $800 per month in a car loan? Buy a rental property (or several rental properties) that will generate $800 per month in income.

Want to send your child to a college that costs $50,000 a year? Buy five rentals that each generate $10,000 per year.

Want a Rolex that costs $10,000? Buy a rental that generates $2,000 per year, and in five years, you've got yourself that shiny new watch.

And in all these cases, even after your "splurge," you still own the house!

What does all this have to do with cash-on-cash return? Well, COC is the best way to determine how much you would need to invest now to generate the monthly or yearly income you need for your splurge.

Let's look at that Tesla example. If you need to generate $800 per month on cash flow to make your car payment, that's equivalent to $9,600 per year (12 × $800). From there, you can plug the numbers into the COC formula to determine either how much you would need to invest to earn that cash flow (if you know the return you can expect) or what COC return you would need to generate (if you know how much you have to invest).

For example, let's say you have $100,000 to invest in order to generate that $9,600 per year. What return do you need to achieve it?

COC = Annual cash flow ÷ Cash invested

COC = $9,600 ÷ $100,000 = 9.6%

You'd need to invest that $100,000 into something that was generating a 9.6 percent cash-on-cash return.

Alternatively, let's say you knew that you could generate 8 percent returns from local rental properties. Flipping the COC formula, you can find that the amount of cash you would need to invest to generate that $9,600 per year return is:

Cash invested = Annual cash flow ÷ COC

Cash invested = $9,600 ÷ .08 = $120,000

You'd need to invest $120,000 at 8 percent cash-on-cash return to afford that $800 monthly car payment.

HONE YOUR SKILLS: CHAPTER 19

- What are the typical inputs used to calculate the cash invested into a deal?
- What is the cash-on-cash return in Year 1 for a deal that has a $40,000 down payment, $7,500 in closing costs, and $12,500 in initial rehab costs, assuming the property has an annual cash flow of $4,000?

CHAPTER 20

AVERAGE ANNUAL RETURN (AAR)

Chapter 20 will help us to answer the question:
■ What is the average rate of return for an investment?

Each of the return metrics we have looked at so far has had its advantages, but they all have the same major drawback: They don't take into account the length of the investment (other than annualized ROI, which, as discussed, is an overly simplistic metric that doesn't provide a lot of information). By now, it should be obvious why not considering time in the investment would be an issue. But let's look an example to make it perfectly clear.

Consider the difference between putting $1,000 into a bank account and having it grow to $1,100 in one year versus putting $1,000 into a bank account and having it take two years to grow to $1,100.

In both cases, the **profit** is $100.

In both cases, the **ROI** is 10 percent.

In both cases, the **equity multiplier** is 1.1.

Additionally, NOI, cash flow, cap rate, and COC are all annual metrics that evaluate the performance of an investment in a single year; none of them are meaningful when presented with data that encompasses longer time periods.

In other words, none of the key return metrics that we've defined so far would consider the fact that in the second scenario, you had to wait an extra year to receive the same amount of money. That second scenario is clearly not as good as the first, despite most of our metrics indicating they are the same! So, how do we account for different investment time frames?

One way is to annualize the calculation. In other words, we can look at what the average return would be for each year of the investment. The simplest way to do this is to take the individual returns for each year in the hold period and divide it by the number of years the investment was held.

We call this calculation the average annual return (AAR), and it's defined as:

#55	Average annual return (AAR)
	$AAR = (ROI_1 + ROI_2 + ... + ROI_N) \div \text{Years held}$

As an example, let's assume you have saved up $10,000. You decide to invest that money into the stock market with a reputable index fund over the course of nine years. As a savvy investor who understands the value of compounding, you reinvest all your profits as soon as you receive them.

As it turns out, over those nine years, the stock market delivered some volatile returns. Some years you have excellent returns; other years, your portfolio loses value.

YEAR	PORTFOLIO VALUE	ANNUAL GROWTH RATE
Year 0	$10,000	
Year 1	$11,500	15%
Year 2	$13,570	18%
Year 3	$11,942	-12%
Year 4	$10,867	-9%
Year 5	$10,324	-5%
Year 6	$9,085	-12%
Year 7	$10,902	20%
Year 8	$12,537	15%
Year 9	$14,041	12%

As the chart shows, the annual return varies from losing 12 percent of your portfolio value in the worst year(s) to gaining 20 percent in your best year.

To determine the AAR, you would simply average the returns for the nine years. You do that by summing them and dividing by nine.

$$AAR = (ROI_1 + ROI_2 + ... + ROI_N) \div \text{Years held}$$
$$AAR = (15\% + 18\% - 12\% + ... + 12\%) \div 9$$
$$AAR = 42\% \div 9 = 4.67\%$$

Quick Tip | **Calculating the Average**

When calculating the average of a set of numbers, we simply add all the numbers up and then divide by the total number of values in the set. For example, the average of the following five numbers: 2, 4, 6, 8, 10 would be:

Average = (2 + 4 + 6 + 8 + 10) ÷ 5
Average = 30 ÷ 5 = 6

The value of the AAR metric is that it provides an estimate of the annual growth seen throughout the hold period of an investment. Not only do you get an idea of how successful this investment was, but you can now also assume that if you hold this investment further into the future, your returns will likely continue along this same trajectory of about 5 percent growth per year. Of course, there is no guarantee that will be the case, but for many investments, long-term average returns are more consistent than what we see in any one year or two.

You may have noticed that we said AAR provides an *estimate* of the annualized growth. That's because AAR is only that—an approximation. We'll discuss this more in the next chapter, but for now, consider that one of the limitations of AAR is that it only provides an estimate of the growth. It also has a couple of additional limitations.

DIG DEEP

AAR VERSUS ANNUALIZED ROI

You may have noticed that AAR seems very similar to annualized ROI. And it is. They are both an approximation (an estimate) of the actual growth rate. In fact, there are many people who consider them the same, and who will use the annualized ROI formula and call it AAR.

The reason we like AAR more than annualized ROI—and the reason we differentiate between the two—is that AAR is going to provide a more accurate estimate of growth rate. Because it looks at the growth rate per year, as opposed to over the entire period, we have more samples to average. And more samples means more accuracy.

LIMITATIONS OF AAR

Clearly, AAR has advantages over other return metrics that don't factor time into their calculation. It also has the benefit of being relatively simple to calculate. But AAR isn't the holy grail of return measures either. It has several limitations that make it less than desirable to use in many circumstances. Let's look at a couple of these limitations and why they will affect our AAR calculations in ways we won't like.

Negative Return Periods

The first thing many people will notice after playing around with AAR for a bit is that it can distort returns for investments that have periods of loss (negative ROI). To illustrate this, let's look at a very basic example.

Let's say we purchased an asset for $10,000. After Year 1, the asset has increased in value by 20 percent, to $12,000. Let's say that in Year 2, the asset decreases in value by 20 percent. Many people might assume that the value is now back to $10,000. But if we do the math, we see that's not the case.

Asset value = $12,000 − ($12,000 × 20%)
Asset value = $12,000 − $2,400 = $9,600

In this case, the value of the asset after Year 2 is $9,600. As anyone who has worked with percentages a good bit intuitively realizes, a percentage gain followed by an equally sized percentage loss results in less money than the original sum.

20% GAIN FOLLOWED BY 20% LOSS

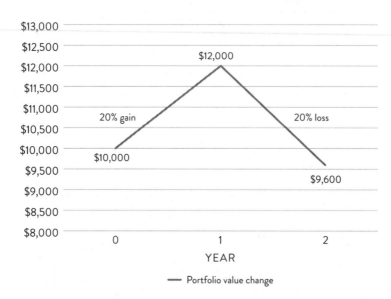

YEAR

— Portfolio value change

Given that, we should expect our AAR calculation for this investment to indicate a loss, right? Unfortunately, it doesn't.

$$AAR = (ROI_1 + ROI_2 + \ldots + ROI_N) \div \text{Years held}$$
$$AAR = (20\% - 20\%) \div 2$$
$$AAR = 0\% \div 2 = 0\%$$

Our AAR implies that we've broken even on the deal, even though the actual numbers make it clear that we've lost money. And when we have a large set of annual returns that mix positive and negative returns, the mischaracterization of the AAR result is compounded further (no pun intended).

Distribution Trends

The second place where AAR breaks down and provides return estimations that are not as expected is when the distribution range of annual returns is large.

To illustrate this, let's look at four scenarios where the starting investment amount is $100,000 and the investment is held for three years.

YEAR	ROI	BALANCE
SCENARIO #1		
0		$100,000
1	10%	$110,000
2	10%	$121,000
3	10%	$133,100
	AAR = 10%	
SCENARIO #2		
0		$100,000
1	15%	$115,000
2	10%	$126,500
3	5%	$132,825
	AAR = 10%	
SCENARIO #3		
0		$100,000
1	20%	$120,000
2	10%	$132,000
3	0%	$132,000
	AAR = 10%	

SCENARIO #4		
0		$100,000
1	30%	$130,000
2	0%	$130,000
3	0%	$130,000
	AAR = 10%	

Notice that the ROIs in each scenario differ across the three years. The first scenario has a nice, even distribution of returns, with a 10 percent ROI in each of the three years of the hold period. In the other scenarios, we see more varied returns, with the ROIs changing from year to year. Yet, for all four of these investments, the AAR across the three-year hold period is exactly 10 percent.

When you look at the Year 3 balance, you can see that despite having the same starting balance and the same AAR, the ending balance is different. Scenario 1 returns $3,100 more than Scenario 4 and is a superior investment, but you wouldn't know that by looking at AAR alone.

DIG DEEP

MISLEADING AAR

While AAR is just an approximation of the returns we can expect in any one year—and there are several more limitations that we'll discuss soon—it is still a common metric used when comparing investment asset classes. In fact, we recently read the following on Investopedia.com:

According to the National Council of Real Estate Investment Fiduciaries (NCREIF), as of Q1 2021 the average 25-year return for private commercial real estate properties held for investment purposes slightly outperformed the S&P 500 Index, with average annualized returns of 10.3% and 9.6%, respectively. Residential and diversified real estate investments also averaged returns of 10.3%

While we can't argue that this data is misleading, it's possible that the comparison is not as meaningful as we might give it credit for, given the limitations of AAR. Without more information about the actual data set (the annual percentage returns), it's impossible to know if commercial real estate has really been a better investment than the S&P 500 over the past twenty-five years.

If there were more (or larger) negative years in one of those asset classes, or if the distribution of return values was much larger in one of the asset classes, then it's quite possible that the AAR has been skewed.

This is especially important given the fact that the comparison values (10.3 percent versus 9.6 percent) are so close. Just a little bit of inconsistent data in data sets (again, negative returns or large differences between years) could easily change those values. For this reason, we're always a bit skeptical when we see people make big assertions like this using AAR as their metric.

Average annual return is an intuitive and useful measure of the annual rate of return of an investment. It can help you quickly benchmark an investment's performance and compare investments against one another. But be careful when using this metric for more than a quick evaluation, because AAR has limitations when measuring losses, or investments with highly variable annual returns. For those cases we'll want to use either compound annual growth rate or internal rate of return—which just so happen to be the subjects of the next two chapters.

HONE YOUR SKILLS: CHAPTER 20

- What advantage does average annual ROI provide over the basic ROI calculation?
- What is the average annual ROI of an investment that earned a 6 percent ROI for the first two years, an 8 percent ROI for the next three years, and a 9 percent ROI for the last year?
- What are the two major limitations of average annual ROI?

CHAPTER 21
COMPOUND ANNUAL GROWTH RATE (CAGR)

Chapter 21 will help us to answer the question:
- What is my annual rate of return when factoring in the effects of compounding?

As we discussed in the previous chapter, AAR gives us a reasonable idea of the annual growth of an asset using a very simple calculation. For some applications, AAR will give a close enough growth estimate that spending more time and energy on further calculations isn't necessary. However, because AAR is just a linear average of annual growth, it's typically not going to spit out a number that's completely accurate.

To see what we mean by that, let's take a fresh look at our example from the last chapter:

YEAR	PORTFOLIO VALUE	ANNUAL GROWTH RATE
Year 0	$10,000	
Year 1	$11,500	15%
Year 2	$13,570	18%
Year 3	$11,942	-12%

Year 4	$10,867	-9%
Year 5	$10,324	-5%
Year 6	$9,085	-12%
Year 7	$10,902	20%
Year 8	$12,537	15%
Year 9	$14,041	12%

Using the data above, we determined that the AAR for this example is 4.67 percent.

This implies that your hypothetical portfolio is growing 4.67 percent per year. This would lead us to believe that if you take your starting value of $10,000 and grow it by 4.67 percent per year, you should end with an account balance of $14,041 after nine years.

Let's see if that really works:

YEAR	PORTFOLIO VALUE	ANNUAL GROWTH RATE
Year 0	$10,000.00	4.67%
Year 1	$10,467.00	4.67%
Year 2	$10,955.81	4.67%
Year 3	$11,467.45	4.67%
Year 4	$12,002.97	4.67%
Year 5	$12,563.51	4.67%
Year 6	$13,150.23	4.67%
Year 7	$13,764.35	4.67%
Year 8	$14,407.14	4.67%
Year 9	$15,079.95	4.67%

No, it doesn't. As we can see, the AAR overestimated your growth rate; if your annual growth was actually 4.67 percent, you should have expected to grow your portfolio to over $15,000 in nine years, when in reality it only grew to about $14,000!

AAR WILL ALWAYS BE HIGHER THAN THE REAL GROWTH RATE

When discussing the limitations of AAR, we mentioned that negative returns are harder to overcome than positive returns. For example, a 10 percent drop from $100,000 to $90,000 requires an 11 percent increase to get back to our original $100,000.

Clearly, a negative return is going to hit our compounded average harder than a positive return will help that average. But because AAR simply averages the positive and negative returns, it counts both of them equally. It treats negative returns as no worse than positive returns—but as you now know, they are!

For this reason, any AAR calculation that has a negative return for at least one period will overestimate the growth rate. In our last example, the AAR is 4.67 percent, but you can now assume that the real annualized growth rate for this investment would actually be lower.

How much lower? Stay tuned...

If AAR isn't an accurate representation of an actual compounded growth rate over a period of time, then what is?

This is where compound annual growth rate (CAGR) comes in. CAGR is defined as:

#56

Compound annual growth rate (CAGR)
CAGR = (Ending value ÷ Starting value)$^{(1 \div n)}$ − 1
Where n = number of periods

To see how this works, let's once again return to the stock portfolio example.

YEAR	ANNUAL GROWTH RATE	PORTFOLIO VALUE
Year 0		$10,000
Year 1	15%	$11,500
Year 2	18%	$13,570
Year 3	-12%	$11,942
Year 4	-9%	$10,867
Year 5	-5%	$10,324

Year 6	-12%	$9,085
Year 7	20%	$10,902
Year 8	15%	$12,537
Year 9	12%	$14,041

Calculating your CAGR, we get:

CAGR = (Ending value ÷ Starting value)$^{(1 \div n)}$ − 1
CAGR = ($14,041 ÷ $10,000)$^{(1 \div 9)}$ − 1
CAGR = (1.4041)$^{(1 \div 9)}$ − 1
CAGR = (1.4041)$^{0.1111}$ − 1
CAGR = 1.0384 − 1
CAGR = 0.0384 (3.84%)

In theory, the CAGR should be giving us a true annualized compounded growth rate. If that's the case, you should be able to start with your initial investment of $10,000, grow it annually at a compounded rate of 3.84 percent, and end with $14,041 after nine years. Let's see if that's the case.

YEAR	ANNUAL GROWTH RATE	PORTFOLIO VALUE
Year 0		$10,000.00
Year 1	3.84%	$10,384.33
Year 2	3.84%	$10,783.44
Year 3	3.84%	$11,197.88
Year 4	3.84%	$11,628.25
Year 5	3.84%	$12,075.16
Year 6	3.84%	$12,539.25
Year 7	3.84%	$13,021.17
Year 8	3.84%	$13,521.62
Year 9	3.84%	$14,041.30

As we hoped (and expected), 3.84 percent is the true annualized compounded growth rate.

CAGR allows us to smooth out investment returns that are more volatile, as well as to determine the actual compound growth rate received over the entire hold period. It's relatively easy to calculate and intuitive to understand. In fact, you only need three inputs to calculate CAGR: beginning balance, ending balance, and term. CAGR is one of the most useful metrics for analyzing returns over time and is a vital tool in every investor's toolbox.

Some common applications of CAGR are:

- Measuring the returns of a stock portfolio
- Measuring property appreciation over time
- Measuring rent growth over time
- Comparing two investments against one another

To demonstrate these common uses, let's imagine that we bought two properties twelve years ago. Property 1 was purchased for $150,000 and is now worth $268,000. Property 2 was bought for $220,000 and is now worth $375,000.

	PURCHASE PRICE	CURRENT VALUE	HOLD PERIOD (YEARS)
Property 1	$150,000	$268,000	12
Property 2	$220,000	$375,000	12

Clearly, both properties have appreciated considerably in the twelve years since we purchased them, but which one had the better rate of appreciation on a compounding basis? Using the formula above (or the RRI formula in Excel) we can measure the appreciation rates and compare these investments against one another.

Property 1:

CAGR = (Ending value ÷ Starting value)$^{(1 \div n)}$ − 1

CAGR = ($268,000 ÷ $150,000)$^{(1 \div 12)}$ − 1

CAGR = (1.7866)$^{(1 \div 12)}$ − 1

CAGR = (1.7866)$^{0.0833}$ − 1

CAGR = 1.0496 − 1

CAGR = 0.0496 (4.96%)

Or, in Excel =RRI(12, 150000, 268000)

Property 2:

CAGR = (Ending value ÷ Starting value)$^{(1 \div n)}$ − 1

CAGR = ($375,000 ÷ $220,000)$^{(1 \div 12)}$ − 1

CAGR = (1.7045)$^{(1 \div 12)}$ − 1

CAGR = (1.7045)$^{0.0833}$ − 1

CAGR = 1.0454 − 1

CAGR = 0.0454 (4.54%)

Or, in Excel =RRI(12, 220000, 375000)

	PURCHASE PRICE	CURRENT VALUE	HOLD PERIOD (YEARS)	CAGR
Property 1	$150,000	$268,000	12	4.96%
Property 2	$220,000	$375,000	12	4.54%

Now, thanks to CAGR, we can compare the appreciation rates of these two properties. Our calculations show us that Property 1's value appreciated at a compounded rate of 4.96 percent per year. Property 2 appreciated more slowly, at a compounded rate of 4.54 percent. If you were evaluating these two properties based on their appreciation alone, Property 1 was the better investment (but, of course, there are factors to consider other than just appreciation).

LIMITATIONS OF CAGR

CAGR is undoubtedly one of the most useful, intuitive, and versatile metrics in the investor tool kit, but like any metric, it has its limitations. As we said at the beginning of this section, no one metric can do it all. So before moving on, let's discuss what CAGR cannot do, in order to ensure you know exactly when to use CAGR and when to use something else.

Representation

CAGR's simple output is what makes it so useful, but this is also its biggest limitation. CAGR simplifies an investment's performance over what can be a long period of time. Unfortunately, most investments have short-term ups and down, meaning CAGR is easily manipulated based on the time period chosen by the person calculating CAGR.

To see what we mean, consider the following example.

Susan makes an investment with an initial input of $50,000 and sees the value of that investment fluctuate over five years, as follows:

Year 1: $50,000
Year 2: $30,000
Year 3: $25,000
Year 4: $50,000
Year 5: $60,000

If Susan were to calculate CAGR for all five years of her investment, she would show a compounded return of roughly 3.7 percent.

CAGR = (Ending value ÷ Starting value)$^{(1 \div t)}$ − 1
CAGR = $(60,000 \div 50,000)^{(1 \div 5)} - 1 = 0.037$ (3.7%)

But perhaps Susan is raising money for a new investment and wants to show her prospective partners how her current investment is performing to demonstrate her track record. Using the same CAGR calculation, Susan could simply choose to calculate CAGR starting in Year 3 (instead of Year 1), which would indicate to her prospective partners a whopping 34 percent CAGR.

CAGR = (Ending value ÷ Starting value)$^{(1 \div t)}$ − 1
CAGR = $(60,000 \div 25,000)^{(1 \div 3)} - 1 = 0.339$ (33.9%)

Susan would not be lying if she said that her investment boasted a CAGR of 34 percent over the last three years. But she would be ignoring the volatility of her investment and the poor performance she experienced in the early years. (Plus, she would arguably be intentionally deceiving potential partners!)

Manipulation of CAGR is unfortunately very easy in the real estate industry. Consider home price appreciation.

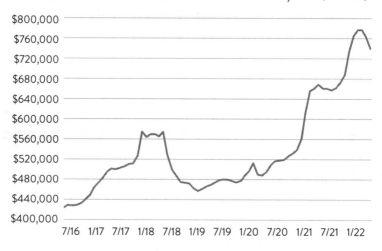

HOUSING INVENTORY: AVERAGE LISTING PRICE IN LAS VEGAS-HENDERSON-PARADISE, NV (CBSA)

Source: Realtor.com; fred.stlouisfed.org

This is a graph that depicts the average listing price of homes in Las Vegas, Nevada, from July 2016 through January 2022.

Using the data from this chart and CAGR, you could tell many different stories about what is going on here.

- July 2016–January 2022 indicates a CAGR of 5.4 percent
- March 2018–January 2022 indicates a CAGR of -2.8 percent
- March 2019–January 2022 indicates a CAGR of 2.8 percent

Which one is correct? All of them! If an investor or agent cited any of the stats above, they would be telling the truth. CAGR is not designed to account for the nuanced fluctuations in the performance of an investment over time. For that, we'll need more advanced tools.

Multiple Inflows/Outflows

The second major limitation of CAGR is again derived from its strength: its simplicity. CAGR asks you only to input a beginning balance and an ending balance. But in practice, many investments are not nearly that clean. Investments often require the investor to input cash at different times, and returns are distributed to the investors over the course of time, not all at once.

Let's use J's first real estate investment as an example, where he:
- Bought the property for $63,500.
- Spent $34,000 in renovation.

- Had the property sit vacant for six months.
- Lease-optioned it for twenty-eight months at $1,000 per month.
- Paid insurance payments on it over the course of two years.
- Pulled $66,000 out in a refi, which cost him $2,300 in fees.
- Sold the property for $120,000 thirty-five months after purchase, which netted $50,000 in cash.

In this scenario, what is J's beginning balance? What is his ending balance?

Confused? You should be! CAGR is not meant to calculate returns on investments with multiple inflows and outflows. For that, we're going to need to use another metric, IRR, which can consider the TVM of many inflows and outflows over the hold period of the investment. We'll do that in the next chapter.

Despite the limitations of CAGR, it remains one of the most useful metrics for real estate investors. It is an annualized rate of return that factors in the effects of compounding, which makes it a great tool to compare investments against one another. It provides a more accurate rate of return than AAR and is very easy to calculate, particularly in Microsoft Excel.

CAGR is well suited to measure the long-term gains from any type of real investment where profits can be reinvested, such as traditional rentals, BRRRRs, short-term rentals, and more. CAGR should be a frequently used metric for most investors.

HONE YOUR SKILLS: CHAPTER 21

- What is the compound annual growth rate of an investment that has a starting value of $80,000 and grows to $210,000 over the course of ten years?
- What is the Microsoft Excel formula that allows you to quickly calculate CAGR?
- What are two of the limitations of CAGR?

CHAPTER 22
CALCULATING INTERNAL RATE OF RETURN (IRR)

Chapter 22 will help us to answer the question:
- What is the time-weighted rate of return of an investment?

We talked a little bit about internal rate of return (IRR) back in Chapter 11. If you recall, the technical definition of IRR is the discount rate that makes a net present value calculation break even (equal 0). And while that is important to understand conceptually, to investors the true value of IRR is as a way to measure returns.

Quick Tip | IRR's Many Names

It's worth noting that you may hear IRR referred to by different names—on your mortgage truth-in-lending statements as "annual percentage yield" (APY) or as the "effective interest rate" of a loan. IRR is a versatile finance metric and, as such, has many applications under different terminologies. And it's certainly not just limited to real estate investing—in many respects, IRR is a great equalizer for comparing investments across asset classes.

At the end of the last chapter, we demonstrated the shortcomings of CAGR by presenting J's first real estate investment. Recall the scenario where he:

- Bought the property for $63,500.
- Spent $34,000 in renovation.
- Had the property sit vacant for six months.
- Lease-optioned it for twenty-eight months at $1,000 per month.
- Paid insurance payments on it over the course of two years.
- Pulled $66,000 out in a refi, which cost him $2,300 in fees.
- Sold the property for $120,000 thirty-five months after purchase, which netted $50,000 in cash.

The multiple inflows and outflows of cash make this example complicated. We know that not having to spend money until later is good, and we know that getting money back earlier is good, but with CAGR, we only use two data points—the starting investment amount and the ending balance. For that reason, CAGR isn't going to help us in a situation like J's.

Luckily, we have IRR. Now, as we mentioned in our previous discussion of IRR, it's nearly impossible to try to calculate by hand. Fortunately, spreadsheets make things easier. Using Excel, we can list the time periods of the investment inflows and outflows alongside the actual cash coming and going, and then apply the XIRR( ) formula to the columns.

We start with the initial investment in Period 0. In the example of J's first property, he had money coming in and going out on a monthly basis, so we choose the regular period to be monthly.

In Month 0, he invested $63,500, which is represented as a negative number (it's an outflow). Because J spent two months renovating, we break his $34,000 renovation budget up over Months 1 and 2 (if we knew the exact amount spent in each month, we could be more specific than just dividing equally). We add all the additional months, with outflows represented by a negative value and inflows represented by a positive value.

For J's investment, the Excel sheet would look like this:

DATE	MONTH #	CASH FLOWS
Aug-08	0	-$63,500
Sep-08	1	-$17,000
Oct-08	2	-$17,000
Nov-08	3	$0
Dec-08	4	$0
Jan-09	5	$0
Feb-09	6	$0
Mar-09	7	$0
Apr-09	8	$0
May-09	9	$1,000
Jun-09	10	$1,000
Jul-09	11	$1,000
Aug-09	12	-$400
Sep-09	13	$1,000
Oct-09	14	$1,000
Nov-09	15	$1,000
Dec-09	16	$1,000
Jan-10	17	$1,000
Feb-10	18	$1,000
Mar-10	19	$1,000
Apr-10	20	$1,000
May-10	21	$1,000
Jun-10	22	$1,000
Jul-10	23	$1,000
Aug-10	24	$62,920
Sep-10	25	$1,000
Oct-10	26	$1,000
Nov-10	27	$1,000
Dec-10	28	$1,000
Jan-11	29	$1,000
Feb-11	30	$1,000
Mar-11	31	$1,000
Apr-11	32	$1,000
May-11	33	$1,000
Jun-11	34	$1,000
Jul-11	35	$50,000
IRR		**16.21%**

(Note that the terms of the lease option were that the tenants would pay all costs associated with the property, including property taxes, maintenance, and utilities. This is why the $1,000 per month income isn't discounted for other expenses.)

Running the XIRR( ) calculation on the two columns, we see that the IRR for this investment over three years is 16.21 percent.

What does that mean? Much like CAGR, this is the average annual compound growth rate over the hold time of the investment. But, unlike CAGR, IRR takes into account the value of the money coming into and going out of the investment at different times.

For example, given the time value of money, that $34,000 spent on renovations in Months 1 and 2 would have reduced J's returns had he needed to invest that money in Month 0, at the very beginning of the project. Likewise, that refinance in August 2010 increased his returns compared to if he had waited until the end of the project to recapture that cash.

As you can probably see, IRR is a tremendously valuable and versatile metric to determine the success—or failure—of your projects. For many investors, particularly those who invest in development projects or rehab properties, IRR is the preferred metric.

INVESTOR STORY
The Cash Flow versus Appreciation Debate

I (Dave) lived in Denver for over ten years at the beginning of my investing career. During that time (2009–2020), I felt that given the macroeconomic climate in Denver, and the monetary policy of the U.S., the market was poised for above-average appreciation.

As such, I didn't focus as much on cash flow metrics as many of my peers. Don't get me wrong—I want and require cash flow in all my deals. But, during the mid-2010s, the conditions were ripe for appreciation, and I was willing to forgo some cash flow to take advantage of the massive appreciation going on in the area. My goal then was (and still is) to maximize my net worth. Because I intend to work full-time for many more years, I didn't care if it came in the form of cash flow or appreciation.

While this strategy ran contrary to other investors, I was confident in my decision-making. Why? Because of IRR.

Using IRR, I was able to determine if the appreciation I was expecting was worth taking a lower cash-on-cash return (and the TVM benefits that come with receiving cash every month). Sometimes I favored deals with more cash flow, and sometimes I favored deals with more appreciation—I just let IRR be my guide.

IRR allowed me to combine the benefits of both appreciation and cash flow (along with expenses and the hold period!) into a single metric with which I could evaluate deals. To me, IRR eliminates the need for the common investor debate, "What is better: cash flow or appreciation?" The deal with the highest IRR is best.

As we've shown, IRR is a powerful tool for investors. But it's also a complicated metric to get right, and it has some limitations.

IRR'S LIMITATIONS

While IRR is clearly one of the most versatile and useful metrics in the world of investing, it too is subject to limitations.

Estimations and Assumptions

IRR is a forward-looking metric and is therefore based on estimates. When used to forecast the success of a project, there are a lot of assumptions that you need to get right.

If that cash flow you expect in Year 1 doesn't come until Year 2, your projections will be impacted. If the projected sale in Year 5 doesn't happen until Year 6, your projections will be impacted. And if the amount of money coming in and going out isn't accurate, your projections will be impacted. The higher the quality of your estimates, the closer your IRR estimate will be to reality.

Project Scope

The IRR calculation gives us a simple rate of return for an investment, but it ignores the size of the project. For example, let's say you could choose between buying a large apartment building that will generate $25,000 per month in cash flow with an IRR of 11 percent, or you could buy a single-family rental that throws off $500 in cash and has an IRR of 15 percent.

The single-family property has a better IRR, but it would take nearly fifty single-family rentals to generate the total cash flow of the apartment building. As an investor, you need to balance rates of return with total return. If your goal is to maximize cash flow, it might be a more effective strategy to pursue the bigger deal with the lower IRR.

Reinvestment Rate

The IRR calculation assumes that all profits that you generate will be reinvested at the same rate as the IRR of the overall project. Unfortunately, in the real world, this isn't always easy (or possible). For example, if you invest in a project that purports to generate a 25 percent IRR over four years, you'll only hit that 25 percent return if you can reinvest all of the cash flow being paid to you at that same 25 percent return. If you can't reinvest at the same rate as the investment itself, by definition, you are not hitting your IRR metric.

In other words, if you invest in a project offering large returns on an annual basis, and you plan to take that annual cash flow and put it in a savings account at less than 1 percent interest, don't expect for the IRR of the overall project to meet—or even come close to—the promises that were made by the operator of that investment. This is the reason why very few projects actually hit their IRR targets. However, by having reinvestment options in place, you can get as close as possible.

Reinvestment Timelines

Not only does IRR assume you'll reinvest cash flow at the same rate as the project is generating, but it also expects that you'll reinvest immediately upon receiving that cash flow. Again, this isn't always realistic or practical. If you receive $5,000 per month in cash flow, you may need to save for several months or years before you have enough cash to reinvest in a desired project. Not reinvesting immediately will reduce your overall returns below the expected IRR.

While you should take care to factor in these limitations of IRR, this metric is still one of the most useful tools an investor has in their arsenal. As we've discussed, IRR is the most sophisticated of all annualized rates of return because it factors in compounding and the time value of money, and it can accommodate multiple inflows and outflows of capital.

IRR is rarely used for smaller real estate investment projects like a single rental property or a flip (although it can be). However, as you progress in your investing career, it's likely you'll start to see IRR used in development, multifamily, commercial, and syndication deals.

HONE YOUR SKILLS: CHAPTER 22

- By what other names is IRR known in the real estate investing industry?
- Consider a property that is purchased for $100,000 in Year 0. It takes all of Year 1 to complete a renovation that costs $50,000. The property then cash flows $5,000 per year for Years 2–4, and then sells for $200,000 in Year 5. What is the IRR of this investment?
- What value does IRR have that CAGR does not?

CHAPTER 23
COMPARING INVESTMENTS

Chapter 23 will help us to answer the questions:
- Which investment better suits my strategy?
- How can I compare two complex investments against each other?

Over the course of Part 3 of this book, we've been building our repertoire of key return metrics. We've seen how these metrics are beneficial when trying to determine whether a particular investment meets our goals. These metrics can also be used to compare two investments against one another.

Let's look at two potential deals that both start with a $1,000 cash outlay. One grows for ten years before being cashed out and the other grows for only seven years. Let's assume that these investments are both completely passive and the profits are immediately reinvested.

The value of each investment looks as follows at the end of each year:

INVESTMENT 1		INVESTMENT 2	
YEAR	ACCOUNT BALANCE	YEAR	ACCOUNT BALANCE
Year 0	$1,000	Year 0	$1,000
Year 1	$1,200	Year 1	$1,200
Year 2	$1,250	Year 2	$1,250
Year 3	$1,400	Year 3	$1,400
Year 4	$1,300	Year 4	$1,300
Year 5	$1,150	Year 5	$1,450
Year 6	$1,600	Year 6	$1,600
Year 7	$1,800	Year 7	$1,900
Year 8	$2,000		
Year 9	$2,100		
Year 10	$2,400		

Let's use a few of the metrics we've discussed to compare and contrast these investments, starting with return on investment (ROI).

ROI = (Ending value – Starting value) ÷ (Starting value)

Using this formula, we see:

Investment 1:
ROI = ($2,400 – $1,000) ÷ $1,000
ROI = 140%

Investment 2:
ROI = ($1,900 – $1,000) ÷ $1,000
ROI = 90%

Using this simplest of metrics, we can see that Investment 1 provides the higher total return. But, as you now know, we cannot rely on ROI alone—it doesn't account for the time frame over which the investments were held. I imagine most of us would happily take a 90 percent ROI over a 140 percent ROI if we were to receive that ROI significantly sooner (and could then reinvest the money for the additional time).

To account for time, let's next look at the annual average return (AAR). This will help us get a better understanding of how our investments have performed on a yearly basis.

The first step in calculating AAR is to figure out the annual ROI for each investment.

INVESTMENT 1				INVESTMENT 2		
YEAR	ACCOUNT BALANCE	ROI		YEAR	ACCOUNT BALANCE	ROI
Year 0	$1,000			Year 0	$1,000	
Year 1	$1,200	20%		Year 1	$1,200	20%
Year 2	$1,250	4%		Year 2	$1,250	4%
Year 3	$1,400	12%		Year 3	$1,400	12%
Year 4	$1,300	-7%		Year 4	$1,300	-7%
Year 5	$1,150	-12%		Year 5	$1,450	12%
Year 6	$1,600	39%		Year 6	$1,600	10%
Year 7	$1,800	13%		Year 7	$1,900	19%
Year 8	$2,000	11%				
Year 9	$2,100	5%				
Year 10	$2,400	14%				

$$AAR = (ROI_1 + ROI_2 + ... + ROI_N) \div \textbf{Years held}$$

Calculating the AAR for each of our investments, we get:

Investment 1:
$$AAR = (20\% + 4\% + 12\% - 7\% - 12\% + 39\% + 13\% + 11\% + 5\% + 14\%) \div 10$$
$$AAR = 9.9\%$$

Investment 2:
$$AAR = (20\% + 4\% + 12\% - 7\% + 12\% + 10\% + 19\%) \div 7$$
$$AAR = 10\%$$

As it turns out, the two investments have the same AAR of 10 percent. Crazy! (It's almost like someone manipulated the numbers to create a compelling example.)

At this point, it should be somewhat hard to tell which investment is best. Investment 1 has the better overall ROI, and the AARs are equal. To break this tie, let's factor in the effects of compounding, which aren't accounted for in either of those first two return metrics.

To account for compounding, we can use CAGR and see which investment performed better.

$$\text{CAGR} = (\text{Ending balance} \div \text{Beginning balance})^{(1 \div N)} - 1$$

Calculating the CAGR for each of our investments, we get:

Investment 1:
   CAGR = ($2,400 ÷ $1,000)$^{(1 \div 10)}$ − 1
   CAGR = 9.15%

Investment 2:
   CAGR = ($1,900 ÷ $1,000)$^{(1 \div 7)}$ − 1
   CAGR = 9.60%

As it turns out, Investment 2 has the better CAGR at 9.6 percent versus Investment 1, which has a CAGR of 9.15 percent.

Using everything we've learned in this section of the book, we can now look at these two examples side by side. Despite Investment 1 having the higher total ROI and an equal AAR, when compounding is taken into account, Investment 2 comes out as the clear winner.

INVESTMENT 1			INVESTMENT 2		
YEAR	ACCOUNT BALANCE	ROI	YEAR	ACCOUNT BALANCE	ROI
Year 0	$1,000		Year 0	$1,000	
Year 1	$1,200	20%	Year 1	$1,200	20%
Year 2	$1,250	4%	Year 2	$1,250	4%
Year 3	$1,400	12%	Year 3	$1,400	12%
Year 4	$1,300	-7%	Year 4	$1,300	-7%
Year 5	$1,150	-12%	Year 5	$1,450	12%
Year 6	$1,600	39%	Year 6	$1,600	10%
Year 7	$1,800	13%	Year 7	$1,900	19%
Year 8	$2,000	11%			
Year 9	$2,100	5%			
Year 10	$2,400	14%			
ROI	140%		ROI	90%	
AAR	9.95%		AAR	9.95%	
CAGR	9.15%		CAGR	9.60%	

Remember that as investors, we want to realize the beneficial impacts of compounding as much as possible, and therefore should rely on CAGR over ROI or AAR in any investment where profits can and are reinvested. In this example, we presumed the reinvestment of profits, and therefore we use CAGR as our defining metric and can confidently determine that Investment 2 is the better investment.

Also keep in mind that every situation is different, and that any one number isn't going to give a definitive answer to the question, "Which is a better investment?" In this case, Investment 2 certainly appears to be a better investment, but we're assuming that after Year 7, the investor will be able to move their money into a reasonable investment. If the $1,900 that comes out of Investment 2 will be put into a savings account at 1 percent interest from Years 8–10, it may not be a better overall investment.

This is why running multiple scenarios is often a great practice. Do you have an idea of what rate of return can be expected for Investment 2 in Years 8–10? If so, you could run a new analysis factoring that in. Additionally, perhaps Investment 1 could be liquidated after Year 7, in which case you might want to compare just the first seven years of Investment 1 against Investment 2.

Remember, the best investors are creative and can look at situations from multiple perspectives. While the metrics we've discussed are all the tools you need, you still have to be skilled at using those tools.

COMPARING INVESTMENTS USING IRR

In the above example, we only put money into the investment once (at the beginning) and only took money out at a single point (at the end). For that reason, CAGR was perfectly suited to tell us our compounded annual return. But what if we're comparing more complex investments that have multiple inflows and/or outflows over their hold period?

To illustrate how IRR can help us compare in a more complex situation, let's assume that we've found a duplex that we intend to buy as a rental and hold on to for ten years. The property is in decent shape, but we're considering rehabbing the property to determine if that would create a better investment for us in the long term.

The obvious upside to renovating the property would be that we could increase rents and generate more cash flow during the ten years we hold the property. But the downside is that the rehab would cost money, and spending money on a rehab has opportunity cost associated with it—we can't use that money for something else.

Let's dig into each of these scenarios a bit deeper and see if IRR can help us determine whether we should do the rehab.

Property Details:
- Purchase Price: $480,000
- Financing: 20 percent down
- Hold Period: 10 years

Scenario 1: Rehab

In Scenario 1, we're going to hold off on renting out our new property for six months while we complete a rehab of the property. The cost of the rehab will be $120,000, and that money will be coming out of our pocket. But we expect that with this significant rehab, we'll be able to raise rents from the current $2,200 per month to $3,600 per month. Furthermore, this renovation will help the property value and rent appreciate faster (3 percent each) than if we do not renovate (1 percent). Lastly, by upgrading the property, we'll keep our expenses (which are heavily impacted by maintenance and repairs) down to $7,500 annually.

To summarize this option:

SCENARIO 1	
Purchase Price	$480,000
Financing	80%
Down Payment	$96,000
Rehab & CapEx	$120,000
Total Initial Investment	$216,000
Rehab Time Frame	6 Months
Current Rent	$2,200
Post-Rehab Rent	$3,600
Rent Growth	3%
Property Appreciation	3%
Annual Expenses	$7,500
Sale Price	$645,079.86

Note that the anticipated sale price assumes 3 percent per year in property appreciation, but it doesn't take into account any selling costs. If you were to do this analysis in the real world, you'd probably want to take those extra costs into consideration.

Scenario 2: No Rehab

In Scenario 2, we buy the house for the same price, but rather than taking six months and spending $120,000 to rehab the place, we rent the property immediately. We do need to invest $10,000 to replace the HVAC system and patch the roof, just as a precautionary measure. As a result, rents stay at $2,200 and the property value and rent only appreciate at 1 percent per year over the ten-year lifetime of our investment. Because we did not renovate the property, our annual expenses are a good bit higher, at $10,000 per year.

SCENARIO 2	
Purchase Price	$480,000
Financing	80%
Down Payment	$96,000
Rehab & CapEx	$10,000
Total Initial Investment	$106,000
Rehab Time Frame	N/A
Current Rent	$2,200
Post-Rehab Rent	$2,200
Rent Growth	1%
Property Appreciation	1%
Annual Expenses	$10,000
Sale Price	$530,218.62

Without doing any math, what does your gut tell you the better deal is? Scenario 1 requires an extra $110,000 in out-of-pocket expenses early in the project, but it also provides significantly more monthly income, and the extra $110,000 in rehab costs is more than recouped at sale.

Luckily, we don't have to rely on our gut anymore. We have the perfect tool to answer the question of whether we should be doing the rehab: internal rate of return. Let's look at the IRR analysis for each of these scenarios.

For Scenario 1, this is what our Excel model would look like. (Note that we've done the math for you for each year to take into account all the inflows and outflows from purchase, rent, expenses, etc.)

	YEAR	CASH FLOWS
Jan-22	0	-$201,900
Jan-23	1	$36,996
Jan-24	2	$38,331
Jan-25	3	$39,706
Jan-26	4	$41,122
Jan-27	5	$42,581

Jan-28	6	$44,083
Jan-29	7	$45,631
Jan-30	8	$47,224
Jan-31	9	$48,866
Jan-32	10	$645,080
	IRR	**25.85%**

And this is what our Excel model would look like to calculate the IRR for Scenario 2:

	YEAR	CASH FLOWS
Jan-22	0	-$102,800
Jan-23	1	$17,192
Jan-24	2	$18,008
Jan-25	3	$18,848
Jan-26	4	$19,713
Jan-27	5	$20,605
Jan-28	6	$21,523
Jan-29	7	$22,469
Jan-30	8	$23,443
Jan-31	9	$24,446
Jan-32	10	$530,219
	IRR	**28.69%**

It turns out that Scenario 2 (not doing the rehab at the beginning of the project) generates a higher compounded return when considering the time value of all the money going into and coming out of the investment. While we obviously make a lot more profit from Scenario 1, the extra money at the beginning of the project combined with the ten-year wait for the bulk of the profit negate the extra cash flow we're receiving over that decade.

As a savvy investor, you could probably think of a lot of additional scenarios that may result in an even higher IRR. For example, what if we did a cash-out refinance in Year 5? Or perhaps we spend an extra $60,000 on the rehab, but turn the property into a duplex to generate even more income. What if we sold the property in Year 6 instead of Year 10? We don't know which of these scenarios might generate better returns, but you now can run those scenarios yourself to see!

IRR WITH DIFFERENT INVESTMENT ACCOUNTS

In the previous example, we ignored the fact that with Scenario 2, we had an extra $110,000 that we didn't use for the renovation. Not putting that extra cash to work for us—for example, letting it sit in a low-interest savings account—will hurt our returns. And Scenario 2 might actually be worse for us overall than Scenario 1 if we're not generating much return off the extra money we're saving on the project.

This is the problem with comparing the IRR of two investments that have different investment amount requirements. To get an apples-to-apples comparison of the scenarios, we need to decide what we'd actually do with that extra $110,000 in Scenario 2 and include the returns from that extra investment in the IRR calculations.

For example, let's say that if we went with Scenario 2 and had the extra $110,000, we would put that money into a passive syndication investment that offered about 10 percent cash flow ($11,000) each year and a 5X return on principal ($550,000) after that same ten years. We could build this secondary investment into our IRR model to see what the resulting blended IRR would be for both investments.

	YEAR	CASH FLOWS
1/1/22	0	$(212,800.00)
1/1/23	1	$28,192.00
1/1/24	2	$29,008.00
1/1/25	3	$29,848.00
1/1/26	4	$30,713.00
1/1/27	5	$31,605.00
1/1/28	6	$32,523.00
1/1/29	7	$33,469.00
1/1/30	8	$34,443.00
1/1/31	9	$35,446.00
1/1/32	10	$1,080,219.00
	IRR	25.69%

In this case, the IRR for Scenario 2 would actually be a tiny bit lower than for Scenario 1. Does that mean Scenario 1 would be a better investment in this situation? Financially speaking, it would. But keep in mind that Scenario 1 also requires a lot of renovation effort, which can be stressful, risky, and time-consuming. Perhaps the loss of 0.16 percent IRR is worth not having to go through all the rehab work laid out in Scenario 1.

While we're huge fans of understanding the math behind all of our decisions, this is the reason why we reiterate that while the math is important, it shouldn't be the only determining factor in our investment decision-making.

Hopefully you can see the power of IRR for both comparing investment options and comparing different strategies within the same investment option. Next time you pick up a rental property, you should run IRR scenarios on different levels of renovation, different hold periods, and other options that may boost your returns higher than whatever your original strategy might have been. But never ignore the nonfinancial aspects of the deal either—for example, the work involved or the additional risk that might be added.

HONE YOUR SKILLS: CHAPTER 23

- What metrics are best suited for investments where profits are reinvested and compounded?
- What limitations exist for all the metrics we've discussed so far?

CHAPTER 24
PROPERTY VALUATION

Chapter 24 will help us to answer the questions:
- How much should I be willing to pay for this future stream of income? (DCF analysis)
- How much is an investor willing to pay for each dollar of NOI? (Cap rate)
- How long would it take for a property to pay for itself? (Gross rent multiplier)

The final chapter of Part 3 is going to stray a bit outside the realm of key return metrics. However, it is a topic that's very much related to the other metrics we've discussed, and in many cases relies on formulas we talked about earlier in this part.

This chapter is going to focus on property valuation—in other words, determining how much an income-producing property should sell for. Understanding the ins and outs of property valuation is important on either side of the transaction. As a buyer, you want to ensure that you're not overpaying for a property; as a seller, you want to ensure that you are maximizing your sale price.

There are several different valuation techniques and methodologies used in real estate, and which one you should be using is often going to be directly related to the type of property you are buying or selling. For example, single-family houses are valued differently than larger multifamily or commercial properties.

COMPARABLE ANALYSIS

For single-family and small multifamily properties—generally fewer than about five units—the value of the property is going to be directly related to the selling prices of similar types of properties, in similar condition, close to the property itself. In other words, if you are interested in finding the value of a three-bedroom, two-bath, one-story renovated ranch house on a half-acre built in 1990, the best way to find that is to look at what other three-bedroom, two-bath, one-story renovated ranch houses on about a half-acre built around 1990 have sold for.

This is what appraisers will do when trying to determine the value of a house you're buying before a bank will give you a loan. If the appraiser can't find enough similar houses, they may have to get creative. Perhaps they can find a house down the street that is very similar, but it has four bedrooms instead of three bedrooms. In that case, the appraiser might assume that your property is worth about the same, minus some amount to account for the one fewer bedroom.

There are a lot of nuances to finding and analyzing comparable properties when determining the value of a single-family or small multifamily property. Again, analyzing those types of deals involves a more subjective—and less mathematical—approach using comparables, so we aren't going to delve into that here (though there are a lot of great resources out there, including J's *The Book on Flipping Houses*). For the remainder of this chapter, we're going to focus on the valuation of larger residential properties and commercial properties, as these are valued in a fundamentally different way.

VALUATION BASED ON INCOME

For larger residential properties and commercial properties, the value of the property is directly related to the income the property will generate. While someone purchasing a house to live in is going to primarily care about the aesthetic qualities of the house—the view, the décor, the finishes, the location, etc.—an investor buys properties for the sole purpose of making money. That's the reason you're reading this book, right?

A savvy investor, which you most definitely are if you've gotten this far into the book, views an investment property simply as a stream of future income. We don't paint a bathroom a specific color because we like that color—we paint it the color that will generate the most income. We don't put in light fixtures we think are awesome—we put in the light fixtures that will appeal to our renters and bump up our rental income. Every decision a savvy investor makes should be related to how much money that decision will ultimately put in the investor's pocket (or keep in the investor's pocket).

Now that we've hopefully convinced you that the value of your next piece of property is directly related to the cash flow it generates, let's look at three common methodologies investors can use to determine property values: discounted cash flow, capitalization rate, and gross rent multiplier.

DISCOUNTED CASH FLOW

We're going to start our discussion of valuation methods with the discounted cash flow method, as we've already discussed the basis for this one back in Chapter 9. If you recall from that chapter, a DCF analysis is a way to determine the present value of a future stream of income. In other words, we use DCF to calculate what a set of future cash flows would be worth in today's dollars if we were to discount them back at a fixed rate.

As we just mentioned, to a buy-and-hold investor, a piece of investment real estate can be thought of solely as a future stream of income. The purpose of a DCF analysis is to take a future stream of income and determine what it's worth in today's dollars. Therefore, if we can figure out what the future stream of income would be from a particular piece of property, we should be able to determine the value of the property today.

Let's look at an example. Assume you are considering purchasing a commercial building, and your goal for owning this building is to hold it for the next five years, generating at least 7.5 percent returns during that period of time. You expect that the property should generate cash flow in each of the five years you hold it ($115,000 in Year 1, then $122,000, $173,000, $154,000, and finally $160,000 in Year 5), culminating in a sale of the property in Year 5 that results in proceeds of $2.38 million.

Using a discount rate of 7.5 percent (your desired return) and the present value (PV) formula we discussed earlier, you can determine the value of the income you generate each future year in today's dollars.

For example, since you expect to generate $115,000 in cash flow in Year 1, you can use the PV formula to determine what that cash flow would be worth today:

$$PV = FV \div (1 + i)^n$$
$$PV = \$115,000 \div (1 + 0.075)^1$$
$$PV = \$106,977$$

You can do the same for the cash flow in Years 2–5, plus the resale proceeds in Year 5.

Discount rate: 7.50%

YEAR	CASH FLOW	PROPERTY SALE	PRESENT VALUE
1	$115,000		$106,977
2	$122,000		$105,571
3	$173,000		$139,258
4	$154,000		$115,315
5	$160,000	$2,380,000	$1,769,259
			Total: $2,236,380

If you add up the present value of all the individual pieces of income you can expect over the hold period, you get $2,236,380. That's the value of the future stream of income from this property, discounted back at your desired rate of return of 7.5 percent.

In other words, if you were to pay $2,236,380 today, and if you were to hit your cash flow and resale targets, your return over the next five years would be exactly 7.5 percent. The value of this property to you, given your desired return and the expected future income stream, is $2,236,380.

DIG DEEP

DISCOUNT RATE FOR VALUING REAL ESTATE

In our example above, we used the discount rate of 7.5 percent for the DCF calculation. We used that number because it was the desired rate of return, and we wanted to know what the value of the property would need to be to hit that return.

But this doesn't answer the question, "What is the fair market value of the property?" If we're trying to determine the fair market value of a piece of commercial property, what discount rate should we choose?

It turns out that's not an easy question to answer. In general, depending on the type of property, the location, the condition, and other factors, it's common to use a discount rate of between 5 and 12 percent to determine fair market value for a piece of commercial property. The higher the risk of the property (considering location, age, condition, tenant risk, etc.), the higher the discount rate is likely to be.

CAPITALIZATION RATE

We talked earlier, in Chapter 18, about cap rate. In that discussion, we addressed cap rate as a return metric, using the formula:

Cap rate = NOI ÷ Value

And while it's true that cap rate can be used as a return metric, this isn't where its power really lies. The true value of cap rate to investors is as a tool to determine a property's value. We can see that by rearranging the cap rate formula like this:

Property value = NOI ÷ Cap rate

While we may think that there are a million little things that factor into the value of an income-producing property, what this formula tells us is that it really boils down to two things:

1. The net operating income (NOI) the property is generating in a given year
2. The cap rate of the property

At the end of Part 1 of this book, and earlier in this part, we talked about calculating NOI. As a reminder, it's simply the income generated by the property minus the operating expenses incurred to keep it running. The NOI is the easy part of this equation.

The more important—and difficult—question here is, "What cap rate should I plug in when using this formula to determine the value of a property?" This is where a lot of investors (including some very experienced ones) get things wrong.

As we discussed in Chapter 18, cap rate isn't something we decide or control. Cap rate is determined by the market, type of property, condition of the property, age of the property, and risk associated with owning the property.

If you are dealing with a large twenty-year-old class B multifamily property in Nashville, Tennessee, the market will define a cap rate. If you're dealing with skyscrapers in Manhattan, the market will define a different cap rate. If you're dealing with a newly built self-storage facility in Boise, Idaho, again, the market will define the cap rate.

Cap rates tell us what investors in a particular market are willing to pay per dollar of NOI for a particular type of property. In some markets, investors are going to be willing to pay more for certain types of properties—and less in others. What investors are willing to pay may change over time as the market changes, the economic conditions change, and so on. Regardless, the cap rate will always be something that is defined for you—not something you define.

With that said, how do we find the cap rate for say, skyscrapers in Manhattan or self-storage in Boise?

Market cap rates are determined by looking at recent sales, and for each sale, dividing the purchase price by the NOI that the property was projected to generate in the following year. If you can look at enough similar property sales in a market from around the same time, you will start to see a typical cap rate emerge.

Unfortunately, most of us probably don't have the resources to find the NOI and sale prices of lots of similar properties in our market. That data just isn't available to us. In fact, at the time of this writing, there are still twelve states that are considered "non-disclosure," meaning they don't make the sale prices of properties publicly available.

While we can't necessarily get access to that data, other professionals in the market often can. For example, income and expense data is available to property managers in that market who deal with that type of property. And sale prices are often available to commercial brokers in that market who buy and sell that type of property. The best way to determine market cap rates is to talk to knowledgeable property managers and brokers in the market and ask them what cap rates they are seeing.

Let's look at an example. We currently own a 150-unit apartment complex in Houston, Texas. At the end of every quarter, we determine what the current value of the property is to decide whether we should consider selling. We just finished our most recent quarter, and it is once again time to determine what the value of the property is.

Here's the P&L for the previous twelve months:

INCOME		
	Avg. Rent	**$1,103**
	# of Units	150
Gross Potential Rent		$1,985,400
- Vacancy		($107,212)
- Concessions, Loss to Lease, Bad Debt		($65,518)
Effective Gross Income		$1,812,670
Other Income		$158,865
Gross Operating Income:		**$1,971,535**
EXPENSES		
Real Estate Taxes		$241,000
Insurance		$105,150
Trash Removal		$10,897
Electric		$17,791
Gas		$13,981
Water and Sewer		$71,697
Repairs & Maintenance		$73,245
Contract & Professional Services		$54,608
General & Administrative		$45,447
Payroll and Benefits		$191,521
Marketing and Advertising		$21,556
Management Fees		$59,146
Replacement Reserve		$49,238
Operating Expenses:		**$955,276**
Net Operating Income (NOI):		**$1,016,259**

As you can see, the NOI for the previous twelve months is $1,016,259.

Given that we keep our pulse on this market, have relationships with several large commercial brokers, and also have a great local property team, we can say with confidence that the market cap rate for these types of properties (150+ units, class B, garden-style apartments in downtown Houston) is about 4.7 percent as of this writing.

Given that, a reasonable estimate of value for the property today is:

Value = NOI ÷ Cap rate
Value = $1,016,259 ÷ 0.047 = $21,622,532

GROSS RENT MULTIPLIER

While not nearly as sophisticated or nuanced as DCF analysis or cap rate analysis, the gross rent multiplier (GRM) is another way to determine an approximate value for a multifamily or commercial property. Much like cap rate, GRM is a value specific to the market and property type that represents how many times gross potential income properties are selling for.

The GRM equation to estimate value is:

#57	**Gross rent multiplier (GRM)** GRM = Value ÷ Gross potential income

If we flip the equation around so we can find the property value (like with the cap rate formula earlier), we get:

Value = Gross potential income × GRM

Instead of cash flow (like DCF) or NOI (like cap rate), the GRM formula is based off the gross potential income of the property.

As an example, let's look again at the P&L for our 150-unit property in Houston. We see that the property has an annual gross potential income of $1,016,259. By talking to local brokers and our property management company, we find that a typical GRM for this type of property in this market today is about 21.

We can estimate the value of the property as:

Value = Gross potential income × GRM
Value = $1,016,259 × 21 = $21,341,439

As you can now see, there are many different methods for valuing real estate. Which calculations and methodologies you use should depend on both the availability of data and the type of property you're trying to buy or sell. When you need to value a prospective deal, return to this chapter and select the best valuation technique for the task at hand.

HONE YOUR SKILLS: CHAPTER 24

- What are the three means of income-based valuation?
- What is the approximate value of a property with a net operating income of $45,000 in an area with an average cap rate of 6 percent?
- What is the approximate value of a property with a gross rent of $82,000 in an area with an average gross rent multiplier of 19?

PART 3
CONCLUSION

I n Part 3, we've covered almost every metric needed to be a successful real estate investor. From simple calculations like ROI to more complex metrics like IRR, you now know how to calculate and interpret the key measurements of any real estate deal.

Once you can calculate these metrics, the trick is knowing what metric to use in what situation. There is a time and place for each of them. As an investor, you cannot come to rely on any one or two metrics. You need to look at the spectrum of tools at your disposal and choose the appropriate tool for the job at hand.

Think of this like the tools used in home construction and maintenance. There are thousands of tools available to build a house, but no one tool can be used in every situation. Each tool has its own purpose. You wouldn't want to use a screwdriver to hammer nails, and you wouldn't use a Sawzall for a precision cut (we hope).

The same thing goes for the spectrum of metrics we've just introduced. Each one has its own purpose and appropriate time of use. As is the theme of this book, you need to start with what question you're trying to answer. Once you're clear about the question, it should become clear which metrics to use.

If you're ever unsure about what metric to use, that's understandable! There are a lot of metrics to remember. That is why we designed this book to serve a reference guide in the future. We hope that you'll return to Part 3 of this book and our Metric Matrix in Chapter 14 whenever you are questioning how and when to use a particular metric.

In this next part of the book, we're going to move on to an important and exciting topic: how to finance real estate deals. After all, to be a great investor, you don't just need to find and analyze great opportunities—you also need to obtain the capital to take advantage of those opportunities. In Part 4, we'll teach you how to do just that.

PART 4
FUNDING AND FINANCING DEALS

O ver the first three parts of this book, we discussed how to craft financial statements for yourself and for your business. We learned about key investing concepts that can help your money grow. And we reviewed metrics that are unique to the real estate investing industry and are an essential part of any investor's tool kit.

Hopefully this has left you excited to land your first deal or to grow your portfolio in a more sophisticated, data-driven way. But to build out a great portfolio, you need more than concepts and metrics. You also need capital to fund your deals.

Each real estate deal comes with its own unique set of costs. Of course, you need capital to fund the property purchase. But you may need capital to cover closing costs, renovation costs, and/or operating costs as well, depending on the deal. As the investor putting together the deal, it's your job to secure the financing needed to get the deal done and make it profitable.

#58	**Financing** refers to all the capital used to purchase an asset, like a business or a real estate investment. Financing can fall into different categories (e.g., debt, equity) and can be provided or obtained from a variety of sources.

When you first learn about financing, it can seem overwhelming. There are a lot of terms and structures that you can use. But it doesn't need to be confusing. In fact, all financing boils down to just two components: equity and debt.

Equity is financing that comes directly from the owners of the deal. Debt is capital that is borrowed from an outside source, like a bank.

We're going to go deep into how both equity and debt work over the coming chapters. For now, you just need to know that the type(s) of financing you select for a real estate deal really matter. Financing is not just a step on your closing checklist. Financing should be strategic. Choosing advantageous financing can help you mitigate risk, scale more quickly, and even boost your returns.

Conversely, if you choose disadvantageous financing options, it can drain cash flow, introduce unnecessary risk, and deplete returns. It's all about knowing what financing best fits your investing strategy.

First, we're going to learn about "capital stacks," a helpful framework to visualize how real estate deals are financed, and will support other discussions in Part 4.

Next, we'll dig deep into equity financing. We'll explain how it works, go over the pros and cons, and give examples of some of the most common forms of equity financing.

From there, we'll turn our attention to debt. Because debt financing is such a broad and important topic, we're going to spend several chapters on it. It may seem like overkill, but it's not. Debt is one of the most powerful tools an investor can wield, and a thorough understanding of it will make you a better investor.

Finally, we'll give you some handy metrics that can help you determine when the right time is to refinance (or sell) your property.

By the end of Part 4, you will be an expert in real estate finance. You will have deep knowledge of the types of funding available to real estate investors, be able to strategically determine what types of funding to use, and, crucially, be able to go out and confidently start raising money for your next deal.

CAPITAL STACKS

Chapter 25 will help us to answer the questions:
- How do I track and visualize the funding for a real estate deal?
- What funding sources take the greatest risk? Which ones take the least risk?

Every real estate deal comes with its own unique set of financing requirements. Some deals will require only the purchase price and closing costs. Others may include rehab costs, operating expenses, regular cash payments to partners, or any number of other capital requirements. Let's start with an example of how financing often works in real estate.

This example is going to follow Brian, a rental property investor who is putting together a deal to buy a property (200 Post Road). The financing requirements are as follows:

200 POST RD.	
EXPENSE	**AMOUNT**
Purchase Price	$250,000
Closing Costs	$5,000
Rehab Costs	$20,000
Operating Reserve	$10,000
Total	$285,000

Brian needs $285,000 for this deal, and he can choose to finance that deal with debt, equity, or a combination of both.

Some real estate deals use only a single source of financing from a single person. For example, if Brian had $285,000 in cash, he could just write a check and finance the entire deal himself. It's a very simple structure where Brian owns 100 percent of the deal and has complete control.

But this type of deal is relatively rare. Most people don't have the means to fund an entire deal themselves; even if someone can afford it, it's not always wise. For these reasons, at some point in their career, almost every investor looks to raise outside capital. In fact, most investors look for outside capital for *every* deal they do. Outside capital is a great way to build a successful real estate portfolio.

However, as you bring in outside capital, the structure of the deal gets more complicated. That's not necessarily a bad thing. Outside capital is vital—it can just get confusing if you don't have a good way to keep track of the various financing sources from whom that capital is coming. That is where "capital stacks" come in.

Let's look at what Brian's capital stack would be if he financed his deal using only his own money.

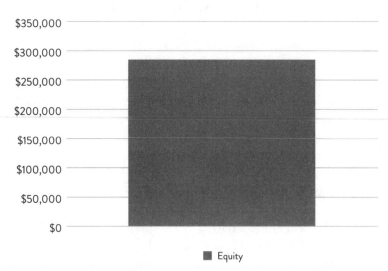

CAPITAL STACK | RENTAL PROP LLC

We mentioned earlier that one type of financing is called equity. Equity is cash put into the deal by one or more of the owners; it entitles them to an ownership percentage. In this case, Brian has contributed all $285,000 using his own cash, and because he is the sole financing source in this deal, he takes on all the risk and he enjoys all the potential reward. He owns 100 percent of the equity in the deal and, as such, will receive 100 percent of the profits or losses it generates.

As we said earlier, this type of structure is rare. So instead, let's pretend Brian is buying 200 Post Road as his primary residence. A common structure for financing primary residences is one in which the property owner puts down about 20 percent in their own cash and gets a mortgage for the remaining 80 percent from a bank.

CAPITAL STACK | RENTAL PROP LLC

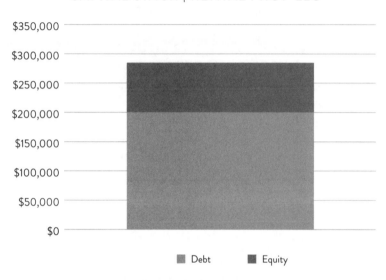

Now the capital stack is a bit more interesting! This financing structure consists of both debt and equity. The debt is the loan from the bank, amounting to about $200,000. The equity is the cash coming from Brian, amounting to the additional $85,000 needed for the deal. Note that because Brian is the only equity holder in this deal, he is still entitled to 100 percent of the profit or loss. But, because there is debt as well, Brian is now required to make regular payments to the lender to keep the property.

The chart above gets this across pretty clearly. But there is more to this chart than meets the eye at first glance. In a capital stack, the financing sources are arranged in a deliberate order that demonstrates the risk/reward profile of each funding source. The lowest-risk financing sources are at the bottom and the highest are at the top.

Debt goes on the bottom because it always gets paid out first. We'll explain debt in more detail later, but for now, just think about what happens when a property is sold. If Brian sells his house, he must pay off the mortgage (the debt source) before he (the equity source) can take any profit.

Since debt gets paid out first, it is the least-risky position in the capital stack. If there's not enough money to pay both the lender and the equity holder, the lender will get all their money first and the equity holder will get whatever is left—if anything.

The equity holder at the top of the stack is paid out second. If there's not enough money from the deal to pay back the equity holder, the equity holder will suffer the loss. Payment is always made starting from the bottom of the stack and finishing at the top. Those lower in the stack get paid first and therefore have less risk; those higher in the stack get paid later and therefore have more risk.

To demonstrate how this might work in this example, let's imagine Brian owns the property he bought for $250,000 for the next two years, and then sells it for $300,000. Because he's paid down some of his loan, let's say he now owes the bank $190,000, rather than the $200,000 he originally borrowed.

In this scenario, Brian would repay the bank its $190,000 first (the bank is lowest in the stack), and the rest ($110,000) would then go to pay back Brian's initial investment of $85,000 plus his profit of $25,000.

Deal Proceeds	$300,000
Loan Balance	$190,000
Owner Equity	**$110,000**
Initial Investment	$85,000
ROI	29.4%
Annualized ROI	14.7%

This deal has worked out for everyone. The bank was repaid in full, and Brian turned a solid profit. He invested $85,000 of his own capital into the deal, and now has $110,000 (a 14.7 percent annualized ROI). In this example, who got paid first didn't really matter because there was enough to satisfy all the payment requirements.

But what happens if the deal didn't turn out so well? What if, instead of selling the property for $300,000, Brian could only sell the property for $260,000?

As always, the lowest entity in the capital stack is paid back first. In this case, it's the debt holder (the bank). Brian would first pay the bank the $190,000 he owes them. Then, he can use whatever is left over to pay the next-higher entity in the capital stack (the equity holders).

Unfortunately for Brian, what is left over is $70,000, less than the initial investment ($85,000) that Brian (the equity holder) put into the deal, and he must take the loss.

Deal Proceeds	$260,000
Loan Balance	$190,000
Owner Equity	**$70,000**
Initial Investment	$85,000
ROI	-17.6%
Annualized ROI	-8.8%

This is why we say that the financing sources at the bottom of the stack are taking on less risk—because they get first dibs on the proceeds of the deal should things go wrong.

But with risk comes reward. If the deal goes well, the financing sources at the top of the stack tend to enjoy the most benefit. Remember our first example where Brian's deal worked out favorably? In that scenario, he enjoyed all the profit from his deal's success. Even though the deal went well, Brian still paid back the bank exactly $190,000—and not a dollar more—and he kept all of the profit.

The positions at the top of the stack risk more, but they also have more potential to gain.

CAPITAL STACK | RENTAL PROP LLC

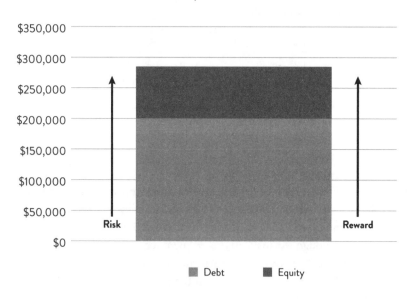

Another way to think of this is to picture the capital stack as a container, like a bucket, and picture the deal proceeds as water. If there is not enough water to fill the bucket, the positions on the bottom will get whatever water is poured in, while those at the top could be left dry. But if there is too much water to fill the bucket, the overflow occurs at the top of the bucket.

So far, we've looked at a very simple example where there are just two sources of funding, but real estate deals can get much more complicated. For example, it's common for commercial real estate deals to have up to four layers in the capital stack: two sources of equity and two sources of debt. And each layer can have multiple people or entities providing a portion of the financing. In the most complex deals, there may be dozens or hundreds of contributors to the debt and equity portions of the capital stack.

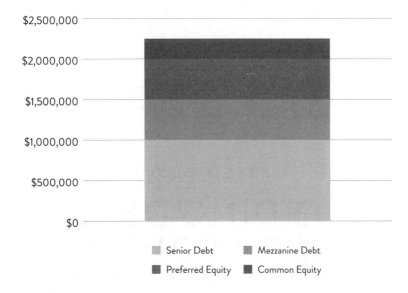

CAPITAL STACK | RENTAL PROP LLC

Senior Debt — Mezzanine Debt — Preferred Equity — Common Equity

For now, you can ignore the names and meanings of each of these financing sources—we'll get into that later—but we want to show you that a capital stack can have many sources and the principles stay the same. The order of payout still goes from bottom to top, and the opportunity for profit is greatest at the top and lowest at the bottom.

We'll continue to see capital stacks throughout this section of the book, but now that we've covered the basics, it's time to learn more about the different types of financing that real estate investors can add to their capital stack.

HONE YOUR SKILLS: CHAPTER 25

- What two things do capital stacks help us visualize?
- Why is debt on the bottom of the capital stack?

CHAPTER 26
FUNDING DEALS WITH EQUITY

Chapter 26 will help us to answer the questions:
- What is equity funding and when should I consider using it?
- What are the pros and cons of using equity to fund a real estate investment?

Let's get something out of the way at the beginning of this chapter. The word "equity" is used a lot in the world of real estate investing. That's because there are several important real estate concepts that include that word. Many experienced investors will refer to any of those concepts as simply "equity" and expect their audience to interpret which concept they're talking about based on context. If you're new to investing, this can be confusing.

We can straighten this out. In the world of investing, the word "equity" refers to "ownership." When someone talks about equity, they are talking about ownership in one way or another. In the context of financing, equity refers to capital that is injected into a deal by the owners of that deal. (And remember, "owner" doesn't necessarily just mean you—it could be an active partner, a passive investor, or even someone else who is trading their non-financial resources for an ownership stake.) That is what we're talking about in this chapter: how to finance real estate deals using equity capital.

The reason that owners exchange their money or resources for equity in a deal is that they want financial growth. If the project goes as planned, the value of the equity (ownership) in the deal should grow over time. That ownership value growth over time is what people are talking about when they say they're "building equity." We can track how much value has been built using something we're going to call "equity value." We'll talk about how to build equity and calculate equity value in future chapters.

QuickTip | Buying Ownership

While many people equate equity with a cash investment into a deal, it's worth noting that there are other ways to "buy" ownership. For example, you might trade ownership in your deal to a contractor in exchange for work they do on the property. You might trade ownership to a credit partner—someone who helps you get a loan by using their good credit history.

While we'll continue to talk about equity as a form of cash, keep in mind that sometimes ownership (equity) is traded for something other than cash that is required to complete the deal.

To summarize, when we talk about *equity* in the context of financing, we're talking about what the owner(s) invested into the deal. For example, if someone were to say, "Jeff put $20,000 of equity into that deal," what that really means is that Jeff traded $20,000 of his cash for some amount of ownership in the deal—likely an amount valued at about $20,000.

When we talk about *equity value*, we're talking about the dollar value of the investment to the owners. For example, if we later were to say, "Jeff's equity is now worth $40,000 after the property was renovated," that means that the ownership stake Jeff has could theoretically be converted to $40,000 if the investment were liquidated.

Now let's talk about some ways to use equity to fund real estate deals.

Recall from the previous chapter the example where Brian funded his deal using 100 percent his own money. That deal was financed entirely with equity because Brian, the owner of the deal, contributed all the capital and there was no lender (debt) involved.

That scenario resulted in a very simple capital stack.

CAPITAL STACK | RENTAL PROP LLC

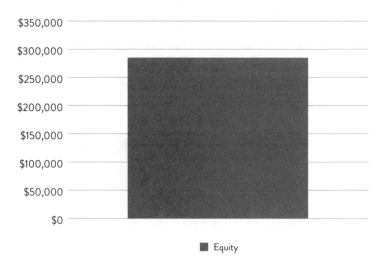

Equity

What if Brian doesn't want to use only his own capital for this deal, but he doesn't want to use debt either? Rather, he wants to finance just half ($142,500) of the deal himself, and he needs to bring in an additional $142,500 in equity to finance his deal. A simple way to raise the needed capital would be to sell a piece of his ownership in the deal.

Remember, equity just means ownership. When Brian needs to raise $142,500 in equity, he's basically selling a piece of the ownership of his deal. Luckily for Brian, he has an investor friend, Melissa, who agrees to purchase 50 percent of Brian's deal in exchange for $142,500.

Brian has gained the capital he needed to fund the deal, but he has lost half of his ownership in it. Melissa is now his partner in this deal, 50/50. The deal is no longer Brian's; it is Brian and Melissa's together.

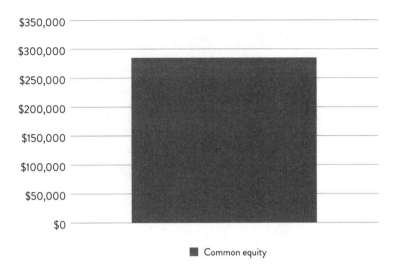

CAPITAL STACK | RENTAL PROP LLC

■ Common equity

This scenario too has a simple capital stack, as you can see above. If you're wondering why the addition of a partner doesn't change the capital stack, it's because Brian and Melissa have the exact same type of equity in the deal. The terms of their ownership are the same. Remember that the capital stack doesn't show any individual person's ownership per se; it shows the order in which different funding sources are paid out. We often call the lowest-priority equity (the equity at the top of the capital stack) "common equity." Common equity typically has the highest potential for upside, but also the most risk because it gets paid last.

In many equity financing situations, different partners will have different terms—perhaps one partner gets more cash flow during the hold period of the investment, but less profit at the end of the project (or maybe more cash flow *and* more profit). For example, let's imagine that Melissa sees Brian's deal as risky. As such, when she buys the equity from Brian, she negotiates terms that entitle her to be paid out first, before Brian. But if things go well, Brian gets to keep 60 percent of the profits and Melissa gets just 40 percent.

CAPITAL STACK | RENTAL PROP LLC

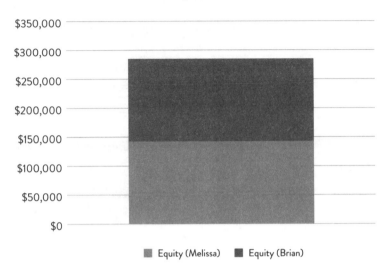

In this case, the capital stack has changed. Melissa has negotiated a less risky position for herself where she gets paid out before Brian. This moves her down the capital stack. Brian is taking on the most risk, but he is given the biggest opportunity for upside. Notice that despite the different terms, the size of Melissa's and Brian's respective investments is the same; therefore, their visual representations on the capital stack are the same size.

We sometimes refer to equity that is lower in the capital stack—and that has a higher priority for payment—as "preferred equity." When profits are paid out, preferred equity gets paid first. And in a situation where the equity holders lose money on the deal and there isn't enough remaining capital to pay back the investors their original investment, the preferred equity holders will get paid first. In the example above, we might say that Melissa holds preferred equity over Brian's common equity.

#59

Preferred equity holders are given preference in the capital stack over common equity holders. Typically, they will receive returns up to a specific amount or percentage (the "preferred return") before common equity holders receive any return. Preferred equity holders have more risk than debt holders but less risk than common equity holders.

While preferred equity adds some complexity, the examples used above still represent fairly straightforward equity deals. In real life, equity partnerships can take on almost any form. If a group of partners can agree on a set of terms, those terms are possible (unless they're illegal, of course). Some of the common variables that are considered in an equity deal are:

- **The number of partners.** There is no limit to the number of partners on a single deal. The person putting together the deal can, however, impose investment minimums.
- **Investment minimums.** Whoever is offering the equity can determine the minimum amount invested by future partners. For example, Brian may not want ten investors each contributing $14,250 because it is too many partners for a small deal. He could then set an investment minimum of $40,000, for example, to limit the maximum number of partners to three.
- **Equity type.** Some equity financing deals will offer multiple types of equity. As we discussed above, common equity and preferred equity are the two types of equity, but even within these two types, we can have different "classes" of equity—meaning different pools of ownership, each with different rights, obligations, and return structures.
- **Compensation for equity.** Our example assumes we are selling equity for cash, which is most common. But it's also possible to trade equity, or even give away equity, depending on the situation. For example, Brian could give away some piece of equity to a contractor in exchange for $10,000 of labor. Or he could give equity to a consultant or adviser for providing expertise that helps grow the business.
- **Buy/sell/reassign.** What happens if one partner wants to sell the property before another? Can they force a sale? Can they resell their equity to someone else? If so, who is allowed to buy it?

There are very few rules about how equity financing is structured, which is one of many advantages to using equity financing. But equity financing does have downsides. As the investor, you need to carefully weigh the pros and cons of equity financing to determine what types of equity and how much of it to use in your deals.

PROS OF EQUITY FINANCING

- **Flexibility.** As we mentioned, equity financing can come in almost any shape or format that partners can agree on.
- **Get started sooner/access to bigger deals.** Pretty much every deal involves some amount of equity. Even if you're buying your own home with an FHA loan, you still must put a minimum of 3.5 percent down in cash (equity capital) to secure a mortgage (debt). Many new and aspiring investors may not have sufficient capital to put toward a deal. Bringing on a partner is a good way for new investors to get

started if they don't have the capital to secure a mortgage, pay for rehabs, etc. Bringing on a partner is also a common way that experienced investors can get into multifamily, commercial, or other large-scale investments that they cannot afford individually.

- **Shared risk.** Adding a partner to a deal spreads the risk proportionally to each partner. When you finance a deal yourself, any losses or cost overruns fall directly to you. Bringing on an equity partner helps ensure that you are not solely responsible for any downside on the investment. A partner may have access to additional capital beyond the initial investment and can add capital to the project if needed.
- **Partner is invested in the deal and may be able to help.** Having a partner can add value to a business beyond just equity. An experienced partner may have connections with great contractors, lenders, or property managers, or be able to provide a host of other services and skills needed to make an investment successful.
- **Don't need to divert funds to make loan payments.** When you take on debt, you must make payments on that debt, regardless of what cash flows or returns your investment is generating. Equity financing does not require that payouts happen at any specific time and can be structured to best suit the investment at hand. For example, financing a flip with equity would allow the flipper to put all their money into the rehab, instead of taking some of their cash and sending it to a lender each month to service their debt.

CONS OF EQUITY FINANCING

- **Giving away more of your profits.** Investors want to be compensated for taking risk. The downside of bringing on a partner who shares your risk in a deal is that partner will want a greater upside for assuming that risk.
- **More oversight.** Having partners means that your decisions will directly impact your partners' finances. As such, equity partners will likely request some oversight of your decisions.
- **Investors will expect more communication.** With debt financing, the bank doesn't really care what you're doing with your time, as long as the loan payments are being made. With equity financing, you're dealing with partners who are depending on your performance for their returns. As such, they will expect regular, professional updates on how the investment is progressing. If those partners are active partners, they will likely require your time in the form of discussions, meetings, and shared updates.
- **Breakups can be messy.** Just like with any relationship, breaking up can create a whole host of issues, particularly if you don't have a well-defined operating agreement in place.

- **May be extra legal work and risk.** Equity arrangements are far more flexible than debt—they can be structured in pretty much any way the partners agree. But that often means lawyers need to get involved to make sure everyone is fairly protected, and there are procedures in place in case things go awry. Even if you're investing with friends and family, it's wise to get legal agreements drafted for any partnerships.
- **Voting rights.** Depending on the structure, equity investors may be entitled to some voting rights, and you can lose some control of your deal.

As with all strategic decisions, the use of equity financing comes with tradeoffs. As you now know, there are great benefits as well as significant drawbacks to equity financing. To maximize the benefits and limit the downsides, it's important to employ a type of equity financing that aligns best with your investing goals.

Before we move on to common forms of equity financing in the next chapter, let's review the fundamentals we've learned here:
- Equity financing is capital (cash) injected into a deal by the deal's owners.
- Equity financing is extremely flexible and can take almost any form.
- The person putting the deal together can sell, trade, or give away equity (ownership) in exchange for cash or other value (e.g., contract work, credit).
- Selling or giving away equity means losing some (or all) control and ownership while spreading risk between partners.
- Equity financing is a great way for investors to invest in properties they cannot afford using their capital alone.

Now, let's move on to explore some of the most common types of equity financing employed by real estate investors.

HONE YOUR SKILLS: CHAPTER 26

- In the world of real estate investing, what does the word "equity" refer to?
- True or false: All equity holders that share the same class of equity are lumped together in the capital stack.
- Name three pros and three cons of equity financing.

CHAPTER 27
TYPES OF EQUITY FINANCING

Chapter 27 will help us to answer the questions:
- What are the different ways to finance deals through equity?
- Which type of equity financing makes sense for my strategy?

Equity financing comes in many forms, each with its own advantages and disadvantages. Depending on your needs and the needs of the equity partners you'll be working with, there are a number of different ways to structure an equity partnership.

In this chapter, you'll find a high-level overview of some of the most common forms of equity partnerships.

ACTIVE PARTNERS

Active equity partners bring capital, effort, and expertise to a real estate deal. Having active partners can increase your odds of success on a given deal. That said, active partners are often a relatively expensive financing option. Partners who work on the deal beyond just contributing capital generally require a greater potential for returns, given their additional investments of both time and expertise.

Active partnerships have large upsides because they can form well-rounded and experienced teams, but they also require some up-front work. Drafting a strong operating agreement with clear roles for each partner is essential at the outset of any partnership.

PASSIVE PARTNERS

Passive partners bring capital to a deal, but do not actively participate in the investment. They contribute money in exchange for some combination of ongoing cash flow and a share of profits, but they do not invest any of their own time into the deal. Passive partners also typically have limited—or no—voting rights. Any time you have passive partners, it's important to ensure that you are structuring the partnership in a way that is compliant with relevant securities laws.

SYNDICATED INVESTMENTS

Syndicated investments are a subset of passive partners, and while they are treated the same legally, we are generally referring to syndications when the pool of passive partners is large and the passive partners are putting in most or all of the capital. Syndications often target large commercial, retail, or multifamily complexes.

TRADE PARTNERS

Trade partners are active partners who contribute labor to a real estate deal. This is an attractive option for smaller investors who don't always have the money to front for various labor tasks on the investment project. With a trade partnership, the partner contributes labor in exchange for some ownership (equity) in the deal. Trade partners may be contractors, professional service providers, or those with expertise (a mentor or coach).

CREDIT PARTNERS

A credit partner brings their credit to a partnership, enabling the partnership to take on more debt than an investor could qualify for on their own. For example, if Sarah has several mortgages in her name and banks are now hesitant to grant her another loan, she could partner with someone who has good credit and less debt in their name. That way Sarah gains access to debt financing she couldn't get on her own, and her partner gains access to Sarah's experience owning several properties already.

DOWN PAYMENT PARTNERS

Down payment partners provide equity to secure debt. Most loans require some sort of down payment, and coming up with cash for a down payment can be prohibitive to some investors (particularly new investors).

A down payment partner can be brought on to provide the cash needed to secure a loan. As an example, let's imagine that Tina wants to purchase a property for $250,000 and the bank is requiring a 20 percent down payment. Tina needs $50,000 to secure the loan, but she doesn't have that on hand. To secure the loan, she brings on a partner who contributes $50,000 to the deal in exchange for a share of the ownership/profits/upside of the investment.

The list of equity financing options above is not meant to be comprehensive and exists to help you understand the scope of what is possible with equity financing. Within each of these categories exists almost limitless structure types. Nearly every deal involves some amount of equity, so it's important to get comfortable with different equity financing formats. Sometimes only a small amount of equity is used to help secure debt, like putting down 20 percent equity to secure 80 percent debt (mortgage). Other times, deals can be funded using mostly—or even entirely—equity capital. It's all up to the investors involved in the deal.

To fully understand when and how to use equity, you need to understand equity's counterpart: debt. In the following chapters, we're going to explore debt very thoroughly. When you've completed these chapters on debt, you will have a well-rounded understanding of real estate financing and know when to use equity, when to use debt, and how to combine them for maximum upside.

HONE YOUR SKILLS: CHAPTER 27

- What is an active partner?
- What is a passive partner?
- True or false: The ways in which you can structure a partnership are very limited and rigid.

CHAPTER 28
INTRODUCTION TO DEBT FINANCING

Chapter 28 will help us to answer the questions:
- How can borrowed money be used in real estate investing?
- What are the pros and cons of using debt to fund real estate investments?

Debt financing is just a formal way of saying "borrowing money." Every debt financing situation involves two parties: a borrower (e.g., a person, business, government entity) and a lender (e.g., a bank, credit union, individual, government). The lender—also known as the "debt holder"— provides capital to the borrower, who uses it to fund their business. In exchange, the borrower pays the lender back the money, with interest, over time.

#60 | **Debt financing** involves borrowing money in the form of a loan and then repaying that money with a predefined amount of interest.

The critical difference between debt and equity is that raising debt financing does not require giving away ownership. The debt holder (lender) does get certain protections and benefits for lending money, like monthly payments and the legal right to foreclose on a property, but the debt holder does not own any piece of the deal.

In real estate, debt is most common in the form of a mortgage, but there are countless types of debt used in other parts of life that you've probably heard of or use regularly. Car loans, student loans, credit cards, and home equity lines of credit (HELOCs) are all examples of debt financing.

Some people, particularly in the personal finance community, simply hate debt. There are some decent reasons for this. It can be very dangerous to rely on debt that you can't easily repay. For example, using credit cards to fund purchases you cannot afford can quickly spiral into a personal financial crisis as the interest on credit card debt compounds at sky-high rates.

But not all debt is bad. Using debt to fund an investment—something that will earn you money and help you repay that debt—is entirely different. Using a student loan to earn a degree that boosts earning potential can be a great investment. If you're starting a property maintenance business and need a truck, getting an auto loan is an investment into your new moneymaking venture.

Real estate is no different. Debt can help fund deals you'd never be able to afford on your own. It can unlock enormous wealth-building opportunities and it can help you scale rapidly.

The trick is being able to identify when debt is helping (boosting your returns) and when it's hurting (draining returns). There are many different types of loan structures and costs, so it's important that you use debt wisely. We're about to show you exactly how to do that.

In Chapters 30–37, we'll break down the math that underpins all loans, and show you several strategies and metrics that will help you determine which types of loans fit your investing strategy.

But first, let's return to the example of Brian to demonstrate how a basic debt financing deal would look. Remember, Brian is seeking funding to purchase and operate a single rental property, 200 Post Road. You may recall from Chapter 25 that Brian needs $285,000 to fund this business.

If Brian were able to fund his entire deal using debt, his capital stack would look as follows:

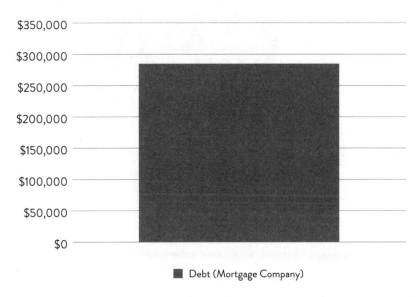

CAPITAL STACK | RENTAL PROP LLC

■ Debt (Mortgage Company)

Simple enough. Brian has taken out a loan for 100 percent of his capital needs. But deals are very rarely funded using 100 percent debt. It can be extremely risky for investors to take on that level of debt (which we'll explain later), and lenders usually won't allow it—they want the owners to have some skin in the game (equity capital).

For these reasons, in a typical mortgage situation, the lender will require at least some equity capital. With most investment properties, lenders will require at least 25 percent equity capital (in the form of a down payment), with the bank providing the other 75 percent or so of the funds.

CAPITAL STACK | RENTAL PROP LLC

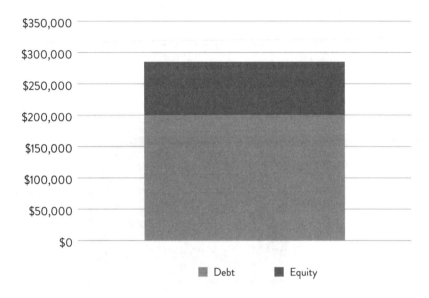

In this capital stack, the bank has provided debt financing for 75 percent of the purchase price of the property ($187,500). Brian has contributed the rest of the financing in the form of equity capital ($97,500). Note that in this example, the bank is only covering 75 percent of the purchase price of $250,000, and none of the additional expenses. Brian is contributing 25 percent of the purchase price ($62,500), plus an additional $35,000 to cover the closing, rehab, and operations expenses. In tabular format, this deal would look like this:

EXPENSE	AMOUNT	DEBT	EQUITY
Purchase Price	$250,000	$187,500	$62,500
Closing Costs	$5,000	$0	$5,000
Rehab Costs	$20,000	$0	$20,000
Operating Reserve	$10,000	$0	$10,000
TOTAL	$285,000	$187,500	$97,500

The above example is a very common structure for real estate financing. Some equity is used to secure debt, which funds most of the purchase price of the deal.

Just like with equity, there can be (and often are) multiple sources of debt.

To demonstrate how this works, let's look at one more scenario with Brian. In this scenario, Brian provides a 25 percent down payment (equity) to secure a mortgage (debt), and he'll also use his own equity capital to cover his closing costs. However, this time around, Brian is going to take on a secondary loan to fund his rehab costs and operating reserve.

EXPENSE	AMOUNT	DEBT #1	DEBT #2	EQUITY
Purchase Price	$250,000	$187,500	$0	$62,500
Closing Costs	$5,000	$0	$0	$5,000
Rehab Costs	$20,000	$0	$20,000	$0.00
Operating Reserve	$10,000	$0	$10,000	$0.00
TOTAL	$285,000	$187,500	$30,000	$67,500

In this capital stack, Debt #1 is at the bottom of the stack. If the deal fails to return sufficient capital to pay out the entire capital stack, this debt would be paid first, then Debt #2 would be paid, and then Brian (the equity holder) would take whatever might be left.

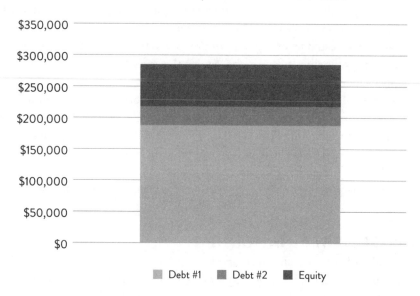

CAPITAL STACK | RENTAL PROP LLC

Because the second lender (Debt #2) in this scenario is higher on the capital stack, this lender has greater risk. Therefore, the interest rate on this loan is likely to be higher than that of Debt #1. Again, as you move from the bottom of the capital stack to the top, the order of payment, risk (chance of not getting paid), and potential reward (returns) all increase.

Hopefully you can see why debt financing is so appealing. Brian is purchasing a property for $250,000, but he only needs to bring $67,500 in equity to the deal—far less than what he would need to bring in an all-equity deal.

But there are trade-offs with using debt. Below is list of the pros and cons of using debt, which should help you understand how to approach the use of debt in your deals.

PROS OF DEBT FINANCING

- **You retain full ownership of the asset.** When taking a loan for your business or for a specific deal, you won't be required to give up ownership to the lender. You can still claim 100 percent ownership in the business entity and/or the investment, and you maintain all rights (subject to the loan agreement) granted to the owner of the business or property.
- **The terms of the agreement are well defined.** When borrowing for a project, the loan terms are typically straightforward and there is little room for confusion. Because the lender has no ownership stake in the project, your obligations are not going to change, regardless of what happens with the deal. Whether you make money on the project, lose money on the project, face complications or a change in investment strategy—your promise to the lender stays the same. Your commitment is simple: Repay the loan on the agreed-upon schedule and at the agreed-upon interest rate.
- **The financing cost is defined up front.** When borrowing, the cost to you as the investor (in the form of interest paid to the lender) is well defined. The only variable is the amount of time it takes you to repay the loan. If you can anticipate how long you'll keep the loan, you can typically anticipate exactly how much you'll pay to the lender. This won't change based on the success (or lack of success) of the project, and it won't change based on the decisions you make as the owner.

CONS OF DEBT FINANCING

- **You absorb all the risk.** The biggest downside to debt financing is that all the risk of loss is on the borrower. Your obligation to repay the loan doesn't change based on the financial results of the project. If the deal goes south and you take a loss on the investment, that won't impact the amount that you owe to the lender. And if the funds from the sale or refinancing of the investment don't cover what's owed to the lender, it's your responsibility to cover the difference out of your own pocket. Debt is lower risk to the provider than equity. Because debt holders (lenders) get paid first in the capital stack, they have a lower risk of not getting paid. In other words, no matter what happens with the performance of the deal, the investor must pay back the debt holder before they take any profits for themselves or for their partners.

- **It takes money from your reserves every month.** Investors want to conserve their capital and spend as little as possible throughout the investment. Lenders will often require monthly payments on the loan. In this struggle between borrowers and lenders, the lenders generally win. You'll probably be writing a check every month to the lender, which will reduce your capital reserves and require more discipline managing your cash flow.
- **It reduces your ability to get additional debt financing.** When a lender makes a loan against a property, the lender will typically have access to the property as collateral for the loan. If you don't repay as promised, the lender will have the ability to take that property to recapture their investment and anticipated profit. Once a lender has the property as collateral, another lender on the same deal will be "second in line" to collect on that collateral. This adds risk to future lenders, and for that reason, having a first loan on a property will make getting additional loans against the same asset difficult.
- **Most debt providers will have a cap on the percentage of the deal they'll finance.** For example, you'll rarely, if ever, see 100 percent debt financing. Most lenders cap out at 75–80 percent of the cost of the deal.

To maximize your use of debt and limit risk, you need to select a debt structure that aligns well with your investing objectives. And there are a lot of types of debt! In the next chapter, we're going to provide a high-level overview of the types of debt and some general guidance on when to use each.

HONE YOUR SKILLS: CHAPTER 28

- True or false: Using debt financing does not require giving away ownership.
- What does it mean for debt to be "senior" to other forms of debt?
- Name three pros and three cons of debt financing.

CHAPTER 29
FORMS OF DEBT FINANCING

Chapter 29 will help us to answer the questions:
- What types of debt are available to me?
- What types of debt best fit my investing strategy and goals?

This section is not meant to be a comprehensive analysis of every type of debt financing on the market. Instead, our goal here is to help you understand which types of financing may be aligned with your personal financial situation and investing goals. We aim to point you in the right direction, but the following is generalized advice. Before making an investment, do more research into the different financing types you identify, and speak to a lawyer, lender, or CPA as appropriate.

TYPES OF DEBT FINANCING

In the world of real estate investing, there are three primary types of debt financing used: term loans, lines of credit, and revolving debt.

Within each of these categories exist different options to be used, depending on your financial situation and investing strategy. Knowing which types of debt are best for a given situation can be tricky, so we've detailed the various types of loans and when to use them in the following section.

Term Loans

A term loan is a form of debt financing where the borrower is lent money for a specific length of time and has a fixed repayment schedule. Common forms of term loans are mortgages, student loans, and auto loans.

All term loans have the same basic format: The borrower agrees to borrow X dollars for Y years at Z interest rate. For example, a common mortgage could be structured as $200,000 for thirty years at a 4.5 percent interest rate. (Note that these are the same inputs we used when calculating interest earlier in the book.) Of course, there are many other variables in each loan, such as the payment frequency, down payment, balloon payments, collateral, loan covenants, and more. But at their core, all term loans follow this basic structure.

Term loans can have either a fixed or an adjustable interest rate. With a *fixed-rate loan*, the borrower pays the same interest rate for the duration of the loan. For example, Sergio gets a mortgage for $330,000 at a fixed 4.5 percent interest rate for thirty years. With a fixed-rate mortgage, Sergio knows exactly what his payment will be for all thirty years of his loan. Typically, interest rates are slightly higher on fixed-term loans because there is less risk to the borrower than an adjustable interest rate.

An *adjustable-rate loan* (when talking about mortgages, it is often known as an ARM, or adjustable-rate mortgage) has an interest rate that changes over the course of the loan. The term of the loan, and the frequency of the adjustments to the interest rate, can vary considerably.

If you've ever heard of a 7/1 ARM, for example, that means that the initial interest rate is locked in for seven years, and then the rate is adjusted every year after that for the duration of the loan.

How much the interest rate changes, and in what direction, is often tied to an index—basically a measurement of how much it costs for the banks to borrow money on the credit markets. This carries both risk and upside for the borrower. If the cost of borrowing goes down, then the borrower is likely to see their interest rate (and therefore their payments) decrease over time. If interest rates go up, however, the borrower is at risk of having their interest rates (and therefore their payments) increase over time. One big benefit of ARMs is that they typically have a lower initial interest rate than fixed-rate loans.

Both fixed-rate and adjustable-rate loans have their uses. If you're buying a rental you intend to hold on to for a long time, and if you can lock in a relatively low interest rate, it likely makes sense to get a fixed-rate mortgage. If you're using a BRRRR strategy and intend to refinance in a year or two, you could get an adjustable-rate mortgage to take advantage of the lower initial interest rate and refinance well before you take on the risk of having your interest rate adjusted.

The type of interest rate, what term, how much you borrow, and what type of fixed-term loan you should consider all depend on your strategy, personal financial situation, and risk tolerance.

Here is a brief overview of some of the more common types of term loans that real estate investors encounter.

Conventional Loans

A conventional loan is a form of mortgage term loan that is offered by a private bank, lender, or credit union. Conventional loans can come with either a fixed rate or an adjustable rate. The term for conventional loans is typically long, with a thirty-year term being the most common. Fifteen- and twenty-year terms are also common, but you can see terms of pretty much any length under thirty years. The shorter the term, the higher your payments will be, but you'll pay less interest (profit to the banks) over the course of the loan. Longer terms mean lower payments, but you'll pay the banks more for borrowing the same amount of money.

Applying for a conventional loan is typically a streamlined process. Banks will have you complete their required paperwork, credit check, and appraisal when they determine whether you're eligible for the loan.

Conventional loans are most used for financing your personal home, traditional rentals, short-term rentals, and BRRRRs.

FHA Loans

An FHA loan is very similar to a conventional loan, except it is made by a federally approved financial institution and is insured by the Federal Housing Administration (which is why it's called an FHA loan). Generally, FHA loans allow borrowers to put less money down than with conventional loans (as low as 3.5 percent), which makes purchasing property affordable for Americans with less income or savings.

FHA loans tend to be riskier loans for the lender, which is why the government must insure the loans—otherwise banks might not choose to lend to this class of borrower. But with the additional insurance comes additional fees. FHA loans come with two forms of "mortgage insurance premium" (MIP). The up-front MIP is due at closing, and as of this writing costs 1.75 percent of the loan amount. The annual MIP varies depending on the size and term of the loan, and it is tacked on to the monthly payment. While FHA loans enable homeownership for millions of Americans, the additional fees can really add up and impact returns.

FHA loans are used exclusively for owner-occupied properties. If you're wanting to buy your next rental and don't plan to move in, forget about an FHA loan. But if you're looking to house hack, do a live-in flip, or simply want to purchase a home to live in, an FHA loan could be a good option, particularly if you don't have savings to put 20 percent down. But remember, FHA loans tend to be more expensive than conventional loans because of the mortgage insurance payments.

Portfolio Loan

A portfolio loan is similar to a conventional loan, but it is issued by a bank that keeps the loan in its portfolio for the lifetime of the loan. Portfolio lenders typically use money from their own depositors/customers to make the loans, so they can define their own criteria for whom they will lend to and the terms of the loans.

This is different from conventional loans, which are often bought and sold on the secondary market, where the lender has to follow strict government rules (which are set up to protect the institutions and investors who buy on the secondary market). For example, you might get a mortgage from a big bank like Wells Fargo, who will then sell it to a different bank or a large institution a few months after closing.

With portfolio loans, the bank has no intention of selling the mortgage on the secondary market, and therefore can set its own internal standards for what loans to make. This often means that portfolio loans have much looser regulations. Portfolios loans can be a great option for people who have poor credit, want to purchase a property that is in poor condition (many investors love these places!), are self-employed, or any of the other reasons you may not qualify for a conventional loan.

Just remember, banks are not going to loosen restrictions out of the goodness of their hearts. To take on the extra risk of a nonconforming loan, they are going to charge a higher interest rate or find other ways to charge the borrower more (for example, charging a higher origination fee).

Hard-Money Loans

A hard-money loan is a type of term loan that is secured by real property. That is, you are using collateral (in real estate, we're pretty much always talking about the property you're using the loan to buy/rehab) to reduce risk for the lender. In fact, the term "hard" in hard-money lending refers to the fact that the loan is secured by a hard asset, like a piece of real estate.

Hard-money loans are not made by banks. Instead, they are traditionally made by individuals or non-bank companies. The advantages of this are that the time to close is reduced drastically, and the lender considers each loan individually (it's not as rigid as a conventional loan process). Also, the lender typically considers the value of the collateral (property) and not the credit of the borrower when deciding which loans to fund.

Typically, hard-money loans are for short periods of time, and because lenders want to make a large profit for this risky undertaking, they charge a high interest rate—sometimes two to three times what conventional loans go for. Borrowers can be asked to put 30–40 percent down given the higher-risk nature of the loan.

This situation creates an interesting dynamic. Sure, the lender would like to get paid back. But if the borrower defaults, the lender simply takes their collateral and resells it. That said, hard-money loans are very useful for certain types of real estate transactions—primarily house flipping or BRRRR projects—really any strategy where the borrower intends to sell or refinance the house quickly. It's often difficult to get a flip financed conventionally, but hard-money lenders will often lend you the money to complete these types of deals.

The speed-to-close and flexibility of hard-money loans make them popular and beneficial for flippers and rehabbers. Just don't get stuck making payments on a hard-money loan for a long time—the high interest rates on these loans can eat into or completely deplete your profits.

Private Loans

Private loans are an all-encompassing category for term loans that are made by private individuals. This could range from a friend or family member to a professional colleague or even a small-time lender who lends within their community. Given that private loans are just between two individuals or two private entities, these loans can take on almost any form. Like hard-money loans, private loans can be originated much faster than loans from banks.

More experienced private lenders will likely have terms they look for, interest rate minimums, repayment terms, and other criteria they have developed over time. However, private loans can come from anywhere, including friends and family (really anyone who has funds to loan can be a private lender).

Private loans are a useful tool because they can be structured in almost any way the lender and borrow can think of. The money can also be used in any way. For example, a new investor with not much cash for a down payment could get a private loan to fund their down payment, and then get a mortgage to finance the rest of their purchase.

When employing a private loan, it's extremely important to make sure there is a proper contract in place that details all the terms of the loan. This is true even if (especially if!) the loan comes from friends or family. Both parties need to know exactly what they are getting into before the loan is made. It will save a lot of headaches, and potentially heartaches, down the road.

Crowdfunding

Crowdfunding is a type of debt where many individuals pool relatively small amounts of money together to make a purchase. For example, an investor may join nine other investors, each of them contributing $10,000 to fund the 20 percent down payment on a $500,000 property.

A number of online crowdfunding platforms have popped up over the past few years, helping investors raise money from "the crowd." These sites help investors vet their deals and present these deals to investors on the platform who are looking for investments backed by real estate. Crowdfunding is quickly becoming a great option for investors who are looking for an alternative to banks or hard-money lenders.

Seller Financing

Seller financing is a situation where the seller of a property is willing to help provide either debt or equity for the buyer of the property. When a seller has a lot of equity in a property—for example, the property is owned free and clear or is worth a good bit more than what's owed in debt—the seller can provide some or all of that equity to the buyer in the form of either a loan or an equity partnership. The seller might allow the buyer of the property to make interest payments for some period of time, or the seller might share in whatever profits the buyer ultimately generates from the property.

This is an attractive option for some sellers because they can get a higher price for their property than they might otherwise; plus, they can either earn interest on the money they are lending or get a split of the profits. Because banks are not involved, this type of loan therefore might appeal to those who have difficulty obtaining bank financing. If you have poor credit, are self-employed, or have too many personal mortgages already, seller financing could be a great opportunity.

Lines of Credit

Lines of credit are a very common form of debt, but are distinctly different from a term loan. Where a term loan is repaid over a fixed amount of time, a line of credit (LOC) is a standing agreement that allows a borrower to borrow and repay money as needed, up to a certain limit. As long as the borrower does not exceed the limit on the line of credit, they can access funds and pay them back as they see fit. When the borrower borrows against the line of credit, interest payments are made on the outstanding debt. Lines of credit work similarly to credit cards, but where there is no interest-free period and where the lender doesn't expect full repayment each month.

As an example, let's say that Maria is thinking about starting a consulting business, but she is unsure how much money she is going to need and when exactly she will need it. Rather than getting a fixed-term loan, she applies for a line of credit from her local bank. Based on her credit history and the needs of her business, she is granted a $75,000 line of credit at a 5 percent interest rate. Now, Maria has access to $75,000 when she needs it. Fortunately, she does not need any of it for the first three months she is running her business, and therefore isn't paying interest unnecessarily.

When her business takes off and she needs to open an office, she needs $50,000 and borrows from her line of credit. At that point, she begins paying interest on the $50,000 borrowed. She still has access to another $25,000 any time she needs it (provided she is making payments as agreed on the $50,000). As she pays down the $50,000 she has borrowed, she regains access to more capital, always up to her maximum of $75,000.

This type of debt is very flexible and useful to investors. If you want to fund a rehab, purchase a new property, or anything else, a line of credit is a low-cost form of debt financing you should consider. But not everyone is eligible for lines of credit. In exchange for the flexibility the bank provides with a LOC, they often look for very creditworthy businesses and individuals, or ask for collateral, like with a home equity line of credit (HELOC). Also, the interest rate on a line of credit will typically fluctuate with broader interest rates, which means that if interest rates rise, you may be paying more interest on your LOC.

Home Equity Line of Credit

A home equity line of credit (HELOC) is a very common financing instrument for real estate investors because it uses the equity you have in your home to secure a line of credit.

When you purchase a home, even with a mortgage, you typically have some equity in that home. For example, if Devon buys a house for $300,000 and puts 30 percent ($90,000) down, Devon now has $90,000 of equity in his home.

A HELOC uses a part of the equity of your home (some part of Devon's $90,000 in our example) to secure your line of credit. Offering your home's equity as collateral means that banks view this type of LOC as less risky, and therefore offer you low interest rates. Often the interest rate offered on a HELOC is similar to that of a conventional mortgage.

Of course, offering your home as collateral does come with its own risks. If you fail to make payments on your HELOC as agreed upon, the bank can foreclose on your house.

Because of the low interest rates, HELOCs are an excellent form of financing for real estate investors. They are a common way to finance rehab projects, flips, and even down payments on rentals. But just like with every form of debt, they need to be used responsibly—failure to do so can result in the loss of your personal residence.

Business Line of Credit

A business line of credit is a loan between a bank and a business that can help a business expand, purchase equipment, manage short-term cash-flow challenges, or nearly anything else related to the business. For a business to qualify for a line of credit, it typically needs to have a good track record of revenue and ideally have some amount of cash flow. Business lines of credit are typically not a good option for businesses looking for startup capital, but they can be a great option for existing and profitable businesses.

Personal Line of Credit

A personal line of credit is a line of credit established between a bank and an individual, but it is not secured with collateral (like a HELOC).

Because this is a relatively risky loan, personal lines of credit are difficult to qualify for, and banks typically charge high interest rates. Thus, personal lines of credit can be helpful to overcome short-term cash-flow challenges, but should not be considered for long-term investments given their high interest rates compared to other forms of debt financing.

Revolving Debt

The most common form of revolving debt is credit cards. Credit card issuers give the borrower access to a certain amount of money that the borrower can use and repay as needed, similar to lines of credit.

Credit cards are very convenient—typically they are interest free for up to a month—but can carry hefty interest rates after that interest-free period. While not recommended for most purposes, credit cards can allow business owners and investors a way to cover short-term cash-flow issues.

Of all forms of debt financing, credit cards tend to have the highest interest rates. As a rule of thumb, you don't want to use credit cards to finance anything that will take you more than a month or two to pay off.

After reading about these debt structures, you may be thinking, "There are so many types of debt—how do I choose which type to use?" And that is exactly what you should be thinking. Picking a debt structure is not a trivial matter. It's a vital decision that will have implications for your deal's risk profile and rates of return. To help you choose from this list of options, we're going to spend the next several chapters on the inner workings of debt, and we'll cover some very useful metrics that enable you to compare different debt types against one another.

HONE YOUR SKILLS: CHAPTER 29

- What is a term loan?
- What is a hard-money loan?
- How is a line of credit different from a term loan?

CHAPTER 30

THE ANATOMY
OF A LOAN

Chapter 30 will help us to answer the questions:
- How does a loan actually work?
- What factors should I examine when considering a loan?

Learning the inner workings of a loan may not be the most exciting topic, but trust us—it's worth it. By understanding how a loan works, you'll be better able to identify financing opportunities that make sense for you.

While it's easy to plug a few numbers into a web-based mortgage calculator and estimate your monthly payments, it's worth the time to learn what's going on behind the scenes. The basic math that underpins a loan will help you find loans that serve your long-term strategy and expose you to the least amount of risk.

PRINCIPAL VERSUS INTEREST

Every loan is primarily made up of two components: principal and interest. Principal is the amount of money borrowed from the lender. Interest is the lender's profit. As you might expect, investors want to pay as little interest as possible, while lenders want to generate as much interest as they can.

When shopping for loans, you will often see numbers for both the interest rate and the APR (annual percentage rate). They are very similar concepts, but the APR builds in any fees and expenses on top of the standard interest rate. For the purposes of explaining the math in this book, we are going to use the term "interest rate." However, APR best shows a borrower the true cost of their loan and should be used to compare loans in the real world.

For example, you may have a credit card that charges an interest rate of 20 percent on any unpaid balance. However, when all the fees are factored in, the amount you wind up paying (your APR) is closer to 23 percent. For obvious reasons, as a consumer, you should care more about that 23 percent APR than the 20 percent interest rate, as it's more indicative of the actual cost of carrying a balance on that credit card.

To help us explain the inner workings of a loan, we're going to use a small but experienced investor, Julia, who is adding a rental property to her portfolio. Julia is looking to purchase a rental for $400,000 and will finance it by putting 20 percent down on a conventional thirty-year mortgage with a fixed 5 percent interest rate.

With just this information, we can determine how much interest and principal Julia will pay over the lifetime of her loan, as well as how quickly she will build equity value in her new property (remember, equity value is the amount of cash the owner could generate from the sale of property, after paying off all debt). Calculating the loan principal is simple. We just determine what percentage of Julia's purchase is being financed by the loan and multiply that by the purchase price.

For example, if Julia is making a 20 percent down payment on the property, then the other 80 percent of the purchase price is coming from the debt (the loan) being provided by the lender.

#61 | **Principal**
Principal = Purchase price × (1 – Down payment %)

In Julia's example:

Principal = Purchase price × (1 – Down payment %)
Principal = $400,000 × (1 – 0.20) = $320,000

The principal on Julia's mortgage is $320,000.

The 20 percent down payment that Julia is making is her starting equity in the property. Keep that in mind—later in this chapter we will show you how to calculate your equity value in a property at any point in time.

Calculating the monthly payment on a mortgage is a bit complex and is best done using an online mortgage calculator. However, if you're curious, the formula is:

#62

Monthly mortgage payments
$$M = P \times [(r (1 + r)^n \div ((1 + r)^n) - 1]$$

Where
  M = monthly mortgage payment
  P = total loan amount
  r = monthly interest rate (Divide your annual interest rate by 12. For a 5 percent interest rate, r = 0.417 percent.)
  n = total number of payments (Multiply the term of your loan in years by 12. For a thirty-year mortgage, n = 360.)

In our example, the monthly payment works out to be approximately $1,717.83 (we're rounding in this example, so if you try to replicate this, your numbers might not turn out identical to ours).

This number combines both the principal and interest Julia is paying to the bank each month. This is often referred to as "P&I" and is the core of any loan payment.

Knowing the total monthly P&I amount, we can calculate the total cost of the loan by multiplying Julia's monthly payment by the total payments.

Total loan cost = Monthly payment (P&I) amount × Total payments
Total loan cost = $1,717.83 × 360
Total loan cost = **$618,418.51**

Our last step now is to calculate the total interest of the loan, which we do by simply subtracting the principal from the total amount of the loan.

Total interest = Total loan amount – Principal
Total interest = $618,418.51 – $320,000
Total interest = **$298,418.51**

In this scenario, Julia is borrowing $320,000 over thirty years and will pay the bank $298,418.51 in interest (the bank's profit) over the course of the loan, on top of the $320,000 in principal she borrowed and must repay. Over thirty years, Julia will pay the bank nearly double the amount she borrowed when factoring in the bank's profit.

AMORTIZATION

It would be reasonable to assume that because Julia's monthly mortgage payments stay the same over the lifetime of her loan, the composition of those payments remains fixed. But that is not the case. The proportion of her payment that goes to paying down her principal—and the proportion going to interest—changes every single month. This concept is known as amortization and is an important factor in generating returns on a real estate investment.

Quick Tip | **Amortization's Other Definition**
The term "amortization" is also used in accounting and refers to the spreading out of capital expenditures over a period. We are not talking about that here.

The reason that the proportion of principal and interest Julia is paying changes each month is due to the way mortgages are structured. Each month the borrower pays interest on the principal balance at the beginning of that month.

When Julia first initiates her loan, she owes $320,000 in principal, as we calculated in the previous section. We also know that the monthly interest rate on her loan is 0.417 percent, which we calculate by dividing the annual interest rate (5 percent) by 12 ($0.05 \div 12 = 0.417$).

Using these two numbers, we can determine that Julia owes the bank $1,333.33 in interest in Month 0 of her loan.

Month 0 interest = Remaining principal × Monthly interest rate
Month 0 interest = $320,000 × 0.00417
Month 0 interest = $1,333.33

Because we already know that Julia's monthly payment is $1,717.83, we can simply subtract her interest from her monthly payment to determine how much principal she is paying down each month.

Month 0 principal = Monthly payment − Month 0 interest
Month 0 principal = $1,717.83 − $1,333.33
Month 0 principal = $384.50

For Julia's first payment to the bank on her $320,000 mortgage, she is going to pay a total of $1,717.83, of which $1,333.33 is interest and $384.50 is principal.

Interest is only paid on the outstanding principal balance of the loan. As the principal balance goes down, the amount of monthly interest owed goes down as well. Because the remaining principal on Julia's loan has changed after her first loan payment (it's gone down by the $384.50 in principal she paid), her interest payment will change for the following month.

To determine next month's payment, we can use the exact same formulas.

Month 1 interest = Remaining principal × Monthly interest rate

Remember, Julia just paid $384.50 in principal in Month 0; we therefore need to subtract that from the starting principal of $320,000.

Month 1 remaining principal = **Month 0 principal balance** − **Month 0 principal payment**

Month 1 remaining principal = $320,000 − $384.50
Month 1 remaining principal = $319,615.50

Julia now owes $319,615.50 in principal. Therefore, her Month 1 interest is:

Month 1 interest = Principal balance × Monthly interest rate
Month 1 interest = $319,615.50 × 0.00417
Month 1 interest = $1,331.73

And her Month 1 principal is:

Month 1 principal = Monthly payment − Month 1 interest
Month 1 principal = $1,717.83 − $1,331.73
Month 1 principal = $386.10

For Julia's second payment, she is still paying $1,718, but now she is paying slightly less interest ($1,331.73 versus $1,333.33) and slightly more principal ($386.10 versus $384.50). This is good! We want to pay less interest and more principal.

AMORTIZATION SCHEDULE

You can conduct this exercise for all 360 payments of the loan (doing this in Excel or another spreadsheet software is a lot easier than doing this by hand), the result of which is called an amortization schedule.

PAYMENT NUMBER	PAYMENT ($)	INTEREST PAID	PRINCIPAL PAID	TOTAL INTEREST PAID	TOTAL PRINCIPAL PAID	PRINCIPAL BALANCE
0	$1,717.83	$1,333.33	$384.50	$1,333.33	$384.50	$320,000.00
1	$1,717.83	$1,331.73	$386.10	$2,665.06	$770.59	$319,615.50
2	$1,717.83	$1,330.12	$387.71	$3,995.19	$1,158.30	$319,229.41
3	$1,717.83	$1,328.51	$389.32	$5,323.69	$1,547.62	$318,841.70
4	$1,717.83	$1,326.88	$390.94	$6,650.58	$1,938.57	$318,452.38
5	$1,717.83	$1,325.26	$392.57	$7,975.84	$2,331.14	$318,061.43
6	$1,717.83	$1,323.62	$394.21	$9,299.46	$2,725.35	$317,668.86
7	$1,717.83	$1,321.98	$395.85	$10,621.43	$3,121.20	$317,274.65
8	$1,717.83	$1,320.33	$397.50	$11,941.76	$3,518.70	$316,878.80
9	$1,717.83	$1,318.67	$399.16	$13,260.43	$3,917.86	$316,481.30
10	$1,717.83	$1,317.01	$400.82	$14,577.44	$4,318.68	$316,082.14
11	$1,717.83	$1,315.34	$402.49	$15,892.78	$4,721.17	$315,681.32
12	$1,717.83	$1,313.66	$404.17	$17,206.44	$5,125.34	$315,278.83
13	$1,717.83	$1,311.98	$405.85	$18,518.42	$5,531.19	$314,874.66
14	$1,717.83	$1,310.29	$407.54	$19,828.71	$5,938.73	$314,468.81
15	$1,717.83	$1,308.59	$409.24	$21,137.30	$6,347.97	$314,061.27
16	$1,717.83	$1,306.88	$410.95	$22,444.18	$6,758.92	$313,652.03
17	$1,717.83	$1,305.17	$412.66	$23,749.35	$7,171.57	$313,241.08
18	$1,717.83	$1,303.45	$414.38	$25,052.80	$7,585.95	$312,828.43
19	$1,717.83	$1,301.73	$416.10	$26,354.53	$8,002.06	$312,414.05
20	$1,717.83	$1,299.99	$417.84	$27,654.52	$8,419.89	$311,997.94
21	$1,717.83	$1,298.25	$419.58	$28,952.77	$8,839.47	$311,580.11
22	$1,717.83	$1,296.50	$421.33	$30,249.27	$9,260.80	$311,160.53
23	$1,717.83	$1,294.75	$423.08	$31,544.02	$9,683.88	$310,739.20

Even though Julia is paying the exact same amount each month, the proportion of her payment that goes to principal versus interest is changing every month. As you can see in the example above, the amount of interest paid goes down every month, and the amount of principal goes up each month.

Take a look at the chart below, which shows what percentage of Julia's monthly mortgage payment is going to interest versus principal. Take note that, rather than showing the dollar amounts (which you can see in the amortization schedule), the left axis here is a percentage.

When Julia begins payment on her loan, around 77 percent of her payment is going to the bank as interest, and only 23 percent is going toward paying down her principal balance.

AMORTIZATION CHART

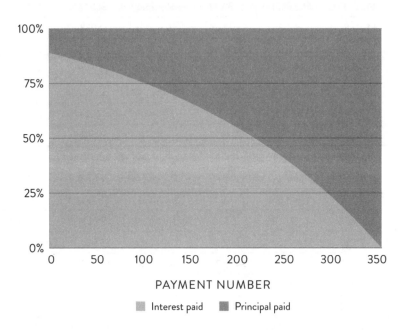

PAYMENT NUMBER

Interest paid   Principal paid

Over time, Julia's payment shifts more toward paying down principal and away from paying interest. That change, as shown in the graph, is often referred to as the "amortization curve."

You might be thinking, "My payment is the same every month, so what does it matter if I am paying principal or interest?" That is a good question. The answer is that paying principal builds equity, while paying interest does not. Every time principal is paid to the bank, that's less money owed should the property be sold, and more money that comes directly to the owner (the definition of equity).

Recall in the beginning of this chapter when we said that Julia's down payment of 20 percent ($80,000) was how much equity she had in the property at the beginning of the investment. That is her starting point. Then, when she makes a payment on her mortgage each month, she gains equity value in the property. The amount of equity value she gains is equal to the amount of principal she pays down that month. Paying down principal generates a return for the investor, which we'll discuss more in Part 5.

At any point, Julia can calculate how much equity value she has in her property by subtracting the remaining principal on her loan from the purchase price. Let's assume she is interested in knowing how much equity she will have by Month 20.

#63	**Equity value**
	Equity value = Property value – Liabilities

In many cases with real estate investors, the primary or only liability held against the property is the mortgage. For this example, we're going to assume that to be true, and we'll use Julia's loan balance as her liability.

In Month 0, the equation would look as follows:

Equity value in Month 0 = $400,000 (property value) – $320,000 (loan balance)

Equity value in Month 0 = $80,000

Using our amortization schedule, we can run through another example and quickly determine Julia's equity in Month 20.

Equity value in Month 20 = $400,000 – 311,997.94
Equity value in Month 20 = $88,002.06

After twenty months of payments, Julia has gained just over $8,400 in equity value. During that time, she has paid the bank over $27,600 in interest. In the early years of her loan, Julia is paying the bank a lot of interest and paying down very little principal. Toward the end of her loan, Julia will owe less interest on each payment and will be gaining proportionally more equity value from each payment she makes. After her 194th payment, Julia finally begins to pay more toward principal than interest.

COMPOSITION OF MONTHLY MORTGAGE PAYMENT

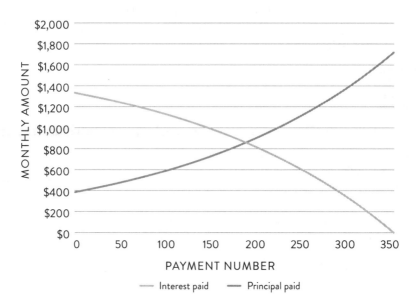

Interest paid — Principal paid

This can all seem like an abstract exercise, but amortization plays a large part in how large of a return you see when you go to sell a property. We'll talk about that more in a future chapter on how principal repayment factors into your profits. For now, just keep in mind that you continuously pay more principal and less interest as the lifetime of your loan progresses.

FULL VERSUS PARTIAL AMORTIZATION (BALLOON)

The above section outlined a traditional or "fully amortized" loan. A fully amortized loan is one where, after the final payment of the loan is made, the principal balance has gone to $0, and no additional money is owed to the lender. The loan has been paid off in equal payments over the life of the loan, and the borrower no longer has any obligation to the lender.

But that is not the only type of amortization. "Partial amortization" (also known as a "balloon mortgage" or "balloon loan") is another form of loan that is particularly common in commercial real estate.

The basic premise of a partially amortized loan is that you start paying down your loan in the same way you do with a fully amortized loan, but after a certain amount of time—an amount of time shorter than what it would take to pay off the entire loan—the loan ends and a lump sum of the remaining principal balance is due to pay off the loan. Typically, the lump sum (or the "balloon payment") is due five to ten years after the loan is initiated.

To fully understand how a partially amortized loan works, we should clarify two terms: amortization period and maturity date.

- The amortization period of a loan is how long your repayment plan is spread out—in other words, how long it would take to pay off your loan in equal payments, from beginning to end.
- The maturity date (sometimes referred to as the term) of a loan is when any remaining principal on your loan is due for repayment.

For a fully amortized loan, these two dates are the same. For example, if you take out a thirty-year mortgage, your payments are spread out over thirty years, and you pay your last dollar of principal down on the loan's maturity date—thirty years after the loan is originated.

In a partially amortized loan, the amortization period and the maturity date of the loan are different. As an example, you often see partially amortized loans that have an amortization period of thirty years, but a maturity date of ten years. In this scenario, the borrower would make payments on their loan for ten years just as if it were a fully amortized loan, but after ten years the remaining principal balance is due. In fact, for the first ten years, the loan payments would be equivalent to the fully-amortized loan example above.

Quick Tip | Amortization Periods

The longer the amortization period of a loan, the less principal that is paid each month. For that reason, a loan with a longer amortization period will always have a lower monthly payment (assuming the same interest rate).

For example, a loan amortized over thirty years—like a typical conventional homeowner loan—will have a lower monthly payment than a loan of the same size and interest rate amortized over twenty years.

This is the reason why many investors will look for loans with the longest amortization period, even if there is a balloon payment associated with it.

That said, keep in mind that when principal payments are reduced and spread over a longer period of time, the total amount of interest paid over the life of the loan increases. For this reason, that thirty-year amortized loan will cost more in interest than a twenty-year amortized loan.

To demonstrate how this works, let's use an example where Alex is purchasing a property for $1 million, is putting 20 percent down, and is getting a partially amortized loan. The loan is amortized over thirty years, has a fixed interest rate of 4 percent, and has a maturity date of ten years.

To determine Alex's payments, we use the exact same formulas as we do for a fully amortized loan. Running those numbers gets us a payment of roughly $3,819 per month. Alex pays that rate for ten years, at which point the remaining principal is due. According to the amortization schedule, this amount is $652,098.

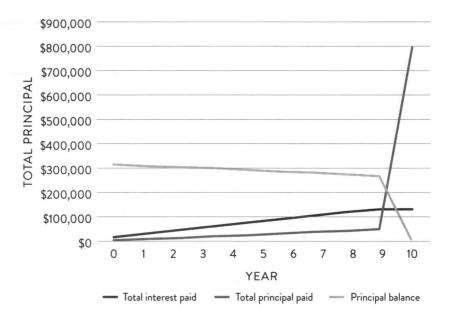

This chart demonstrates exactly how this works. Alex gets to enjoy low monthly payments for ten years, and then one day, everything comes due all at once.

For example, if you were to borrow $100,000 at 5 percent, interest only, your monthly payment would be:

Monthly interest = Principal balance × Monthly interest rate

Monthly interest = $100,000 × (5% ÷ 12) = $416.67

Because each payment consists only of interest, the principal balance of the loan doesn't change as payment are made. If you borrowed $100,000 today and made interest only payments for ten years, you'd still owe $100,000 in ten years to pay off the loan.

As you can probably guess, this means that an interest-only loan is always a partially amortized loan, and there must be a balloon payment at some point. This balloon payment will consist of the entire principal amount of the loan.

It is sometimes helpful to think of an interest-only loan as being amortized over an infinite period of time. Remember, the longer the amortization period, the lower the monthly payment; with interest-only loans, the monthly payment is as low as it can possibly get, since no principal is being paid as part of the payment.

BENEFITS OF PARTIALLY AMORTIZED LOANS

It might seem confusing why anyone would accept a loan like this. Who would want to pay off $652,098 all at once? But there are two very significant benefits to this type of loan: relatively low monthly payments and less total interest.

Low Monthly Payments: Partially amortized loans allow Alex to act, for ten years, as if he is going to be making payments for thirty years, keeping his payment to $3,819. However, in reality, he is borrowing the money for just ten years. If he borrowed $800,000 for ten years with a fully amortized loan, it would cost him about $8,100 per month. By using a partially amortized loan, Alex is keeping his payments low and boosting his cash flow by over $4,000 per month for the first ten years while his investment gets up and running. That's a huge savings!

This is the primary reason that partially amortized loans are common in commercial lending. Banks are willing to accept lower monthly payments to help a large-scale investment, like an apartment complex, get up and running and start generating cash flow. By doing so, they allow the business to generate more cash flow, helping it afford the balloon payment at the maturity date of the loan.

Less Interest: Partially amortized loans cost less overall to the borrower, plain and simple. To highlight this point, let's look at the amortization schedule for Alex's partially amortized loan:

YEAR	PAYMENT ($)	INTEREST PAID	PRINCIPAL PAID	TOTAL INTEREST PAID	TOTAL PRINCIPAL PAID	PRINCIPAL BALANCE
1	$3,819.32	$2,623.69	$1,195.63	$31,743.58	$14,088.29	$787,107.34
2	$3,819.32	$2,574.98	$1,244.34	$62,913.18	$28,750.56	$772,493.78
3	$3,819.32	$2,524.28	$1,295.04	$93,485.41	$44,010.20	$757,284.84
4	$3,819.32	$2,471.52	$1,347.80	$123,435.94	$59,891.53	$741,456.27
5	$3,819.32	$2,416.61	$1,402.71	$152,739.45	$76,419.89	$724,982.82
6	$3,819.32	$2,359.46	$1,459.86	$181,369.56	$93,621.65	$707,838.21
7	$3,819.32	$2,299.98	$1,519.34	$209,298.85	$111,524.23	$689,995.11
8	$3,819.32	$2,238.08	$1,581.24	$236,498.75	$130,156.19	$671,425.05
9	$3,819.32	$2,173.66	$1,645.66	$262,939.57	$149,547.25	$652,098.41
10	$652,098.41	$0.00	$652,098.41	$262,939.57	$800,000.00	$0.00

Over the course of ten years, Alex can borrow $800,000 and pay just $262,940 in interest.

If he used a fully amortized loan instead, the total interest paid would be much higher. According to the following thirty-year amortization schedule, Alex would pay $574,956 in interest over those thirty years. By using a partially amortized loan, Alex will pay less than half of the interest that he would have if he'd used a fully amortized loan.

YEAR	PAYMENT ($)	INTEREST PAID	PRINCIPAL PAID	TOTAL INTEREST PAID	TOTAL PRINCIPAL PAID	PRINCIPAL BALANCE
1	$3,819.32	$2,623.69	$1,195.63	$31,743.58	$14,088.29	$787,107.34
2	$3,819.32	$2,574.98	$1,244.34	$62,913.18	$28,750.56	$772,493.78
3	$3,819.32	$2,524.28	$1,295.04	$93,485.41	$44,010.20	$757,284.84
4	$3,819.32	$2,471.52	$1,347.80	$123,435.94	$59,891.53	$741,456.27
5	$3,819.32	$2,416.61	$1,402.71	$152,739.45	$76,419.89	$724,982.82
6	$3,819.32	$2,359.46	$1,459.86	$181,369.56	$93,621.65	$707,838.21
7	$3,819.32	$2,299.98	$1,519.34	$209,298.85	$111,524.23	$689,995.11
8	$3,819.32	$2,238.08	$1,581.24	$236,498.75	$130,156.19	$671,425.05
9	$3,819.32	$2,173.66	$1,645.66	$262,939.57	$149,547.25	$652,098.41
10	$3,819.32	$2,106.61	$1,712.71	$288,590.36	$169,728.33	$631,984.38
11	$3,819.32	$2,036.84	$1,782.49	$313,418.94	$190,731.61	$611,050.87
12	$3,819.32	$1,964.22	$1,855.11	$337,391.82	$212,590.60	$589,264.50
13	$3,819.32	$1,888.64	$1,930.69	$360,474.12	$235,340.16	$566,590.52
14	$3,819.32	$1,809.98	$2,009.35	$382,629.58	$259,016.58	$542,992.77
15	$3,819.32	$1,728.11	$2,091.21	$403,820.42	$283,657.60	$518,433.61
16	$3,819.32	$1,642.91	$2,176.41	$424,007.35	$309,302.54	$492,873.87
17	$3,819.32	$1,554.24	$2,265.08	$443,149.46	$335,992.30	$466,272.78
18	$3,819.32	$1,461.96	$2,357.36	$461,204.20	$363,769.43	$438,587.93
19	$3,819.32	$1,365.92	$2,453.41	$478,127.25	$392,678.25	$409,775.15
20	$3,819.32	$1,265.96	$2,553.36	$493,872.50	$422,764.86	$379,788.50
21	$3,819.32	$1,161.93	$2,657.39	$508,391.99	$454,077.25	$348,580.14
22	$3,819.32	$1,053.67	$2,765.65	$521,635.76	$486,665.35	$316,100.31
23	$3,819.32	$940.99	$2,878.33	$533,551.84	$520,581.13	$282,297.20
24	$3,819.32	$823.72	$2,995.60	$544,086.14	$555,878.70	$247,116.90
25	$3,819.32	$701.68	$3,117.64	$553,182.36	$592,614.35	$210,503.29
26	$3,819.32	$574.66	$3,244.66	$560,781.91	$630,846.67	$172,398.00
27	$3,819.32	$442.47	$3,376.85	$566,823.82	$670,636.62	$132,740.23
28	$3,819.32	$304.89	$3,514.43	$571,244.63	$712,047.69	$91,466.75
29	$3,819.32	$161.71	$3,657.62	$573,978.28	$755,145.90	$48,511.72
30	$3,819.32	$12.69	$3,806.63	$574,956.05	$800,000.00	$3,806.63

DRAWBACKS OF PARTIALLY AMORTIZED LOANS

While the low monthly payments and lower overall cost of a partially amortized loan have true benefits, this loan structure also comes with significant risks. Put simply, if you cannot afford your balloon payment at the maturity date of the loan, you can face losing your investment, and even bankruptcy.

Many investors mitigate this risk by assuming they can refinance into a different type of loan—and that often works. If your business is doing well, and if macroeconomic conditions make debt easy to come by, it can be a great option to refinance and push out or completely avoid the balloon payment (your loan will start over, though, meaning you'll pay more interest overall). But that doesn't always work, and entering a partially amortized loan assuming you can refinance out of your balloon payment comes with significant risk.

DIG DEEP

PARTIALLY AMORTIZED LOANS AND BALLOON PAYMENTS

Partially amortized loans with balloon payments are most common in the commercial world. When taking out a large commercial loan from a big bank, these loans are often structured with a twenty- or thirty-year amortization period (and are sometimes interest-only), but with a ten-year maturity date, or term. Many lenders will even provide very short-term loans of two or three years on properties that need renovation. The expectation is that the owner of the property will refinance or sell in that window of time.

Additionally, it's common for portfolio lenders—small local or regional banks that also lend to mom-and-pop investors on single-family and small multifamily rentals—to use partially amortized loans. In many cases, the loans are amortized over fifteen to thirty years (remember, the longer the amortization, the lower the monthly payment), but have a maturity in three, five, seven, or ten years.

For each of these partially amortized loans, the borrower must be prepared to make the balloon payment by the maturity date, either by refinancing, selling, or coming up with the cash.

HONE YOUR SKILLS: CHAPTER 30

- What is amortization?
- What are the pros and cons of a partially amortized (balloon) loan?
- What is the difference between amortization period and maturity date?

CHAPTER 31
KEY DEBT METRICS: LTV, LTC, AND DSCR

Chapter 31 will help us to answer the questions:
- How do lenders evaluate risk?
- How can I get the best possible rate from a lender?

Starting in Chapter 32, we're going to explain how to use debt to boost your real estate returns. But before we do that, let's go on a brief foray into three metrics: the loan-to-value ratio, the loan-to-cost ratio, and the debt service coverage ratio. These metrics are primarily used within the lending industry, which is precisely why it's important for investors to understand them. If you can understand how lenders operate and think about risk versus reward, you can better position yourself to apply for loans.

LOAN-TO-VALUE RATIO

The loan-to-value ratio (LTV) is a simple calculation that measures what percent of a property purchase will be covered by a loan. It is determined as follows:

#64	**Loan-to-value ratio (LTV)** LTV = Loan amount ÷ Property value

For example, if Luis is buying a home that is valued at $300,000, and he takes out a $240,000 mortgage, his LTV would be 80 percent.

LTV = Loan amount ÷ Property value
LTV = $240,000 ÷ $300,000 = 0.8 (80%)

This metric plays a huge part in applying for a mortgage. Lenders will factor LTV into whether they approve a loan, the interest rate for any loan approved, and whether the borrower will be required to pay private mortgage insurance (PMI).

Typically, mortgage rates are lowest for borrowers whose LTV is less than 80 percent. Or, put another way, borrowers who put at least 20 percent down (1 − Down payment % = LTV) get the best interest rates.

The LTV range that a lender will accept is dependent on the strength of the borrower (e.g., credit score, investing experience, total assets), the type of loan in question, and the lender's own strategy and risk appetite.

The maximum LTV for conventional mortgages in the U.S. is about 97 percent, meaning some borrowers can put as little as 3.5 percent down toward a home (like with an FHA loan, as discussed in Chapter 29). But in addition to having a loan with an LTV greater than 80 percent that carries a higher interest rate, borrowers will likely also have to pay PMI, further raising the cost of the loan. Again, borrowers with an LTV of 80 percent or less tend to get the best economics for conventional mortgages.

Hard-money lenders, private lenders, or lenders of other loan types that are less rigid can, in some cases, approve a 100 percent LTV (meaning the borrower does not put any money down).

LOAN-TO-COST RATIO

The loan-to-cost ratio (LTC) compares the loan amount of a deal to the actual cost of the investment. For example, in the case where an investor is interested in purchasing a property and performing renovations on that property, some lenders may be willing to lend against the total cost of the project. This is common in the new-construction space, where lenders will often lend against a percentage of both the purchase cost of the land and the construction cost of the newly built property.

#65   **Loan-to-cost ratio (LTC)**
LTC = Loan amount ÷ All-in costs

As an example, let's say you want to build a duplex, can purchase the land for $150,000, and will need to spend $350,000 to construct the building. Further, let's assume that your lender is willing to fund $400,000 of the total costs, with you bringing the additional $100,000 as a down payment. The LTC for this loan would be:

LTC = Loan amount ÷ All-in costs
LTC = $400,000 ÷ $500,000 = 0.8 (80%)

The LTC for this deal is 80 percent.

The higher the LTC, the higher the risk for the lender. Lenders typically don't want to fund 100 percent of a construction project; as we discussed earlier, they want the owners to contribute equity and have some skin in the game.

DEBT SERVICE COVERAGE RATIO

The debt service coverage ratio (DSCR) measures how well an investment's available cash flow can cover its debt obligations. In real estate, DSCR is most used by lenders when underwriting loans on investment properties. It's also a quick way for real estate investors to estimate the cash-flow prospects of a given property.

To calculate DSCR, we need just two inputs: net operating income (NOI) and total debt service (TDS).

#66	**Debt service coverage ratio (DSCR)** DSCR = Net operating income ÷ Total debt service

We've already discussed net operating income, but as a quick reminder, NOI equals revenue minus all operating expenses (not including debt service).

Total debt service refers to any debt obligations in the coming year. When applying for a mortgage, TDS will be equal to one year of payments on the mortgage.

As an example, if Jose is looking to buy a property with an NOI of $30,000 per year and his annual mortgage payments are $24,000, his DSCR would be:

DSCR = Net operating income ÷ Total debt service
DSCR = $30,000 ÷ $24,000 = 1.25

A DSCR of 1 means the property will essentially break even after paying its debt service. A DSCR of greater than 1 means the property should expect positive cash flow. And a DSCR of anything less than 1 implies that the property's cash flow will not cover the property's debt obligations. In general, the higher the DSCR, the lower the risk for both the lender and borrower, because a high DSCR implies greater potential cash flow.

Most commercial lenders will look for a DSCR of at least 1.2 to 1.3.

Debt service coverage ratios are not just for lenders, though. As an investor, you can use DSCR to compare the cash-flow prospects of multiple properties against one another. The higher the DSCR, the more potential for cash flow.

Below, you can see an example of two properties. While Property 1 has the higher NOI, it also comes with higher debt and has a DSCR of just 1.2. Meanwhile, Property 2 has a lower NOI, but given its lower debt obligations, it has the better cash flow potential (as demonstrated by the higher DSCR of 1.5).

	NOI	TDS	DSCR
Property 1	$25,000	$21,000	1.2
Property 2	$22,000	$15,000	1.5

While there isn't enough information here to determine whether Property 1 or Property 2 is the better investment, the DSCR provides insight into the risk the buyer and lender are taking with respect to the cash flow available to service the debt.

HONE YOUR SKILLS: CHAPTER 31

- What is the loan-to-value ratio, and why is it so important?
- What is the LTV of a property purchased for $488,000 with a down payment of $73,200?
- What is the DSCR of a deal with an NOI of $120,000 and a total debt service of $105,000?

CHAPTER 32
THE LOAN CONSTANT

Chapter 32 will help us to answer the questions:
- How much is my debt costing me?
- Which loan option is the most cost effective for me?

Now that we've covered the details of how debt works and how lenders think about debt, it's time to learn how to select the best loans for your deals. We're going to start with the *loan constant* in this chapter and then build through Chapter 39 to give you a full understanding of how you can boost your investing returns using debt. This is one of the most important concepts in real estate investing and is one of the reasons why so many savvy investors get into real estate in the first place. Let's jump in.

The loan constant (sometimes called the mortgage constant) is a number that signifies the relationship between a loan and the payments on that loan. It helps us understand the cost of debt and is the foundation for several other important debt-related metrics.

#67

The **loan constant** (or **mortgage constant**) is a ratio that indicates the relationship between a loan and its monthly payment. The ratio (percentage) is the cash paid to service a loan in one year divided by the total amount owed on the loan.

Loan constant = Annual debt service ÷ Loan amount

The loan constant can be calculated by taking the total loan payments for a given year and dividing it by the principal balance of the loan.

For example, a twenty-year, fully amortizing loan of $100,000 with a 6 percent interest rate would require debt service of $716.43 per month. Over the course of one year, the debt service would be about $8,597.

The loan constant for this loan would be:

$$\$8,597 \div \$100,000 = \mathbf{0.08597} \text{ (or about } \mathbf{8.6\%)}$$

First, notice that this number is larger than the interest rate. This is typical and will be important later in this section.

The loan constant has a lot of uses when it comes to analyzing and evaluating both loans and the investments they finance. Loan constants were originally used before we had financial calculators or computers, as they make it easy to determine the monthly payment on a fixed-rate loan (multiply the loan constant by the total loan amount and divide by 12).

In addition, the loan constant can help you rank loans in terms of which are more or less costly. Generally speaking, the higher the loan constant, the more the loan costs you, regardless of the interest rate. When you have multiple debts—whether it be mortgages, car loans, or student debt—and you are deciding in what order to pay them off, you should focus on those with the higher loan constants first.

QuickTip | **Loan Constants**

The loan constant is the return the lender is getting on the loan. The higher the loan constant, the more money the lender is siphoning from our deal as profit; the lower the loan constant, the more of our investment profits we are keeping.

Loan constants have some important uses in the investing world. In addition to telling us exactly how much our borrowed capital is costing us, the loan constant can derive other important numbers that can help us make smart investing decisions like estimating cap rates and calculating breakeven cash flow.

BREAKEVEN CASH FLOW

Another feature of the loan constant is that it can help us determine how much of a loan we can take out against a property before we go from positive cash flow (making money each month) to negative cash flow (losing money each month).

Here's the formula to determine the loan amount where cash flow goes from positive to negative.

#68 — Breakeven loan value is the amount you can borrow using a specific loan for a specific property where the cash flow transitions from positive to negative.

Breakeven loan value = NOI ÷ Loan constant

Let's look at an example.

Let's assume we have a property that we're considering purchasing for $100,000 with a cap rate of 8 percent. Further, let's assume we're getting a fifteen-year, fully amortized loan at a 6 percent interest rate.

From the cap rate formula we discussed in the last part of the book, we know that our NOI will be the purchase price times the cap rate, or $8,000 ($100,000 × 8%).

As for the loan constant, we can go back to our formula:

Loan constant = Annual debt service ÷ Loan amount

If we enter the loan information into a loan calculator, we'll find that for a loan of $100,000 at the previously mentioned loan conditions, our monthly payments are about $844, which is about $10,130 per year.

Adding in the annual payments, we know the loan constant for this loan is:

Loan constant = $10,130 ÷ $100,000 = 10.13%

Using the NOI for this property and the loan constant for this loan, we can now determine our breakeven loan value:

Breakeven loan value = $8,000 ÷ 10.13% = $78,973

So, for this property and this loan, if we borrow less than $78,973, we'll have positive cash flow; if we borrow more than that, we'll have negative cash flow; and if we borrow that exact amount, we'll break even on our cash flow. This a very handy calculation when determining what size loan to take out on a prospective deal.

Quick Tip | **Loan Constant Limitations**

The loan constant does have some limitations. For loans that don't have fixed interest rates or for loans that are interest only, the loan constant will not provide very useful information. Typically, for loans that are not fixed interest, using the highest interest rate during the loan period to calculate the loan constant should provide a conservative value with which to do your calculations.

DERIVING CAP RATE

One common use of the loan constant in the commercial real estate industry is to help estimate cap rates of properties in a particular market. As we discussed earlier, cap rates are a peculiar animal—it can be difficult to determine what the cap rate is for an area, and we often have to rely on local investors or brokers to provide the information based on their experience.

But there is a more indirect way to do this as well, based on sampling what lenders are charging and what investors are demanding for their returns. By surveying lenders to determine the loan constant for their typical commercial loan and by surveying investors to determine the returns they demand on their equity investments (their cash-on-cash returns), we can weigh those two numbers to derive a local cap rate.

Here's an example.

Let's say we are interested in purchasing a self-storage facility in Atlanta, Georgia, and we want to estimate the current cap rates for such an investment in that area right now.

We survey a bunch of lenders and determine that to lend on such an investment, the typical loan would be a twenty-five-year, fully amortized loan with a 6 percent interest rate (and with a 75 percent LTV). On a $100,000 loan at these terms, the monthly payment is $644.31. The loan constant for this loan would be:

Loan constant = (12 × $644.31) ÷ $100,000
Loan constant = 0.077316 (or about 7.73%)

A survey of a number of self-storage investors in the area indicates that, on average, these investors are looking for cash-on-cash returns of about 15 percent for these investments.

If we weigh those two numbers using the loan-to-value ratio (percent of the purchase that is bought using debt versus equity), we get the following:

Estimated cap rate = (75% × 7.73%) + (25% × 15%)
Estimated cap rate = 0.0955 (or 9.55%)

Based on this information, we can deduce that an estimated cap rate for self-storage in this area at this time is about 9.55 percent. We can then use that number as a starting point to evaluate deals and make offers.

Now that we understand how the loan constant tells us the price of borrowed capital and how the loan constant is applied in the real world, let's move on to a discussion of whether the cost of borrowed capital will help or hurt our investment performance.

HONE YOUR SKILLS: CHAPTER 32

- What is the loan constant for a property with an annual debt service of $30,000 and a loan amount of $380,000?
- What is the breakeven loan value of a property with an NOI of $25,000 and a loan constant of 7 percent?
- What are some limitations of the loan constant?

CHAPTER 33
LEVERAGE
(AS A CONCEPT)

Chapter 33 will help us to answer the questions:
- Why should we consider using debt when purchasing investment properties?
- What are the benefits and drawbacks to using debt when investing?

Many investors think of finding financing as a burdensome hurdle required to invest in real estate. In many cases, particularly for new investors, it can be a real obstacle to find enough equity to use as a down payment or to find a lender who will lend to you. If you're having trouble securing any financing at all, we recommend you read either Scott Trench's *Set for Life* (to help get your financial house in order) or Brandon Turner's *The Book on Investing in Real Estate with No (and Low) Money Down* (to learn creative ways to get to your first deal).

Our purpose here is to demonstrate that financing can be much more than an annoying obstacle or simply a box to check when securing a deal. In fact, financing your investments strategically can boost your returns by using the concept of leverage.

You've probably heard the term "leverage" before. In a nutshell, leverage is the concept of borrowing or making use of other people's money to benefit you in the purchase of an investment. We use the word "concept" here to differentiate another definition of leverage that we'll discuss later in this book.

Leverage (the concept) is the use of borrowed capital for an investment with the intent to generate a return on the borrowed capital that will be greater than the interest paid to secure the capital.

Debt financing (getting a loan) is the most common form of leverage when buying cash-flowing real estate, like residential rental property or commercial property. You use some of your own money for the down payment, and you borrow money to cover the rest of the cost of the investment.

BENEFITS OF LEVERAGE

There are two major financial benefits to using leverage for your cash-flowing properties.

1. **Leverage allows you to use less of your own money for the purchase of your investments.** The most obvious benefit to using leverage to purchase an investment is that you can use less of your own cash to invest. This means that you might be able to purchase an investment that you otherwise couldn't have purchased—because you didn't have access to the funds—or it may mean that you can save the funds you would have used for other investments or other purposes.

   While too much leverage is risky (we'll talk about that in a minute), you can often find lenders who are willing to loan 75 percent or more of the total cost of the investment, limiting your own cash contribution to a small percentage of the total price. In fact, in some cases, if the deal is good enough, you may be able to get a lender to provide 100 percent of the funds for the investment.

2. **Leverage can boost your returns on an investment.** In some cases, using leverage will actually increase the return on your investment into the deal. That is what we should all strive to achieve—financing that benefits us, the investors, instead of solely benefitting the lender. We'll talk about this in much more detail in an upcoming chapter.

DRAWBACKS OF LEVERAGE

In addition to those two big benefits of leverage, there are several drawbacks and risks.

1. **Leverage adds cost to your investment each month.** When you purchase an investment using all your own cash (no loan), the monthly cost to keep the property is lower. For example, if you own a rental property and a tenant moves out, the monthly cost to keep the vacant property is going to be relatively low—you will owe taxes (which are typically not paid each month), insurance (also not paid each month), and perhaps utilities. If it takes three months to get a new tenant into the property, the out-of-pocket costs won't be fun, but they likely

won't bankrupt you. However, if you have a $400 or $500 mortgage payment each month, that adds significant out-of-pocket costs when a unit is empty (or, worse yet, when you have a tenant who isn't paying and you're going through an eviction). Leverage is a drain on your cash reserves each and every month.

2. **Leverage can destroy liquidity.** Imagine a situation where you need some quick cash. For example, you have an emergency expense, your child is about to go to college, you have medical bills, or you need a new car. Let's say that you own a house and want to sell the house to get that cash. If you paid all cash for a property, you could sell it regardless of whether the market has increased, decreased, or stayed the same since your purchase. You might have to take a loss on the investment, but you can still sell without anyone stopping you. But imagine you have a loan on the property for 80 percent of the value, and imagine that the market value has dropped 30 percent since your purchase (this happened in many places back in 2007–2008); you now owe more on the loan than the house is worth! (This is also known as "being underwater" on a loan.) If you don't have extra cash sitting around to pay the difference between what you owe and what you can sell the house for, the lender won't allow you to sell the house.

3. **Leverage can cause bankruptcy.** As we discussed in the last chapter, there are several different types of loans—for example, fully amortizing versus balloon payment, and fixed rate versus adjustable rate. If you have a balloon loan and/ or an adjustable-rate loan, there will come a time when you'll either owe a big chunk of cash (balloon payment) or your interest rate may increase, making your monthly mortgage payment higher. In either/both of these situations, if you're not prepared, you may find yourself in financial trouble. If the market has gone up, you always have the option to sell the house and get out of the loan. But if the value of the house has decreased to the point where you owe more than the house is worth, you could find yourself facing foreclosure…or, worse yet, bankruptcy.

4. **Leverage can reduce your returns on an investment.** Just like we mentioned that leverage can, in some cases, increase the return you get on your investment, leverage can also do the opposite—in some cases, it can reduce your ROI instead. We'll talk about this in greater detail in an upcoming chapter.

HONE YOUR SKILLS: CHAPTER 33

- What is the concept of leverage?
- What are the two primary benefits of leverage?
- What are the drawbacks of leverage?

CHAPTER 34
POSITIVE AND NEGATIVE LEVERAGE

Chapter 34 will help us to answer the question:
- Is my debt helping or hurting my returns?

In the last chapter on leverage, we mentioned in our benefits list that when used properly, leverage can boost your returns on an investment. In our drawbacks list, we mentioned that, when used improperly, it can reduce your returns.

When leverage increases your investment returns, we call that *positive leverage*.

#70	**Positive leverage** occurs when the use of borrowed capital generates higher returns on an investment than would be attained by paying for that investment with non-borrowed funds.

When leverage reduces your investment returns, we call that *negative leverage*.

#71	**Negative leverage** occurs when the use of borrowed capital reduces the returns on an investment compared to if that investment were purchased with non-borrowed funds.

To put this into perspective, let's look at three scenarios. In each, let's assume we are purchasing a $100,000 single-family property that generates $1,200 per month in rental income. Finally, let's assume half of that income ($600) is used for all our expenses (e.g., taxes, insurance, maintenance).

This means that at the end of every month, we have $600 left over as our cash flow before taxes (let's just call it "cash flow," for simplicity), assuming we don't have a mortgage and therefore don't have to make a loan payment. When we do have a mortgage, our loan payment will be subtracted from that $600 to determine our cash flow.

SCENARIO #1: ALL-CASH PURCHASE

In our first example, let's assume that we purchase this property solely using our own cash. In other words, we don't get a loan to help finance the purchase.

In this case, each month we earn $1,200 in rent and spend $600 on expenses. This translates to $600 per month in cash flow, or $7,200 per year (12 × $600).

	MONTHLY	ANNUAL
Rental Income	$1,200.00	$14,400.00
Expenses	$600.00	$7,200.00
Net Operating Income	$600.00	$7,200.00
Debt Service	$-	$-
Cash Flow	$600.00	**$7,200.00**

A simple ROI calculation of dividing the profit into the total cash investment ($7,200 ÷ $100,000) tells us that our ROI on this property is:

ROI = $7,200 ÷ $100,000 = **7.2%**

You might have noticed that the ROI in this case is equivalent to the cap rate of the property—it's the return we get when we pay all cash.

SCENARIO #2: LOAN AT 4.5 PERCENT INTEREST

In our second scenario, let's assume we purchase the same $100,000 property with a typical loan: We put down a 20 percent down payment ($20,000) and borrow the other 80 percent ($80,000). In this scenario, let's assume the loan is repaid over thirty years with a 4.5 percent interest rate.

Plug the information into a mortgage calculator and you'll see that our monthly payment on this loan would be $405. That $405 would be subtracted from our $600 per month in cash flow, resulting in a new cash flow of $195 per month, or an annual cash flow of $2,340 (12 × $195).

	MONTHLY	ANNUAL
Rental Income	$1,200.00	$14,400.00
Expenses	$600.00	$7,200.00
Net Operating Income	$600.00	$7,200.00
Debt Service	$405.00	$4,860.00
Cash Flow	$195.00	**$2,340.00**

Because we need to make a loan payment each month, our cash flow has decreased a good bit, from $7,200 (Scenario #1) to $2,340. But our total investment into the deal also decreased significantly, from $100,000 of our own cash to just $20,000.

Our ROI now looks like this:

ROI = $2,340 ÷ $20,000 = **11.7%**

We've increased our ROI from 7.2% to 11.7% just by borrowing money! That's positive leverage.

Scenario #3: Loan at 7 Percent Interest

In this final scenario, let's assume that instead of borrowing the $80,000 at a 4.5 percent interest rate, we instead must pay 7 percent interest on the money. Everything else stays the same.

Plugging the numbers into a mortgage calculator again, we get a monthly mortgage payment of $532 on that thirty-year, 7 percent interest rate loan. Again, our cash flow before the loan payment was $600 per month, and in this case, we subtract the $532 loan payment to get $68 per month in new cash flow, or $816 per year.

	MONTHLY	ANNUAL
Rental Income	$1,200.00	$14,400.00
Expenses	$600.00	$7,200.00
Net Operating Income	$600.00	$7,200.00
Debt Service	$532.00	$6,384.00
Cash Flow	$68.00	**$816.00**

As we should expect, with the higher interest rate mortgage, our annual profit has dropped even more. And if we run our new ROI calculation, we get:

ROI = $816 ÷ $20,000 = **4.1%**

Our ROI has dropped to 4.1 percent. In this example, borrowing money has *decreased* our ROI, from the 7.2 percent return we were getting without a loan to 4.1 percent with these loan terms.

Here's a summary of the three scenarios:

	NO LOAN	LOAN @ 4.5%	LOAN @ 7%
Purchase Price	$100,000.00	$100,000.00	$100,000.00
Loan Amount	0	80000	80000
Down Payment (DP)	$100,000.00	$20,000.00	$20,000.00
Interest Rate	N/A	4.50%	7.00%
Cash Flow	$7,200.00	$2,340.00	$816.00
ROI (Cash Flow/DP)	7.20%	11.70%	4.10%

Going from no loan on the property to the thirty-year loan at 4.5 percent increased our ROI—that's an example of positive leverage.

However, going from no loan on the property to the thirty-year loan at 7 percent interest decreased our ROI—an example of negative leverage.

Clearly, going with the first loan would be a good financial decision. It would allow us to save our cash for other deals *and* generate better returns. But if we were to go with the second loan option, we'd generate lower returns on our investment. Perhaps we might decide that being able to purchase the investment with less of our own cash would outweigh the drawback of negative leverage, but this is still a red flag.

It took a decent amount of work to figure out if we had positive or negative leverage on our deal. We also aren't coming away with a clear picture about where exactly our return and cash flow are coming from.

Luckily, we have a better way of looking at the benefit of our leverage that also provides some insight into exactly how we're generating our returns and where our cash flow is coming from.

Quick Tip | **Leverage and LTV**

If you have a positive leverage loan, it will be positive leverage for any loan LTV, up to 100%. In other words, for a positive leverage loan, you can borrow up to the entire amount you paid for the property, and it will still provide positive cash flow—or, worst case, exactly zero cash flow.

Conversely, any loan that provides positive cash flow at a lower LTV and negative cash flow at a higher LTV is a negative leverage loan.

HONE YOUR SKILLS: CHAPTER 34

- What is the difference between positive and negative leverage?
- True or false: If your loan has positive leverage, it will be positive for a loan with any LTV up to 100 percent.

CHAPTER 35
LEVERAGE (THE VALUE)

Chapter 35 will help us to answer the questions:
- What ROI have I earned on my debt?
- Is my debt generating positive or negative leverage?

In the last two chapters, we defined leverage as a concept—the concept of using other people's money to fund our investments. However, there's another definition of leverage that is less commonly used, but probably even more important.

This definition of leverage is a ratio (a percentage value), and it indicates the ROI we will gain or lose on any borrowed funds. We calculate the Leverage (we're going to use a capital L to differentiate the ratio from the concept) by subtracting the loan constant of the loan we're using from the cap rate of the investment (the return we receive assuming we don't have a loan).

#72 Leverage (the value) is the difference between the cap rate of an investment and the loan constant of a particular financing option for that investment.

Leverage = Cap rate − Loan constant

This value is also the ROI that will be generated by the borrowed funds from that particular loan. If this is confusing, just stick with us—we promise things will become clearer soon enough.

Let's take a look at an example.

Assume we are purchasing a property for $1,000,000 and it generates $100,000 per year in NOI. Further, let's assume that we get a fully amortized loan against the property for $1,000,000, with a monthly payment (P&I) of $6,666.67. What is the Leverage on this loan for this investment?

First, we can calculate the property's cap rate as follows:

Cap rate = NOI ÷ Value (Price)
Cap rate = $1,000,000 ÷ $100,000 = 0.1 (or **10%**)

Next, we can calculate the loan constant for the loan.

Loan constant = Annual debt service ÷ Loan amount
Loan constant = (12 × $6,666.67) ÷ $1,000,000 = 0.08 (or **8%**)

Using the Leverage formula, our Leverage for this investment and this loan is:

Leverage = Cap rate − Loan constant
Leverage = 10% − 8% = **2%**

Our Leverage for this deal is 2 percent. In the next chapter, we'll show you how to use Leverage to calculate your rate of return on borrowed funds. But for now, let's discuss how we can use it to help us analyze the leverage we'll receive from a specific loan on a specific property.

REVISITING POSITIVE AND NEGATIVE LEVERAGE

In the previous chapter, we calculated the cash flow and ROI for three scenarios to determine whether a potential loan would provide positive or negative leverage. While this method works, it can be cumbersome to calculate cash flow and ROI numbers for different loans and scenarios.

With the Leverage ratio, we now have another way to determine if a loan option is going to provide positive or negative leverage.

Determination of positive or negative leverage is done by looking at the Leverage value. If Leverage is a positive number (the cap rate is higher than the loan constant), the loan will provide positive leverage. If Leverage is a negative number (the cap rate is lower than the loan constant), the loan will provide negative leverage.

Let's go back to our scenarios in the last chapter and use this new method to confirm our previous results.

In Scenario #1 (all cash), our ROI for this particular property was:

ROI = $7,200 ÷ $100,000 = **7.2%**

Because that scenario assumes an all-cash purchase, this is also our cap rate for the property.

For Scenario #2 (4.5 percent loan), we can calculate the loan constant by taking our annual loan payments and dividing by the loan amount. The monthly loan payments of $405 equal $4,860 per year (12 × $405). The loan constant would be:

Loan constant = $4,860 ÷ $80,000 = **6.1%**

We can determine the Leverage value for this loan using the formula we provided:

Leverage = Cap rate – Loan constant
Leverage = 7.2% – 6.1% = **1.1%**

Leverage is a positive number, so a 4.5 percent loan on this property will provide positive leverage.

For Scenario #3 (7 percent loan), the monthly loan payments of $532 equal $6,384 per year (12 × $532). And the loan constant would be:

Loan constant = $6,384 ÷ $80,000 = **8.0%**

The Leverage value for this loan is:

Leverage = Cap rate – Loan constant
Leverage = 7.2% – 8.0% = **-0.8%**

The Leverage value is negative, which confirms our previous conclusion that this loan would provide negative leverage against this property. In just a few simple steps, we can use the loan constant and Leverage value to determine if a loan is beneficial or damaging to our deal.

In addition to telling us whether a loan is positive leverage or negative leverage, the Leverage value gives us an indication of how strongly a particular loan will impact our returns. For example, a Leverage value of 3.2 percent is more beneficial to a deal than a Leverage value of 1.1 percent. Conversely, a Leverage value of -2 percent is more harmful than a Leverage value of -1.3 percent.

This is important, as it can allow us to compare several different loan options to quickly determine which is more beneficial to our investment returns.

To pull this discussion of debt and leverage together, in the next chapter we'll talk about how returns on leveraged properties work and why the Leverage value impacts returns.

HONE YOUR SKILLS: CHAPTER 35

- What is the Leverage (value) for a deal with a cap rate of 5.5 percent and a loan constant of 6 percent?
- How do you interpret the Leverage value?

CHAPTER 36
BOOSTING RETURNS WITH LEVERAGE

Chapter 36 will help us to answer the questions:
- What is my ROI on my various funding sources?
- How can I maximize my returns using leverage?

We want to round out your understanding of leverage by providing a framework in which to think about returns on your leveraged properties. When viewing leverage through this framework, you'll get a better understanding of how leverage works and why certain loans are better (or worse) than others.

To restate a point we've made several times: For any property that is bought with a loan, there are two types of financing.

1. Equity, or the cash we put into the property (typically referred to as the down payment)
2. Debt, or the cash infused by borrowed funds (typically referred to as the loan amount or the leverage amount)

PROPERTY FINANCING

DOWN PAYMENT + BORROWED FUNDS

Additionally, we will generate some amount of positive or negative cash flow on our properties from each of these two sources of funds.

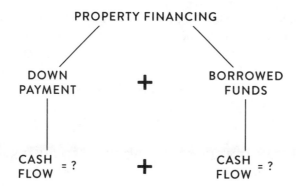

PROPERTY FINANCING

DOWN PAYMENT + BORROWED FUNDS

CASH FLOW = ? + CASH FLOW = ?

If we purchase a property for all cash, we know that our return is going to equal our cap rate. And because we don't have a loan, our cash flow will be the same as our NOI.

Let's go back to the three scenarios that we used in the previous two chapters and see how Scenario #1, where we pay all cash for a property, would look.

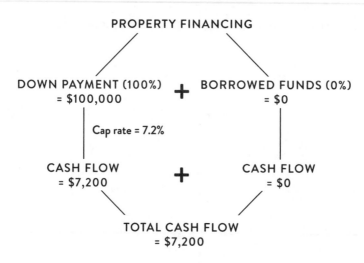

PROPERTY FINANCING

DOWN PAYMENT (100%) = $100,000 + BORROWED FUNDS (0%) = $0

Cap rate = 7.2%

CASH FLOW = $7,200 + CASH FLOW = $0

TOTAL CASH FLOW = $7,200

Because all the financing for the project is coming from the 100 percent down payment, and because our return is the same as our cap rate, our cash flow will be the same as our NOI and will be the cap rate times the purchase price:

NOI = Purchase price × Cap rate
NOI = $100,000 × 7.2% = **$7,200**

This matches what we determined earlier and shouldn't come as a surprise. But how about when we add a loan into the mix—how does that impact where our cash flow is coming from?

Let's jump into Scenario #2 (4.5 percent interest). In this case, we put 20 percent of the purchase price down ($20,000) and have a loan for 80 percent of the purchase price ($80,000).

PROPERTY FINANCING

DOWN PAYMENT (20%)   +   BORROWED FUNDS (80%)
= $20,000   = $80,000

Just like in our 100 percent down payment scenario, the down payment amount we are making in this scenario will generate cash flow at a rate equal to the cap rate. But in this case, we're only putting $20,000 down (not $100,000), so only $20,000 will be generating cash flow at the 7.2% return.

Cash flow on down payment = $20,000 × 7.2% = **$1,440**

That down payment generates one part of our cash flow:

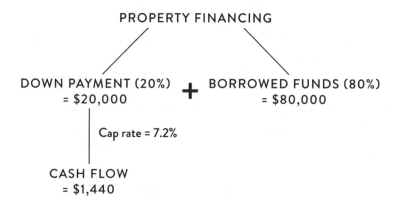

The borrowed funds are also generating a return. In other words, for every dollar that we've borrowed, we're either gaining or losing cash flow. And it turns out that the rate at which we gain or lose cash flow on the borrowed funds is equal to the Leverage value.

Remember that in this scenario, the Leverage value was 1.1 percent (see the last chapter if you've forgotten how we determined that). That means the cash flow being generated by the $80,000 in borrowed funds is:

Cash flow on borrowed funds = Borrowed funds × Leverage
Cash flow on borrowed funds = $80,000 × 1.1% = **$880**

Adding the cash flow generated by the down payment to the cash flow generated by the borrowed funds, we expect our total cash flow on this property and with this loan to be about $2,320.

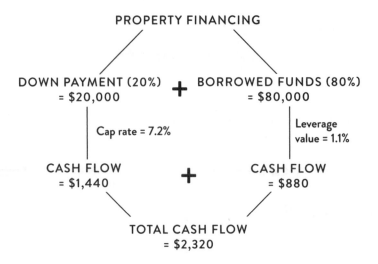

PROPERTY FINANCING

DOWN PAYMENT (20%) **+** BORROWED FUNDS (80%)
= $20,000   = $80,000

Cap rate = 7.2%   Leverage value = 1.1%

CASH FLOW **+** CASH FLOW
= $1,440   = $880

TOTAL CASH FLOW
= $2,320

Note: You might notice that our cash flow here ($2,320) doesn't match exactly to the cash flow amount we calculated in the previous chapter ($2,340). This is because we rounded our monthly loan payment to $405—it's actually $405.35. We also rounded our loan constant to 1.1 percent when, more precisely, it's 1.119 percent. If we used those more precise numbers, we'd find our cash flow values to be equivalent in both chapters and would be approximately $2,335.

You're probably wondering why the return on the borrowed funds is equal to the Leverage. Here's why.

Remember that the cap rate is the return we're earning on the cash we put into the property; the loan constant is the return that the lender is making on their loan; and Leverage is the difference between these two numbers.

In our scenario above, we're earning 7.2 percent (the cap rate) on the property for every dollar of our own cash that we put in, but when we borrow funds, the lender is "stealing" away 6.1 percent (the loan constant) of that as *their* profit. The 1.1 percent difference is the return that is ours to keep and applies to every dollar that is borrowed.

This is why when the Leverage value is positive, we're generating positive cash flow on every dollar that we borrow (positive leverage). The lender is stealing away part of our return, but they're not taking all of it—the remainder is ours to keep.

When the Leverage value is negative, we're giving up cash flow on every dollar we borrow (negative leverage). The lender is taking all of our return, *plus more*, and is causing us to lose return on each dollar we borrow.

To illustrate that last point, let's take a look at Scenario #3 (7 percent interest). We determined earlier that this is a negative leverage scenario, and we now know that this means we're losing cash flow for each dollar we borrow. And we know that the rate of that loss is equal to the Leverage.

Here's what this cash-flow scenario looks like:

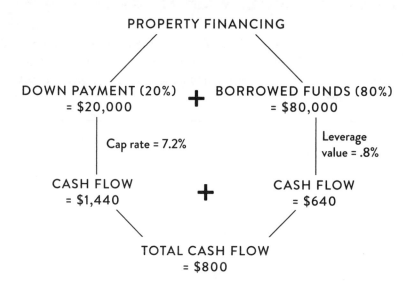

PROPERTY FINANCING

DOWN PAYMENT (20%) = $20,000 **+** BORROWED FUNDS (80%) = $80,000

Cap rate = 7.2%   Leverage value = .8%

CASH FLOW = $1,440 **+** CASH FLOW = $640

TOTAL CASH FLOW = $800

As expected, when breaking down our cash flow, the aggregate remains about $800. Again, note that the cash flow we've calculated here is about $16 less than what we calculated previously, simply because we rounded the monthly payment and the loan constant in the previous chapters.

When you start thinking about the fact that our cash flow is generated both by the cash we infuse into the investment and the funds we borrow, it becomes a lot clearer why our cash flow is so much more significant when we make large down payments and why some loans will treat our cash flow so much better than others.

While this chapter may seem academic in nature—and it is—we believe it's important to understand where your returns are coming from or getting lost. This should go a long way toward helping you understand the value of your equity, as well as the potential value of your debt. (Or, in some cases, the negative value your debt is causing.)

Long story short, we recommend that you always calculate the Leverage you'll be getting from your particular financing options, and use that to help determine which loans are more likely to contribute positive leverage. If you determine that none of your loans will provide positive leverage, use the understanding gained in this chapter to make better decisions about how much debt to take. In other words, you shouldn't always just put the minimum amount down on every deal (although that is often a good strategy); instead, you should be thinking critically about what your goals are, and find a loan product that best meets those goals.

- For a property purchased with a loan, what are the two types of financing?
- What is the cash flow generated from equity on a property purchased for $300,000 with a 25 percent down payment, which has a cap rate of 6.8 percent?
- What is the cash flow from borrowed funds for the same property if the leverage is 1.9 percent?

RETURN ON EQUITY (ROE) AND REFINANCING

Chapter 37 will help us to answer the questions:
- What return is my equity generating for me?
- Should I refinance or sell a property to improve my returns?

A great way to measure the performance of your equity (and leverage) in your portfolio over time is with a metric known as return on equity (ROE). ROE is a great way to understand the profitability of a real estate investment, but it is curiously underused. Publicly traded companies often use ROE to measure profitability, but when it comes to real estate, most investors tend to evaluate their portfolios in terms of other metrics, like cash-on-cash return or IRR.

But ROE shouldn't be overlooked, as its utility goes beyond simply measuring return. It can also help investors answer critical portfolio management questions, like when to refinance or sell a property to maximize the return generated for each dollar of equity invested.

Like most metrics in this book, the calculation for return on equity is relatively simple and requires just two inputs: cash flow and equity value.

As a brief reminder, equity value is the dollar value of the deal to the deal's owners. Put another way, if you were to sell the property and everything of value associated with the deal, and then use the proceeds of those sales to pay off your liabilities, what you have left over is your equity value.

Equity value = Property Value – Liabilities

For example, if we had a deal that we could sell and generate $300,000, but we have a $200,000 loan balance to repay, our equity value would be $100,000 ($300,000 – $200,000 = $100,000).

Because ROE is a measure of profitability, the higher the ROE, the better. You can interpret the results of ROE as the answer to the question, "How much annual cash flow will each dollar of equity I have invested produce?"

For example, let's say that Stephen just purchased a property for $400,000, where he put 20 percent down, and he expects it will produce $8,000 in cash flow.

At the time of purchase, Stephen's equity in the deal is equal to his down payment, which in this case would be $80,000 ($400,000 × 20% = $80,000). Stephen's ROE would then be:

ROE = Cash flow ÷ Equity value
ROE = $8,000 ÷ $80,000 = 0.1 (10%)

	TIME OF PURCHASE
Property Value	$400,000
Down Payment	$80,000
Interest Rate	4%
Loan Balance	$320,000
Equity ($)	$80,000
Equity (%)	20%
Cash Flow	$8,000
Return on Equity	**10%**

In this example, for every dollar of equity that Stephen has invested into this property, he can expect a 10 percent annual return. Or at least that is what he can expect at the time of purchase—ROE will change continuously, and it is important to recalculate it often.

In fact, over the lifetime of a rental property investment, both inputs into this formula—cash flow and equity value—will likely change. As we discussed at the beginning of this book, cash flow from a rental property is primarily a function of gross income (rent) and expenses. If you're doing a good job of maintaining your properties and consistently improving management efficiency, hopefully your rents are increasing faster than your expenses.

Equity can change in two ways: appreciation and amortization.

- When the value of a property increases due to market forces, improvements to the property, or other factors like inflation, it increases the owner's equity—that is appreciation.
- As we discussed when breaking down the anatomy of a loan, making payments on an amortized loan grows your ownership of a property over time because you're paying down the principal—that is amortization.

To demonstrate this point, let's fast-forward five years from Stephen's purchase. Stephen's cash flow has grown from $8,000 to $10,000 per year, and his property has increased from $400,000 to $450,000 in value (appreciation!). After five years of mortgage payments, Stephen now owes the bank about $290,000 on his loan, down from the original $320,000 (amortization!).

As a result, Stephen's equity has grown to $160,000—his $80,000 initial down payment, plus the difference in property valuation from the time of his purchase until now ($50,000) and the amortization he's accrued on his loan ($30,000).

	TIME OF PURCHASE	5 YEARS LATER
Property Value	$400,000	$450,000
Down Payment	$80,000	$80,000
Interest Rate	4%	4%
Loan Balance	$320,000	$290,000
Equity ($)	$80,000	$160,000
Equity (%)	20%	36%
Cash Flow	$8,000	$10,000
Return on Equity	**10%**	**6%**

Stephen appears to be doing well on this deal. His equity has doubled in five years, so why is this measure of profitability going down? Why has his ROE decreased from 10 percent to 6 percent?

It's because Stephen is building equity at a faster rate than his cash flow is increasing. His cash flow grew 25 percent in five years, which is great! But he *doubled* his equity during that time, so proportionally, each dollar of equity he has invested into the deal makes him less cash flow.

A declining ROE isn't necessarily a bad thing. After all, Stephen doubled his equity and is now generating $10,000 per year in cash flow, which is excellent. Stephen should be very happy with his investment's performance. But it begs the question: Can he do better? Is there a way that Stephen can generate more return for each dollar invested; in other words, can he make his money work harder for him?

Stephen has two strategies to consider that can potentially boost his ROE: selling or refinancing.

DIG DEEP

RETURN ON EQUITY VERSUS CASH-ON-CASH RETURN

Both return on equity and cash-on-cash return measure how much cash flow is produced for each dollar invested into a deal. But which one should you use, and when?

As we said in Part 3 of this book, COC is a great metric to evaluate cash flow at the time of purchase. As a quick refresher, COC = annual cash flow ÷ cash invested. It's best used at the time of purchase because it factors in up-front costs like your down payment and any initial out-of-pocket expenses you incur to improve the property. It's an excellent snapshot of how much you're spending out of pocket, as well as what you can expect in return for that investment in the first year or so.

But over time, COC loses its utility. As we've demonstrated in this chapter on ROE, sophisticated investors see the amount they've invested in a deal not just as the out-of-pocket expenses they incurred at the time of purchase, but also the equity value that has built up in a deal.

Returning to the example of Stephen—he would have enjoyed a COC of about 9.1 percent. He had a cash flow of $8,000 and invested $88,000 ($80,000 in down payment, and we'll assume closing costs of $8,000). $8,000 ÷ $88,000 = 9.1 percent.

Five years later, Stephen's COC would have shot up to 11.4 percent. This improvement reflects that his rent income has increased from $8,000 to $10,000, while his cash invested has not changed.

But is Stephen generating cash flow at a more efficient rate five years into the investment? A savvy investor will recognize that after five years, the amount Stephen has invested into the deal goes far beyond what he paid for out of pocket at the time of purchase. At this point, Stephen has $160,000 in equity in this deal that he could use for other investments were he to sell.

Therefore, five years into the deal, it's better to measure cash-flow production by how much equity you have in a deal, not how much you paid out of pocket at the time of the initial purchase. Therefore, we recommend using ROE to evaluate your portfolio over time, while COC is the better metric to use at the time of purchase and to evaluate your first-year returns.

SELL

The simplest way to improve ROE is to simply sell an existing investment and trade up to an investment that has a better ROE.

Using our example from above, recall that Stephen started with a ROE of 10 percent, but his ROE dropped to 6 percent over the course of five years.

To improve the rate at which his equity produces cash flow (ROE), Stephen can start analyzing prospective deals and see if he can find a better deal.

	TIME OF PURCHASE	5 YEARS LATER	NEW PURCHASE
Property Value	$400,000	$450,000	$600,000
Down Payment	$80,000	$80,000	$120,000
Interest Rate	4%	4%	4%
Loan Balance	$320,000	$290,000	$120,000
Equity ($)	$80,000	$160,000	$120,000
Equity (%)	20%	36%	20%
Cash Flow	$8,000	$10,000	$13,500
Return on Equity	10%	6%	11%
Cash Out			$40,000

In this hypothetical scenario, let's say Stephen scours the market and finds a deal for $600,000 that could generate a ROE of 11 percent. If Stephen's sole goal is to maximize ROE, this would be a great deal, as he would improve his ROE from 6 percent to 11 percent.

But even with this more expensive deal, Stephen is only using $120,000 of the $160,000 he would generate in profit from selling his initial purchase. A savvier move would be to find a way to reinvest all his profits into a new purchase (or even two new purchases). Remember from earlier in the book that if you want to build wealth as quickly as possible, you need to reinvest your profits.

Perhaps a better example of how Stephen might optimize his portfolio for ROE would be to sell his initial property and upgrade to two properties.

This example would allow Stephen to fully reinvest his equity, grow his portfolio, optimize ROE, and reduce risk by spreading his equity into two investments rather than one.

	TIME OF PURCHASE	5 YEARS LATER	NEW PURCHASE 1	NEW PURCHASE 2
Property Value	$400,000	$450,000	$420,000	$380,000
Down Payment	$80,000	$80,000	$84,000	$76,000
Interest Rate	4%	4%	4%	4%
Loan Balance	$320,000	$290,000	$84,000	$76,000
Equity ($)	$80,000	$160,000	$84,000	$76,000
Equity (%)	20%	36%	20%	20%
Cash Flow	$8,000	$10,000	$8,000	$7,000
Return on Equity	10%	6%	10%	9%

Of course, selling a property is not always an ideal solution. For example, you may find that the market has changed for the worse since your purchase, and you can't currently sell for a price that would make sense for your overall goals. Or maybe you want to hold on to this particular property for its longer-term appreciation potential. Plus, selling a property comes at a price—commissions, closing costs, and potential tax implications.

Selling isn't always the best way to boost ROE. In these cases, an alternative is through a refinance.

REFINANCE

Refinancing a property allows the owner to essentially "reset" their mortgage. There are two ways to do it: traditional refinance or cash-out refinance.

Traditional Refinance (Rate-and-Term Refinance)

The traditional refinancing option that property owners take advantage of when mortgage rates decline is often called a "rate-and-term refinance." This is where a property owner can reset their mortgage with a new interest rate and a new loan term, without extracting any additional cash from the property.

For example, say your primary residence has a mortgage with a 5 percent interest rate and a thirty-year term. Due to market forces, interest rates drop to 4 percent two years after you purchased the property. You may consider refinancing into a new thirty-year loan with a 4 percent interest rate to save you money each month. On the downside, this refinance also resets the amortization schedule on the loan, adding back the two years you had accrued in loan paydown, and restarting the thirty-year clock.

Rate-and-term refinance is a solid strategy investors should consider if they want to increase cash flow and if they can lock in a lower interest rate without too much up-front cost. A traditional refinance, however, is not generally a great way to improve ROE. For that, you need a cash-out refinance.

Cash-Out Refinance

A cash-out refinance is the same idea as a rate-and-term refinance, but it allows the borrower to withdraw some of the equity they have built in the home in the form of cash. Let's go back to Stephen to see how this might work.

After five years of ownership, Stephen has amassed an impressive $160,000 in equity. But his ROE is declining, and he wants to make sure that his equity is generating returns at the best possible rate. Therefore, he considers a cash-out refinance.

Determining the impact of a cash-out refinance is straightforward.

Stephen's property is now worth $450,000. Just as when he purchased the property, Stephen needs to keep some equity in the property as a guarantee on the loan. When he bought the property, he put 20 percent down; let's assume that after the refinance, the bank will require the same loan-to-value ratio of 20 percent. This means that Stephen must keep 20 percent of the new value ($450,000 × 20% = $90,000) of equity in the deal to secure a new loan from the bank.

Remember, Stephen has $160,000 in equity value. If he has $160,000 and only needs to keep $90,000 in the deal, what happens to the other $70,000? He can take that out as cash! That is the "cash-out" part of the cash-out refinance.

Look at how this works:

	TIME OF PURCHASE	5 YEARS LATER	REFINANCE
Property Value	$400,000	$450,000	$450,000
Down Payment	$80,000	$80,000	$90,000
Interest Rate	4%	4%	4%
Loan Balance	$320,000	$290,000	$340,000
Equity ($)	$80,000	$160,000	$90,000
Equity (%)	20%	36%	20%
Cash Flow	$8,000	$10,000	$9,000
Return on Equity	**10%**	**6%**	**10%**
Cash Out			**$70,000**

When Stephen closes on his new loan, a few things happen.

- He has kept $90,000 in equity in the property (you can think of this as the down payment on the new loan).
- His loan balance increases to $360,000 because his mortgage is starting over: He again has equity of 20 percent, just like at the time of the original purchase.
- His cash flow has decreased because the monthly payments on his mortgage have increased (a mortgage on a $450,000 property is more expensive than a mortgage on a $400,000 property).
- He has withdrawn $70,000 from the deal that he can do whatever he wants with.

For Stephen, a cash-out refinance restored his ROE to its former level and is now generating cash flow more efficiently. This works because Stephen has reduced his equity in the deal from $160,000 down to $90,000, but he still gets to take advantage of increased income he has generated over the past five years.

In other words, the cash that Stephen has invested in the property is once again working hard for him, with each dollar in equity once again generating a 10 percent return.

INVESTOR STORY
Dave's First Deal

My first deal was a fourplex in Denver in 2010. It's hard to believe now, but at that time you could buy a four-unit building for under $500,000, which is what I did with the help of several partners.

The property was $467,000 and generated about $15,000 in cash flow per year at the time of the initial purchase. I'll be honest—at that point I had no idea what return on equity meant. I was just excited that my property was cash flowing and the Denver market was appreciating.

Over the course of the next several years, I became a more sophisticated investor and started to understand why ROE was so important. I wanted to build my portfolio, but I had a lot of equity tied up in this deal. I needed to get money out of this deal to invest in new deals.

Don't get me wrong, the deal was a big winner. But over time I was no longer generating efficient returns given how much I had invested into the deal. My ROE had dropped from 16 percent at the time of purchase to about 10 percent.

I considered both selling and refinancing, but ultimately, I decided to sell. The Denver market had appreciated massively, and it felt like the market for small multi-family properties was going to flatten out in coming years as rental growth slowed. The building needed some major repairs, and I didn't have the time to oversee the process properly, as I was working full-time and in graduate school. Additionally, with several partners in the deal, it felt like time to walk away while we were ahead.

We listed the house and sold it very quickly, and I was then free to use the equity I built over eight years to get into two new deals. I used a 1031 exchange to purchase a rental property in a different neighborhood in Denver, and I used the rest of my proceeds to purchase my first short-term rental property in a different town in Colorado.

By trading out of my first deal, I was able to exceed my initial ROE (the average for the two new purchases was about 17 percent), and I increased my total cash flow by about 35 percent. I was sad to part with the deal that got me into real estate investing in the first place, but I'm happy that I did the analysis, saw that this deal was no longer working for me the way it once did, and moved on to bigger and better things. It seems fitting that my first-ever purchase was also my first-ever sale.

As you can now see, using a cash-out refinance is an excellent way to improve the ROE of a current investment. It's a tool that every investor should be familiar with, particularly those who are interested in the BRRRR (buy, rehab, rent, refinance, repeat) strategy, given that one of the four R's stands for refinance!

When running a BRRRR deal, you typically invest a good chunk of equity into the acquisition of the property and the rehab. Additionally, when rehabbing a property, you tend to focus on generating forced appreciation (we'll discuss this at length in Part 5, but forced appreciation is the strategy of driving up the price of a property by rehabbing and improving the property).

If you invest a lot of equity into a deal, and then successfully drive up the value of the property through forced appreciation (building even more equity in the process), you will likely have a lot of equity in proportion to the cash flow the property produces. Again, this isn't a bad thing—you're generating returns—but it leaves you in an inefficient place equity-wise.

That's why a core tenant of the BRRRR strategy is to refinance—to pull equity out, improve ROE, and give the investor more equity with which they can do another deal. We'll discuss BRRRR analysis in more depth in Chapter 47.

It's important to note that refinancing a property does have drawbacks.

- When resetting your loan, you pay more interest to the bank and build equity through amortization at a slower rate.
- Your cash flow may decrease due to higher mortgage payments (depending on how much equity you extracted and how much rates have decreased).
- If your cash-out refinance occurs at a time when interest rates are higher than the existing loan, the two drawbacks above will be even more dramatic: You will pay more in interest and your cash flow will decrease more than if you refinance at the same interest rate (like we did in the example above).

Due to the inherent trade-offs in refinancing, it's important to continuously evaluate the ROE for each property you own. We recommend that each year, you sit down and calculate ROE for every property in your portfolio. Then, compare those ROE rates to what you could get from refinancing or selling your properties, and determine whether you could deploy your equity more efficiently.

HONE YOUR SKILLS: CHAPTER 37

- What is the return on equity of an investment with cash flow of $12,000 per year and equity value of $135,000?
- What is the equity value of a deal that sells for $475,000 and has liabilities of $366,000?
- What are two strategies to improve your return on equity?

PART 4
CONCLUSION

Over the course of Part 4, we've explained how you can finance any real estate investment, and we hope you can now see that financing should be a major part of your strategy—not just a hurdle to overcome.

When approaching a new investment, it's important to start at the beginning and determine which types of financing best suit the investment's goals and details. Will you use all equity? Mostly debt? Or a more complicated structure that involves multiple levels of debt and equity? Remember, the answers to these questions will likely change for each deal you do based on deal strategy, your own investable assets, interest rates, and many other factors. At any time in your investing career, feel free to return to Chapter 26 (on equity) and Chapter 28 (on debt) to review the list of pros and cons for each financing type.

If you choose to use equity from outside investors, remember there are many formats in which you can raise equity: active partners, passive partners, contractor partners, and more. If you need a refresher, return to Chapter 27 to see our overview of equity financing types.

Regardless of what type of equity financing you choose, it's important to remember that raising equity financing from outside investors is just an arrangement between two or more investors. This means there are very few formal processes you must follow, but that doesn't mean you shouldn't formalize your agreements—quite the opposite. Whatever equity financing structure you choose, we recommend you find a qualified attorney to help you draft the appropriate documentation to outline the terms of the deal. This will help you avoid any confusion or hurt feeling over the course of the deal, even if (especially if!) you're just raising capital from friends and family.

If you choose to use debt financing, as almost every investor will over the course of their career, it's important to shop around and find the right type of loan. The best type of loan is likely to vary considerably, depending on the investment strategy. You won't want to use a hard-money loan for a long-term hold, and you may not need a conventional loan for a flip. In Chapter 29, you can review our overview of loan types and some general guidelines on when each type of loan is best used.

Before you settle on any particular loan, make sure you research different lenders so you can get the terms, rate, and structure that are best for your investment. You do that by talking to many lenders and getting a lot of quotes. Once you have quotes in hand, you should calculate the cost of each loan using the loan constant formula you learned, and then determine the Leverage value of each loan, so you can understand if the loan will boost or hurt your investment's returns. This will allow you to compare different loan options against one another.

Unlike with equity financing, most lenders will have a documented and formal process for working with investors. Review those documents carefully and make sure you understand all the terms of a loan before signing anything. Chapter 30 ("The Anatomy of a Loan") should help you understand the terms of almost any loan, but don't hesitate to reach out to an attorney, CPA, or trusted investor friend if there is still something you don't understand.

Now that you've gained an expert understanding of how to strategically finance your investments, it's time to put together all the knowledge you've acquired so far in this book. In Part 5, we'll dive into deal analysis, and you'll put to work everything you've learned about financial statements, financial concepts, return metrics, and financing through the first four parts of this book. This is where things get fun!

MAKING IT WORK
FOR YOU

We've spent the bulk of this book discussing how to evaluate business performance, measure investment returns, and think about all the numbers and metrics around investing. In Part 5, we're going to introduce some concepts that will help you think about money, investing, and wealth in ways that you may not have considered before. In addition, we will provide real-world examples of how we can use these concepts, along with the metrics we've introduced previously, to analyze investment deals, and ultimately determine if those deals will allow us to achieve our financial goals.

It would be nice if we were able to provide a step-by-step process that any investor could use as a checklist to say, "This is a good deal" or "This is a bad deal." But in reality, it's rarely as simple as saying that a deal is good or bad.

Instead, deals that may be good for one investor might be very bad for another. Some deals may be bad for nearly all investors but good for one specific investor who has a unique financial situation or need—and vice versa. Some deals might look great on paper but not satisfy the specific needs of an investor who has a nontypical financial goal.

Instead of asking the question, "Is this a good deal?" we would challenge you to instead start asking the question, "Is this a good deal *for me?*"

To do that, you need to understand what your personal financial goals are; in other words, what you're trying to achieve with your investments. For example, a twenty-two-year-old recent college graduate with no money—but tons of time and energy—is likely going to have different goals than a sixty-year-old executive working eighty hours per week with $5 million in the bank who's looking to invest that cash and retire in five years.

When it comes to time and money, most of us fall somewhere in between those extremes.

In order to answer the question of "Is this a good deal *for me?*" there are two things you should consider:

1. What *type* of deals are right for me to achieve my goals?
2. What *returns* do these deals need to offer for me to achieve my goals?

Again, it would be impossible for us to provide a step-by-step process or checklist to answer these questions. However, what we *can* provide are some frameworks for how to think about investing to achieve your individual financial goals.

Over the next several chapters, we're going to discuss three of these frameworks that you can use to help clarify your personal financial goals and lay out an investment plan that makes sense for you. Then, we'll dive deep into some case studies that will teach you how to analyze various types of deals to determine whether they would allow you to achieve those goals.

The first framework will address the types of deals available to us. The second framework will address the returns generated by these different deals. And the third framework will take a more holistic view of how we can use different types of investing and compounding returns over many deals and many years in order to build wealth.

From there, we will dig into the nitty-gritty of deal analysis and evaluation, so that we can be confident that we're actually on track to generate the returns that we want and need.

TRANSACTIONAL (ACTIVE) VERSUS RESIDUAL (PASSIVE) INCOME

Chapter 38 will help answer the questions:
- What type of deals are out there and on what types of deals should I be focused?
- What are the differences between transactional and residual income?

The first question most new investors (and even seasoned investors) ask themselves is "What type of deals should I be focused on making?" This is a logical place to start, but to properly answer that question, we need to start with another, more basic question: "What types of deals are there?"

Intuitively, most new investors have an idea of the answer to that question, even if they haven't thought about it in the same terms as we will. However, the foundation of this question is encapsulated in what is probably one of the most common questions we get from new investors: "Should I start by flipping houses or buying rentals?"

Given that these are the two most common real estate investing strategies, and given that there are a lot of appealing aspects of both, it's not surprising that this is the first question to go through many people's heads. It was certainly a question that crossed our minds when we started investing. (Note that J started with flipping while Dave started with rentals.)

Time and experience have shown us that "flipping versus rentals" isn't the right way to think about how and where to start investing. And with a little context, we think that you'll start to view flipping, rentals, and other investing strategies in a whole new light.

Let's start at the beginning.

Most of us aren't born wealthy. At some point, we need to start earning money to survive. And the most common way of doing that is to trade our time and effort to get it. In other words, we get jobs.

Jobs are—for the most part—transactional. We agree to provide our work in exchange for a lump sum of money. That lump sum may be in the form of hourly compensation, a salary, a fixed fee (like consulting), or a commission (getting paid based on performance and results). But the commonality among most jobs is that you are trading your time, effort, knowledge, and experience for money.

If we work hard, we may find that our jobs turn into careers or blossom into entrepreneurial pursuits. Perhaps we start our own business. Perhaps we become full-time consultants. Perhaps we create or invent things that we can license or sell. Regardless, for most of us, earning money is purely transactional—we trade our time and effort to make money that allows us to pay the bills, and hopefully to start saving and enjoying as well.

This is what many of our financial lives look like for a good bit of time:

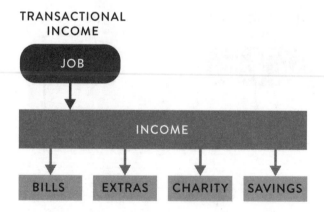

Unfortunately, the issue with transactional income is that if we ever decide to stop devoting our time and effort to these money-generating tasks, the money stops coming in. As employees, if we stop working for longer than our allotted vacation time, our employer stops paying us. If we're self-employed small business owners or consultants, we may stop getting paid the minute we leave the office.

As we recognize this pitfall of "working for a living," we may start to think longer term and come to realize that, while it allows us to live, trading time and effort for money isn't the best way to accumulate and compound wealth. We notice others who are taking some of their hard-earned money and putting it into investments like the stock market or buy-and-hold real estate. And we see them getting ahead while we're still trading our valuable time and energy for our weekly or monthly paycheck.

This is how they are living their financial lives:

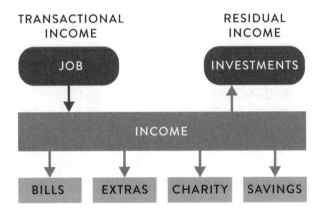

And for those who are using their investments to generate recurring (residual) cash, they start to supplement their income month after month, year after year:

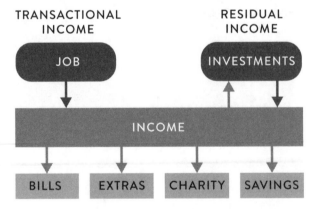

When they stop working (perhaps they get laid off from a job or need to take an extended leave from their career), while the transactional income might stop, the residual income keeps coming in. That residual income will likely be small at first—maybe a couple hundred bucks a month. And it certainly won't feel life changing.

However, if we continue with these investments that are generating residual income, allowing both time and compounding to take effect, we'll find that the residual income generated by these investments will increase to a meaningful amount, and that monthly residual income may eventually surpass the transactional income we're generating from our jobs and careers.

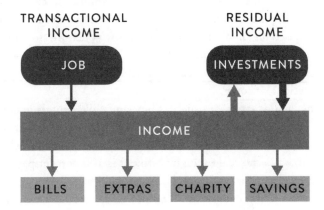

In fact, if we invest purposefully and consistently enough, we'll eventually get to the point where the residual income we're generating from our investments will be enough to cover all of our bills, our vacations, and anything else we need money for. As long as we're not spending at a faster rate than our investments are growing, we can find ourselves living off of our investments for the rest of our lives, and then passing those investments on to the next generation.

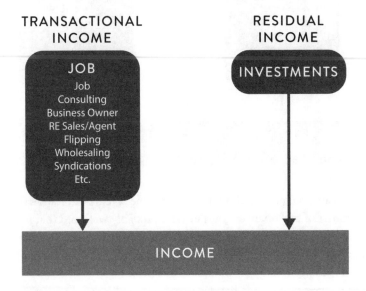

This is financial freedom.

Now, after all that, you may be wondering: "What does this have to do with a decision between flipping houses and buying rentals? Or any other type of real estate investing, for that matter?"

Well, using the framework supplied above, it should be clear that investing strategies such as flipping houses are transactional. The cash from flipping houses is generated once, based on an input of time and effort. When we stop flipping houses, the income stops, no different from our 9-to-5 jobs. In fact, unlike our 9-to-5 jobs, we don't even get paid sick time or vacation time! Flipping houses is simply a job that generates transactional income.

On the other hand, strategies such as buy-and-hold rentals generate residual income—recurring revenue month after month and year after year that can be used to grow your income and net worth without a significant continued investment of time. (Yes, we recognize that no real estate investment is 100 percent passive, but when structured correctly, rental investing and other strategies can come close.)

So, instead of thinking in terms of "flipping versus rentals," we should instead be thinking in terms of "transactional income versus residual income."

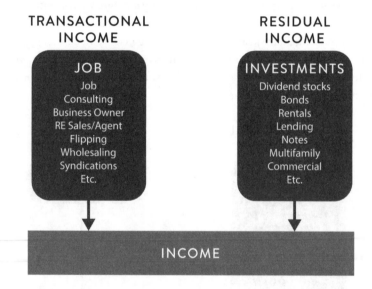

Most of us are going to need both types of income. We'll need transactional income at the beginning of our financial journey (and probably well into that journey). And once we've accumulated some cash from our transactional effort, we will want to use that extra cash to start generating residual income. Hopefully we'll continue to use that residual income strategy for the rest of our lives.

Instead of trying to decide between transactional income and residual income (flipping or rentals), our recommendation is to pick at least one primary method of generating transactional income and at least one primary method of generating residual income.

Either or both may be real estate related.

Remember, time is our most limited asset—we can't make more of it. For transactional income, we encourage you to focus on doing whatever (within reason, of course) will maximize your hourly income. Oftentimes, this means doing what you're best at—or what you can become the best at. Perhaps that's working at a job or in a career that you're trained or well suited for. Maybe that's being a consultant or small business owner. Or perhaps that's flipping houses or some other form of transactional real estate.

Once you've maximized your transactional income, take as much of that income as you possibly can and start allocating it into whatever residual income strategy you've chosen. Perhaps you've decided that you want to own cash-flowing rental properties. Or you want to lend or buy notes. Maybe you'd prefer to stick with dividend-paying stocks. Or maybe you'd like a combination of tactics.

Regardless, pick one or more residual income strategies and start to move as much transactional income as you can into this residual income "machine," allowing time and compounding to build that residual income and set you on a path to financial freedom.

HONE YOUR SKILLS: CHAPTER 38

- What is the difference between transactional income and residual income?
- What are three examples of real estate–focused transactional income strategies?
- What are three examples of real estate–focused residual income strategies?

CHAPTER 39
THE FOUR WAYS THAT REAL ESTATE GENERATES RETURNS

Chapter 39 will help answer the questions:
- Specifically, how does real estate help me achieve financial freedom?
- When I invest in real estate, where are my returns really coming from?

For many newer real estate investors—and for many seasoned investors as well—cash flow is considered the holy grail of investment returns. Whether the goal is to achieve cash flow to live on, to purchase more investments with, or to pay for our toys and vacations, generating income from our investments provides us with short-term security and flexibility.

But cash flow isn't the only benefit that real estate investing provides. As our financial situations and our life priorities change, we often find that these other benefits of owning real estate become as important as—or even more important than—the cash flow itself.

While there are dozens of benefits of investing in real estate, they all essentially boil down to these four:

- Cash flow
- Appreciation
- Amortization
- Tax benefits

Understanding these benefits will provide the foundation you need when analyzing deals to determine whether a deal meets your financial goals.

Let's examine each of these in more detail.

CASH FLOW

As we discussed in Part 1, cash flow is simply the spendable profit an investment creates while you own that investment. Most of us are familiar with the cash flow generated by a rental property: You rent out the property, pay the expenses, and at the end of the month (or year...or decade), you have a bunch of leftover money—your profit—to spend or reinvest (after you pay taxes, of course).

Now, there are lot of non–real estate investments that also generate cash flow. Simply sticking your money in a savings account or Certificate of Deposit will generate a small amount of cash flow from the interest they pay you. Certain stocks pay quarterly or annual dividends—that's cash flow. And there are plenty of other examples as well.

But cash flow from real estate is different. Unlike those other cash-flowing investments, when you invest in real estate, you have the ability, to some extent, to affect the amount of cash flow you're receiving. When you put your money in a savings account, you might get your 0.005 percent interest; that's nonnegotiable. When you put your money in a dividend-paying stock, you get your 3 or 4 percent dividend offered by the company; that's nonnegotiable.

With real estate, nobody is fixing the return on your investment. If you are good at finding undervalued properties, you can generate higher returns. If you're a good negotiator, you can generate higher returns. If you're good at managing your properties efficiently, you can generate higher returns. If you do your research and buy in the right place at the right time, you can position yourself for higher future returns. If you renovate your properties correctly and attract great tenants, you can create higher returns.

Unlike most other cash-flowing assets, the returns you get from real property are directly related to you—your motivation, your persistence, your efforts, your abilities, and the decisions you make. They're directly related to how good you are at finding and engineering great deals.

Not only that, but the cash flow you receive from real estate is different from most other investments in that you can often use leverage to increase the percentage returns you receive on your investments. A rental property that you purchase for cash might generate 8 percent annualized returns, but if you were to get a loan for 80 percent of the value of that property, you might be able to increase the returns on the amount you still have invested to 10 percent or more. (See our discussion of positive leverage in Chapter 34 if it's not clear why this is.)

Between your ability to control the amount of cash flow you generate by finding and engineering great deals and your ability to boost returns on that cash flow through the use of leverage, cash flow from real estate is a tremendously powerful way to generate income.

By the way, rental property investing isn't the only way to generate cash flow in the real estate world. You can lend money to real estate investors and create monthly cash flow from the interest your borrowers pay you. You can seller-finance property and generate cash flow from the interest your buyers pay you. You can partner or buy into a larger syndication and generate cash flow from your equity stake in someone else's deal. There are lots of ways to generate cash flow in the real estate game.

Cash flow is the first fundamental way to generate income from real estate. But again, it's not the only way.

APPRECIATION

The second way in which real estate investing can generate income is appreciation. Most people think of appreciation as buying a property; holding it for five, ten, twenty, or thirty years while the market goes up; and then selling it for more than it was purchased for, thanks to market values increasing over time.

This form of appreciation is known as *market appreciation.*

But there's another form of appreciation that real estate investors use, often referred to as *forced appreciation.*

As the name implies, this form of appreciation is more deliberate, requiring active (transactional) involvement from the investor. Rather than just waiting for time to increase the value of a property, investors can force the increase in value through their input of time, knowledge, and effort.

Both market appreciation and forced appreciation can contribute to the same positive outcome for investors—selling a property for more than you bought it for and pocketing the difference. That said, the time frame, predictability (and risk), and ways in which we calculate ROI are very different between market and forced appreciation, and we should consider them separately.

Market Appreciation

We've all heard stories of relatives or friends who purchased real estate decades ago, and now that property is worth many, many times more than it was purchased for. In fact, without digging into the numbers, it appears that the natural increase in value of property over time is a significant incentive to purchase real estate.

Unfortunately, when we do dig into the numbers, we often find that this isn't the case. Certainly, there are parts of the country where the ROI from simply purchasing and holding property over years or decades will generate ridiculous returns (think of places like Palo Alto, California, where the average value of a single-family home increased from $600,000 in 1998 to nearly $4 million in 2021).

But these locations are outliers. For many regions across the country, market appreciation historically hasn't outperformed inflation by much, if anything.

What about all the stories we hear of someone buying a piece of real estate in 1970 for $50,000 that is now worth $350,000? That's a tremendous increase in value based on market appreciation, right?

Well, it's not. If you put these numbers into a compound interest calculator, you'll find that a property like the one in this example barely outperformed inflation over that same time period. In other words, the spending power of the $50,000 used to purchase that property in 1970 is actually worth about $330,000 in today's dollars. That property did better than inflation, but just barely so.

VALUE OF $50,000 IN 1970 DOLLARS

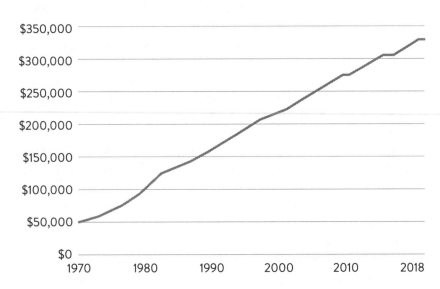

This book is being written in 2022, when inflation is at its highest rate in decades and real estate appreciation has been extremely high. It's unclear at this point whether this rapid value growth will continue long term or if this is a short-term anomaly that will revert back to more historic value trends. Regardless, we don't like to assume that short-term trends will necessarily become the norm, so we're hesitant to assume that market appreciation is going to continue to outperform inflation over the next decade.

All of that said, we don't want to err too far on the other side either. Many successful real estate investors will completely discount market appreciation and say that it's not a way to make money. This isn't true; market appreciation, especially coupled with leverage, can provide a lot of equity creation over long hold periods.

While it can be a winning strategy to knowingly accept lower cash flow to make calculated bets on appreciating markets, we wouldn't recommend forgoing cash flow altogether, especially for new investors. It is risk to do a deal where market appreciation is the sole benefit.

If you want to invest in a market you believe will appreciate, we recommend you still have enough cash flow to cover all expenses, with plenty of cushion and at least some excess cash flow. This is what we do. We both love deals that have an appreciation upside, but we look for deals that have adequate cash flow and can deliver other desired returns, even if no market appreciation materializes. We buy fundamentally sound deals in specific locations where we believe appreciation might occur, and if everything goes well, market appreciation can turn a strong deal into an incredible one.

Forced Appreciation

The other type of appreciation is the type that we, as shrewd real estate investors, create ourselves. Forced appreciation is, simply put, the act of forcing value increase of a property through our own efforts. This might be through making physical improvements to the property or improving management efficiency to reduce annual expenses.

The most common example of forced appreciation in real estate investing is house flipping. An investor purchases a property for $X, forces a value increase, and sells for $Y. If the investor can ensure that $Y is sufficiently more than $X, then they get to keep a portion of that increased value as their profit.

As an example, let's say Tina purchases a single-family home for $100,000. She renovates the entire home for a total cost of $50,000 over the course of four months, and then sells the property for $200,000. Tina has "forced" the property to appreciate by $100,000 in just four months, and because it only cost her $50,000, she gets to keep the other $50,000 in profit. (Yes, we're ignoring a bunch of other costs and details here for simplicity's sake, but you get the idea.)

While flipping may be the most common form of forced appreciation, it's not the only way to force value increases in our real estate assets. There are plenty of other real estate strategies that generate forced appreciation as well.

Let's look at buy-and-hold real estate. We know that the value of a larger property is equal to the amount of income it generates (NOI) divided by the cap rate of the property. Remember, a property's cap rate is the return an investor would expect to achieve for an all-cash deal on that type of property, in that location.

If we have a property that generates an NOI of $10,000 per year, and the property has a cap rate of 10 percent, the value of that property is probably about $100,000 ($10,000 ÷ 10%).

But what if we can increase the income that the property generates? Maybe we raise rents to market value, or start charging for laundry facilities and preferred parking spaces. At the same time, we improve management and reduce overhead in order to decrease expenses. Maybe we negotiate better terms with our vendors, petition the city to reduce our property taxes, and start buying our materials in bulk to reduce their cost.

Let's say that our hard work allows us to increase our net operating income from $10,000 per year to $15,000 per year. Using our value formula, the new value of the property is $150,000 ($15,000 ÷ 10%). We've forced the value of this property to increase by $50,000 through our targeted efforts!

The same idea also applies to other types of real estate investing. Many investors buy nonperforming notes—meaning the borrowers aren't paying their loans as they're supposed to—at prices far below what the note would be worth if the borrower were paying. If those investors are successful at getting their borrowers to start paying (often by restructuring the note in creative ways), that note suddenly becomes much more valuable than the amount it was purchased for. Again, the shrewd investor was able to force appreciation of that note.

Quick Tip | **Real Estate Notes**
A real estate note is simply the IOU a lender holds when making a loan against a piece of real estate. Often called a promissory note (it's a promise to repay the loan), we generally refer to *performing notes* as those where the borrower is actively repaying the loan per the terms of the note. We refer to *non-performing notes* as those where the borrower has stopped paying, or is behind on payments.

Too many investors think that forcing appreciation is just for house flippers, but as you can see, that's not the case. For example, forced appreciation could be finishing a basement with an extra bedroom to bring value to a rental property. Or it could be dividing up a commercial space to provide multiple, smaller income-producing offices or retail outlets. And we'll bet if you were to think about it a bit more, you could think of plenty of other places in real estate where smart investors can make a lot of money by forcing appreciation.

A few years ago, I (Dave) found a market I believed was primed for success in the short-term rental space. I purchased some data about the area and found that homes with four or more bedrooms were generating excellent returns for the owner. Properties with three bedrooms earned, on average, about $350 per night, whereas properties with four or more bedrooms often earned $500 per night or more. Best of all, the price difference between three- and four-bedroom homes was relatively small, so I looked exclusively for properties with four or more bedrooms.

As I looked, however, I couldn't find a deal in a good location with more than three bedrooms. I kept coming up empty. So, I changed my search parameters and instead looked for properties with three bedrooms that also had a lot of square footage, where I could create a fourth or even fifth bedroom.

Eventually, I found one. It was a three-bedroom house with almost 4,000 square feet—plenty of room to add bedrooms and still have several nice living areas. I wound up adding two extra bedrooms, at a cost of about $20,000.

By adding those rooms, my average daily rate went from about $350 to $450 in a couple of weeks. With approximately 120 nights of occupancy per year, that took my gross revenue from $42,000 to $57,600. Presuming a cap rate of 6 percent, my property value soared from $700,000 to about $960,000.

Forced appreciation is a powerful force for real estate investors. It does take more work than market appreciation, but it's predictable and can be maximized by mastering your craft and being a great investor.

Between market appreciation and forced appreciation, an increase in the value of investments through time and effort is the second way that real estate generates returns for investors.

AMORTIZATION

That brings us to the third way in which real estate generates returns for us: amortization. As discussed in Part 4, amortization is just a fancy way of referring to the principal paydown of a loan over time.

When you purchase a property with debt, your tenants will hopefully be paying enough money every month to cover all of your expenses, plus your monthly mortgage payment. Part of that mortgage payment is interest—the extra amount paid to the lender as the lender's profit. And part of that mortgage payment is principal—this is the part of the payment that reduces the total amount you owe to the lender.

For every dollar in principal paid to the lender, that's another dollar of equity you build. And when you sell or refinance the property, every dollar of equity turns into a dollar of profit in your wallet. In other words, every time one of your tenants pays rent, and part of that rent payment goes to pay your mortgage, the tenant is putting additional profit in your pocket. This is profit over and above any appreciation you created with the property, and over and above any cash flow you're getting from the property.

Amortization is especially powerful in situations where interest rates are low, as this means less of each mortgage payment is being used to pay interest and more is being used to pay down the principal. In a low interest rate environment, you will gain more in equity and give away less in interest with each mortgage payment.

Let's look at an example. Let's say you purchase a property for $200,000 and get a mortgage for 75 percent of the purchase price, or $150,000. Let's also say that the interest rate is 4 percent, amortized over twenty years. In the first year alone, you will pay down enough principal to reduce your loan payoff to $145,000; that $5,000 in principal reduction is equity you've built, and it will be captured when you sell or refinance the property in the future.

In Year 5, you'll be accruing over $6,000 per year in principal reduction, and by Year 10, you'll be accruing over $7,000 per year. Over the twenty-year amortization period of the loan, you will build the full $150,000 in equity, which—if you still own the property at that point—is an average of $7,500 per year in equity generated by your tenants' payments. Just by paying your mortgage with your rental income, you're generating a solid return.

DIG DEEP

AMORTIZATION BENEFITS

This discussion of amortization is somewhat simplified, and when we dig a bit deeper, we realize that there are a lot of nuances to the amortization benefit. First, it's important to note that the principal we pay down every month isn't free money being generated by our owning the property. We are actually trading monthly cash flow in return for the equity we're building.

Think of it this way: If we didn't have a loan, that equity being generated through principal paydown would be money going into our pocket each month from the rent we're collecting—it just wouldn't be flowing out of our pocket to the mortgage company. Plus, there's a cost to that equity buildup, namely the interest we're paying on the loan.

Some people might even argue that amortization is not a benefit, because if we didn't have a mortgage payment, that extra cash could be immediately reinvested. But there are a number of benefits to having a loan that far outweigh the reduction in cash flow every month.

1. We are getting access to cash at the time we take out the loan, and that cash can be reinvested. For example, on a $100,000 loan, we get $100,000 on Day 1, as opposed to paying $100,000 extra for the property in cash, and then waiting for that money to come to us as cash flow over the following years. As we know from our discussion of the time value of money, having this $100,000 now is more valuable than getting it over time in the future.

2. Leverage allows us to magnify our appreciation. For example, let's say our $400,000 property appreciated 5 percent this year. That's $20,000 in appreciation. On a $400,000 cash purchase, we have just earned 5 percent growth through appreciation. However, if we were to get a $300,000 loan and only put $100,000 down on that same property, the $20,000 in appreciation represents 20 percent growth ($20,000 ÷ $100,000 = 0.2).

3. Assuming we have positive leverage, our cash-on-cash return is increased for every month we have the loan.

4. We have the ability to diversify. The cash we receive from the loan can be used to diversify our equity into other asset classes. For example, paying $400,000 for a house ties $400,000 of our cash to equity in one asset. But getting a $300,000 loan against that $400,000 house gives us $300,000 that can be used to diversify our equity across other assets or asset classes.

5. Inflation allows us to arbitrage our future debt payments. What we mean by this is that borrowing money today, with the ability to pay it back in the future after inflation has eaten away at the value of the dollar, is a financial benefit in itself. As an example, if inflation causes the cost everything to double over the next twenty years, it will likely also drive incomes up by about double—but our mortgage payment stays the same. We could be earning twice as much but still have the same mortgage payment; the payment essentially costs half as much as it did when we originally got the loan.

Long story short, amortization isn't necessarily as beneficial as some may make it out to be, but there are a lot of indirect benefits to amortization that make it a major driver of potential investment growth.

TAX BENEFITS

Many real estate investors—especially newer investors—don't appreciate the value of tax benefits from real estate. This is understandable. Many newer investors are younger and don't have a high enough income that lower taxes would make a big difference to their bottom line.

While many newer investors are thinking about all the money they can make in real estate, most of them aren't thinking about how much they can keep. Even for those investors who have high incomes outside of real estate, taxes are just a cost of doing business—we tend to think that paying a lot in taxes is good, as it means we're making a lot of money!

In our experience, the older people get, the more their income increases. And the more experienced they become as investors, the more important the consideration of lowering their tax burden becomes. In fact, for a lot of experienced investors, the opportunity to decrease their taxes is the single most important aspect of investing in real estate. This is evidenced by the fact that many real estate investment funds are structured to provide tax benefits first and foremost.

Real estate can provide a wide range of tax benefits, as we discussed in detail back in Chapters 12 and 13. To recap a few of the most common benefits:

- **Depreciation:** Literally speaking, depreciation means a reduction in the value of an asset over time. The physical structure in a real estate investment (as opposed to the land it sits on) will deteriorate over time. The IRS recognizes that there is a cost associated with maintaining the physical asset, and they compensate investors in the form of a tax deduction known as depreciation. If you own a piece of real estate, a percentage of the value of the physical structure can be used as a deduction against the property's income each year. In many cases, this deduction can completely (or nearly completely) offset the income that the investment is generating, making that income tax free (or nearly so).
- **1031 exchange:** Named after Section 1031 of the U.S. tax code, this IRS regulation allows you to sell certain real estate investments and use the gains to purchase a similar property, deferring the taxes on those gains. Normally, when you sell a property, you pay taxes on the profit generated by the sale; with a 1031 exchange, you can push those taxes off into the future. If you recall our discussion on the time value of money, you understand why this is so beneficial.
- **Tax-free borrowing against equity:** There aren't many situations in this world where you can put a big chunk of cash in your pocket without owing any taxes… ever! But there is one common situation in real estate where this is possible. The cash pulled out of a piece of real estate during a refinance is nontaxable. For example, if you have a property that you purchased for $100,000 ten years ago and is now worth $300,000, you can potentially refinance and pull out $200,000 or more in cash absolutely tax free.
- **Interest deduction:** The interest you pay on your mortgage on investment properties is fully deductible against income.

- **Capital gains exclusion on the sale of a primary residence:** For those who purchase a primary residence with the intent to benefit from appreciation (forced or market), it's often possible to avoid taxes on gains when the property is sold. If you live in the property for at least two years, and if the amount of the gain is below certain thresholds, you can literally earn up to hundreds of thousands of dollars on a sale without owing anything in taxes.

On top of these common tax benefit strategies, there are plenty of other less common but very powerful ways that real estate can be used to legally defer, avoid, or shelter taxes. We're not going to go into great detail in this book about tax strategies—that's an entirely separate book. We recommend you work with a great accountant, CPA, and/or tax adviser.

Cash flow, appreciation, amortization, and tax benefits are the four ways in which real estate generates income for investors. *Good* real estate investors can use any one of these methods of income production to create a profitable real estate business. *Great* real estate investors will use many of these methods of income production to create a profitable real estate business. And the *best*, most innovative real estate investors will put these methods of income production together in new and creative ways to devise real estate strategies that have not yet been fully explored and exploited.

HONE YOUR SKILLS: CHAPTER 39

- What are the four ways you can generate returns from real estate?
- What is the difference between market appreciation and forced appreciation?
- True or false: Cash flow is the most important of the four ways real estate generates returns.

CHAPTER 40

THE COMPOUNDING MACHINE: PLANNING YOUR FINANCIAL FREEDOM

Chapter 40 will help answer the questions:
- How do the returns generated by investments lead to financial freedom?
- What specifically do I need to accomplish with my investments to achieve my financial goals?
- What are the various levers I can pull to achieve my goals in an optimal fashion?

Now that we have a better understanding of the two different types of deals we tend to see (transactional versus residual) and now that we know where returns are coming from (cash flow, appreciation, amortization, and tax benefits), let's take a look at how we can use this information to create a plan that will help us map out our road to financial freedom.

We refer to this framework as "the compounding machine," as that's what we're ultimately trying to achieve with our investments—a set-it-and-forget-it mechanism for generating compounded returns that will continue to grow long after we have stopped actively working for them, creating enough income and cash flow to set us financially free.

We like to think of the compounding machine as having (1) a slot where you stick money in at regular intervals and (2) a crank that you can turn at different speeds for as long as you want. The money going into the slot is the active income you're generating and dedicating to growing your nest egg. The crank represents your ability to generate residual returns through relatively passive investments. The harder you turn the crank, the higher your returns on the money you stick in the slot, and the more quickly your nest egg grows. And the longer you turn that crank, the bigger it grows.

Want to build the biggest pot of cash as quickly as possible? It's as simple as putting lots of money in the slot and then turning that crank as hard and long as you can.

How fast and how big that nest egg grows depends on three factors:

1. How much income are you adding to the machine each week, month, or year?
2. How large of a return are you generating (and reinvesting) on your total investment?
3. How long are you allowing that return to compound?

The cool thing about the compounding machine is that we can use it to plan our financial freedom. If we fill in two of those three parameters above, we can use some simple calculations to generate the third.

For example, perhaps you know how much you can add to your nest egg each month and you know what types of returns you can expect by investing those funds—in that case, you can easily calculate how long it will take for the machine to achieve your financial goals.

Or perhaps you know what level of return you can expect to generate through your investing, and you know how long you have until retirement—now you can calculate how much you need to put into the machine each month to hit your target nest egg.

Finally, perhaps you know how much you can contribute to your nest egg each month and you know how long you're willing to continue working to make those contributions—now you can calculate what level of return you'd need to achieve to hit your target net worth in the allotted amount of time.

Let's look at an example.

When I (J) was first creating my plan for financial freedom, I decided that I could realistically earn and stash away $5,000 per month into my investment pool. This was back in the early 2000s, and at the time, I was fairly certain that I could figure out how to generate a 12 percent annualized compounded return on this cash. (Remember, back in 2001, it was possible to earn 6 percent in a no-risk certificate of deposit backed by the U.S. government!) Finally, I knew that I needed $2 million in total net worth to achieve my goal of financial freedom.

I had two of the parameters: how much I was putting into the machine ($5,000 per month) and how hard I was able to turn the crank (12 percent annualized returns). This allowed me to calculate how long I would need to turn that crank to hit my $2 million target.

STARTING AMOUNT	MONTHLY CONTRIBUTION	ANNUALIZED COMPOUNDED RETURN	YEARS OF COMPOUNDING	NET WORTH TARGET
$0	$5,000	12%	?	$2,000,000

Plugging these numbers into an online compound interest calculator (we've added a Dig Deep at the end of the chapter if you'd like to know how to do this by hand), I was able to determine that it would take just under fourteen years, starting from nothing, to achieve my financial freedom number.

STARTING AMOUNT	MONTHLY CONTRIBUTION	ANNUALIZED COMPOUNDED RETURN	YEARS OF COMPOUNDING	NET WORTH TARGET
$0	$5,000	12%	14	$2,000,000

If we know how much we can contribute and at what rate we can compound our investment, we can determine how long it will take to hit our financial goal.

Let's look at another example.

Let's say you are starting with $80,000, you have a high-paying job and know you could generate $7,500 per month to contribute to your nest egg, and you decide that you only want to work another eight more years before you hit your target of $1.2 million in your nest egg. What level of compounded return would you need to meet your goal?

STARTING AMOUNT	MONTHLY CONTRIBUTION	ANNUALIZED COMPOUNDED RETURN	YEARS OF COMPOUNDING	NET WORTH TARGET
$80,000	$7,500	?	8	$1,200,000

Again, putting these numbers into a compound interest calculator, you can determine that you would need to generate about 8.8 percent annualized compounded returns to achieve your goal.

STARTING AMOUNT	MONTHLY CONTRIBUTION	ANNUALIZED COMPOUNDED RETURN	YEARS OF COMPOUNDING	NET WORTH TARGET
$80,000	$7,500	8.8%	8	$1,200,000

Now that you know you need 8.8 percent annualized compounded return, this gives you a reasonable idea of what types of investments are likely to work for you. Historically, investing in an S&P index fund has returned about 8 percent annual compounded return, adjusted for inflation. So, that would get you close. And there are many relatively passive real estate investments that could get you those numbers as well.

Of course, you cannot always achieve whatever annualized compound return the compounding machine spits out. If you put in an aggressive goal and aggressive timeline, you may find your needed annualized compounded return to be unachievable, or perhaps so high that it would require taking on a good deal of risk. In these scenarios, it can be wise to revise your goal or timeline rather than pursue unnecessarily risky investments.

Finally, let's assume that you know that your residual income stream could generate a specific return and that you had a time frame in mind for when you wanted to retire. You could use that information to determine how much you would have to contribute to your investments each month in order to hit that time goal. In this situation, you could create a target monthly savings amount that would allow you to achieve your goals.

For example, if you knew that you could consistently generate 12 percent compounded returns by investing passively in syndications with the $1 million you currently had, and if you knew that you wanted to retire in fifteen years with an additional $5 million in net worth, the compounding machine could tell you how much you'd need to invest each month to achieve that goal.

STARTING AMOUNT	MONTHLY CONTRIBUTION	ANNUALIZED COMPOUNDED RETURN	YEARS OF COMPOUNDING	NET WORTH TARGET
$1,000,000	?	12%	8	$6,000,000

Again, plugging these numbers into a compound interest calculator, you'd be able to determine that you would need to contribute an extra $7,500 per month to your passive investments to achieve your goal.

STARTING AMOUNT	MONTHLY CONTRIBUTION	ANNUALIZED COMPOUNDED RETURN	YEARS OF COMPOUNDING	NET WORTH TARGET
$80,000	$7,500	12%	8	$1,200,000

While achieving financial freedom or accumulating enough wealth to retire can seem complex, this simple framework demonstrates that it's not. At the end of the day, there are three factors to consider: how much you are contributing to your investments, what rate of return you can expect, and how long you are investing for.

COMPOUNDING WITH REGULAR ADDITIONS

For the sake of simplicity, we suggested earlier you plug your numbers into an online compound interest calculator. But there's no reason we couldn't do that math ourselves. The formula for calculating the compounded result when making regular contributions into an investment (like we are doing above) is:

Total value = Contribution × ((((1 + Interest)^{Periods}) − 1) ÷ Interest)

Let's use this formula to verify what learned in the first example above—that it would take just under fourteen years to accumulate $2 million if we were to contribute $5,000 per month to our investments, earning 12 percent annual returns.

Contribution = $5,000

Interest = .01 (it's 12 percent per year, but we'll assume we're compounding monthly along with our contributions, so 1 percent monthly)

Periods = 168 (twelve monthly periods per year over fourteen years)

Let's solve for the total value:

Total value = $5,000 × ((((1 + .01)^{168}) − 1) ÷ .01)

Total value = $5,000 × ((((1.01^{168}) − 1) ÷ .01)

Total value = $5,000 × (4.3209 ÷ .01)

Total value = $2,160,484

As expected, contributing $5,000 per month with a 12 percent annual return (compounded monthly) over fourteen years generates about $2 million.

HONE YOUR SKILLS: CHAPTER 40

- What are the three variables that impact your "compounding machine"?
- If you make an initial investment of $25,000 and contribute $1,000 per month, with an estimated rate of return of 8 percent, what will your net worth be in thirty years?

CHAPTER 41
ANALYZING DEALS

There are simply too many different types of real estate deals—and too many nuances among those deals—to cover every possible analysis situation in this book. However, if we use the frameworks we've laid out as our guide, we can dig into the analysis of several example deals that will cover many of the situations you're likely to experience throughout your career as a real estate investor.

In fact, when looking at deals from the 10,000-foot level, we like to think about them in the exact terms we laid out earlier: Some deals are transactional and others are cash-flowing. The transactional deals generate returns almost exclusively from forced appreciation, while the cash-flowing deals may generate all four types of returns we discussed.

When analyzing deals, we refer to this chart, which describes exactly what metrics we look at to determine if the deal is good:

TYPES OF DEALS	CASH FLOW	APPRECIATION	AMORTIZATION	TAX BENEFITS
Transactional	✗	✓	✗	✗
Residual	✓	✓	✓	✓

Of course, not every deal fits nicely into a bucket. You may have some transactional deals that generate cash flow during your hold period, or a residual deal that generates no amortization benefits (for example, if you pay cash for a property, you won't get any amortization benefits).

For that reason, the analysis techniques we will discuss may have to be massaged and modified to fit your specific situation. But if you think about deals as being transactional, residual, or a combination of both, and if you think about returns as falling into the categories of cash flow, appreciation, amortization, and tax benefits, you should be able to figure out a reasonable analysis strategy for any transaction you do.

Over the next several chapters, we will dig into some examples that will provide an analysis framework for you to use on your own deals.

CHAPTER 42
ANALYZING TRANSACTIONAL DEALS

Chapter 42 will help answer the questions:
- How is a transactional deal different from a deal that generates residual income?
- How do I determine the profit potential of a transactional deal?

As you saw from the chart in the previous chapter, the returns for transactional deals generally fall into just one of the four return-generating categories: appreciation.

Remember, there are two types of appreciation: market appreciation and forced appreciation. Market appreciation is the result of holding an asset long enough for inflation and other market forces to drive the price up. Forced appreciation is the act of increasing the value of an asset through knowledge and effort—specifically, by buying an asset below market value or by adding value to the asset before you resell.

We often see this forced appreciation in the real estate investing world with wholesalers and house flippers. Wholesalers buy properties below market value and resell them to investors at a marked-up price, keeping the difference as their profit. House flippers do renovations to increase the value of a property, and then resell to homeowners at a higher price, keeping anything above their costs as profit.

Keep in mind that transactional deals don't just apply to physical properties. Note investors will often buy a note below market value—or even "rehabilitate" a note by working with the borrower—and then resell the note at a profit. Nearly any asset can be used to generate profit if you can buy it below market value and/or add value before resale.

Long story short, most transactional deals generate returns through forced appreciation. This is why when we analyze transactional deals, we typically start with *profit* as our key return metric. But profit is just one metric, and it doesn't tell the whole story. We also have to take into account the cost and time that will be expended on the project.

Once we determine our expected profit, we can then apply other common return metrics to determine whether the profit justifies the cost of the deal—metrics such as return on investment (ROI), average annual return (AAR), and internal rate of return (IRR). If you don't remember these terms, we would suggest going back to Part 3 of this book and brushing up on these metrics.

DETERMINING PROFIT

As we mentioned, when analyzing transactional deals, we will generally start by determining the profit (or expected profit) of the deal. Without knowing the expected profit, we won't be able to apply the other metrics that will tell us whether the time and money we spend is worth the profit we're receiving.

The expected profit on any transactional deal can be computed as follows:

#75	**Profit**
	Profit = Sales price – Purchase price – Expenses
	
	Where
	    Sales price is the conservative estimate of what you can sell the property for at sale.
	    Purchase price is the expected cost to acquire the property.
	    Expenses are the expected total costs associated with buying, renovating, holding, and then reselling the property.

In this definition, we are assuming that the deal is being considered, and we are estimating our sales price, purchase price, and expenses; if a deal has already been completed, then the actual costs of those items should be used.

Sales price and purchase price should be pretty straightforward. But we want to dig into the expenses a bit more, as many investors (even seasoned investors) often fail to account for all the expenses associated with a deal.

Expenses fall into four categories; let's look at each of these in a bit more detail.

PURCHASE COSTS

Purchase costs refer to those fixed expenses that contribute to the purchase of a property. The major contributors to purchase costs include:

- **Inspection costs.** If you hire a property inspector before or after purchase, that cost would be factored in here.
- **Closing costs.** Each purchase comes with a fixed set of closing costs paid by the buyer. This might include title search fees, attorney fees, state-specific transfer taxes, mailing fees, and recording fees.
- **Lender fees.** Lenders often charge up-front costs for providing financing for a deal. These costs might include a loan origination fee, appraisal, underwriting fee, flood certification, document preparation fee, processing fee, and credit report fee.

Even if the deal doesn't involve a physical property (for example, buying a note or a contract), there may be other due diligence costs associated with making that purchase.

RENOVATION COSTS

If you are planning to renovate the property during your hold period, you will likely incur the following two sets of costs:

- **Labor costs.** These are the costs for paying contractors to perform renovations on your property.
- **Material costs.** These are the costs of the materials purchased for use during your renovation.

Again, even if the asset being purchased and sold isn't a property, there still may be some rehabilitation costs associated with the deal.

HOLDING COSTS

Holding costs refer to those expenses that add up between the time you acquire the property and the time you sell the property. Here are a few of the most common:

- **Mortgage payments.** If you've financed the purchase, you likely have monthly principal and interest payments to your lender.
- **Property taxes.** You will pay property taxes for the period in which you hold the property. These taxes may be paid in advance at purchase, during the hold period, or at sale.
- **Utilities.** Assuming you need utilities at the property during your hold period, you will incur the monthly utility costs.
- **Insurance.** Will you insure your property during the hold period? Make sure you factor in this cost.

SELLING COSTS

Selling costs refer to those fees and commissions that are paid as part of the disposition (sale) of the property. The most common costs associated with property sale are:

- **Commissions.** If you're using a listing agent to sell your property, or plan to sell to a buyer represented by an agent, you will likely incur a cost of between 3 percent and 6 percent of the sales price to compensate the agent(s).
- **Closing costs.** Each sale may come with a set of closing costs paid by the seller. This might include title search fees, attorney fees, state-specific transfer taxes, mailing fees, and recording fees.

Quick Tip | Estimating Expenses

Estimating expenses is a key step in analyzing a transactional real estate deal. Estimating rehab costs is particularly important and can also be very tricky, especially for newer investors. There's too much to cover on that topic in this book, but luckily, J has written *The Book on Estimating Rehab Costs*, which covers that topic in detail. In this book, we're going to stick to the formulas and concepts that will help you analyze deals like a pro. But pick up J's rehab estimation book if you'll be doing any renovations/remodeling over your investing career.

Let's look at a couple of examples.

ANALYZING A FIX-AND-FLIP DEAL (USING LEVERAGE)

Perhaps the most common type of transactional deal in the real estate world is the fix-and-flip. This is where an investor purchases a property—generally at a discount to the market value—renovates the property, and then resells it to a homeowner or another investor.

Since many house flippers don't have hundreds of thousands of dollars lying around, the house flipper often will rely on debt (a loan) to make the project feasible. In this example, we will assume that the house flipper is getting a loan as part of the transaction.

A good house flipper will run through an analysis of the deal *before* they decide to move forward, in order to determine whether the deal makes sense from a financial standpoint. Let's assume we are house flippers looking at a potential deal and we want to determine whether or not it's a deal that makes sense.

For this potential deal, let's make the following assumptions:

- The property would be purchased for $100,000 on January 1.
- The investor would get an interest-only loan against the property for 80 percent loan-to-cost (LTC), or $80,000.

- The property would require $40,000 in renovations and can be resold for $200,000.
- The property would be sold on April 30. (So the entire process, from purchase through sale, would take four months.)

In order to calculate the profit that would be generated by this deal, we need the three pieces of information from our profit formula: purchase price, sale price, and expenses.

- **Purchase price:** We know the purchase price to be $100,000.
- **Sale price:** We know the sale price to be $200,000.
- **Expenses:** For each investor and each situation, the expenses will be different, but here's a sample breakdown of expenses that many house flippers might encounter:

PURCHASE COSTS	
Appraisals	($450.00)
Loan origination costs	($1,750.00)
Inspections/surveys	($500.00)
Closing costs	($1,000.00)
TOTAL	**-$3,700.00**
REHAB COSTS	
Contractor/labor	($24,000.00)
Materials	($16,000.00)
TOTAL	**-$40,000.00**
HOLDING COSTS	
Interest payments	($2,000.00)
Property taxes during hold	($350.00)
Insurance	($500.00)
Utilities	($250.00)
Lawn care	($200.00)
TOTAL	**-$3,300.00**
SELLING COSTS	
Commission to agents	($12,000.00)
Closing costs	($1,000.00)
TOTAL	**-$13,000.00**
TOTAL EXPENSES	**($60,000.00)**

In this example, the total expenses for the project are $60,000.

We now have enough information to determine our expected profit using our profit formula.

Profit = Sales price – Purchase price – Expenses
Profit = $200,000 – $100,000 – $60,000
Profit = $40,000

We now know that we would likely make $40,000 on this deal. Keep this deal in mind as we look at another example.

ANALYZING A FIX-AND-FLIP DEAL (WITHOUT LEVERAGE)

In the last example, we used leverage (a loan) to reduce our out-of-pocket expenses on the fix-and-flip deal. If you recall from Part 4 of this book, leverage has two primary benefits: First, it reduces your out-of-pocket expenses, and second, it can improve your returns.

We can already see that in our original fix-and-flip example, leverage reduced our out-of-pocket expenses. The $80,000 loan was $80,000 that we didn't need to come up with ourselves.

But did that leverage also serve to boost our returns? And if so, by how much?

Let's look at the same example, with one assumption changed—no leverage. In this example, let's assume we're fortunate enough to have the extra $80,000 sitting around, so that we don't have to get a loan and can use all of our own cash to finance the deal.

Again, to determine our projected profit, we need three numbers: purchase price, sale price, and expenses.

In this example, the purchase price is unchanged at $100,000.

The sale price is unchanged at $200,000.

But the expenses are changed. Because we have no loan, we have no loan costs at purchase and no interest payments during the hold period. Removing these two expenses reduces our total expense cost from $60,000 to $56,250.

PURCHASE COSTS	
Appraisals	($450.00)
Loan origination costs	$0.00
Inspections/surveys	($500.00)
Closing costs	($1,000.00)
TOTAL	**-$1,950.00**
REHAB COSTS	
Contractor/labor	($24,000.00)
Materials	($16,000.00)
TOTAL	**-$40,000.00**
HOLDING COSTS	
Interest payments	$0.00
Property taxes during hold	($350.00)
Insurance	($500.00)
Utilities	($250.00)
Lawn care	($200.00)
TOTAL	**-$1,300.00**
SELLING COSTS	
Commission to agents	($12,000.00)
Closing costs	($1,000.00)
TOTAL	**-$13,000.00**
TOTAL EXPENSES	**($56,250.00)**

As you might guess, the reduced expenses will serve to increase our profit.

Profit = Sales price – Purchase price – Expenses
Profit = $200,000 – $100,000 – $56,250
Profit = $43,750

In this example, our expected profits are $43,750—just a little higher than the $40,000 we generated when we were using leverage.

Calculating profit for a transactional deal is relatively simple from a mathematical perspective. You only need to know the purchase price, expenses, and expected sales price. However, it takes experience and practice to be able to estimate accurate inputs for the expenses and expected sales price parts of the equation. This calculation is only as good as the estimates you put in. So, if you're new to this, take your time, get input from experienced investors, and make sure your assumptions are sound before taking action.

Now that we've covered how to calculate profit, the simplest metric for transactional deals, it's time to apply some of the return metrics we learned in Part 3 of this book to our examples and understand our deals in more depth.

HONE YOUR SKILLS: CHAPTER 42

- What are the four broad cost categories for transactional deals?
- What is the profit on a fix-and-flip deal (no leverage) with a purchase price of $250,000, a sales price of $400,000, purchase costs of $5,000, rehab costs of $55,000, holding costs of $9,000, and selling costs of $24,000?
- How does the analysis of a fix-and-flip deal change when leverage is used versus when leverage is not used?

CHAPTER 43
ANALYZING TRANSACTIONAL RETURNS

Chapter 43 will help answer the questions:
- How does the profit from a transactional deal relate to my overall returns?
- Does a particular amount of profit on a deal make it a good deal or bad deal?

In the two examples from the previous chapter, we saw potential profit of $40,000 and $43,750. But, as we mentioned earlier, those numbers don't tell the whole story.

Is $40,000 a good or bad amount of profit?

Is $43,750 a good or bad amount of profit?

Does leverage really only provide a small benefit? (In this case, $3,750.)

To create a little perspective, let's start with the first two questions. Is $40,000 (or $43,750) a good or bad profit for a fix-and-flip deal?

We'll bet if we told you that you could generate this $40,000 in two days with no money out of your own pocket, you'd think this was a pretty good deal. But if we told you it would take you ten years and $1 million out of your pocket to generate this $40,000, you wouldn't be nearly as happy with that number.

That's where time and out-of-pocket investment come in. Luckily, after reading the previous chapters of this book, you now have the tools to analyze these deals more deeply, accounting for the time and cost that went into generating them.

RETURN ON INVESTMENT (ROI)

The first metric we often like to look at is return on investment (ROI). As we discussed earlier in the book, ROI leaves a lot to be desired, as it doesn't consider the amount of time the project took or when the money went in or came out.

But ROI does give a general idea of how much profit was earned relative to the amount of personal capital the investor needed to put into the deal. If you recall, ROI is a catchall return metric that compares the ending value of our investment to the beginning value of our investment in order to determine a percentage gain in value.

We define ROI as:

ROI = (Ending value − Starting value) ÷ (Starting value)

In this case, the starting value is the total amount of cash that we needed to invest in this deal, and the ending value is the total amount of cash that we had at the conclusion of the deal.

Let's look at how we would calculate ROI for our first fix-and-flip example above—the deal that used leverage to reduce our out-of-pocket expenses.

Let's start with what we know about the starting value (the amount of money we put into the deal):

- The purchase price of the property was $100,000.
- We received a loan for $80,000, which offset much of the purchase price.
- We needed to pay for a lot of the expenses as well—the purchase costs, renovation costs, and holding costs. In total, we had $60,000 in expenses.
- However, the selling costs never came out of our pocket, as they were simply deducted from the sale price of the property at closing. The other expenses—purchase, renovation, and holding costs—totaled about $47,000.

Put all this together, and the total amount of cash that we needed to have on hand to complete this deal was the $100,000 in purchase price plus the $47,000 in expenses minus the $80,000 that the lender provided—for a total out-of-pocket cost of $67,000.

- Purchase Price: $100,000
- Expenses: $47,000
- Loan: -$80,000
- Out-of-Pocket Costs: $67,000

As you can see, calculating your out-of-pockets costs isn't always straightforward, and you shouldn't assume that the entire purchase amount or the entire list of expenses will have to come out of your pocket. Ultimately, though, our out-of-pocket costs (our starting value) for the ROI calculation is $67,000.

Our ending value is simpler. At the end of the project, after selling the property, paying our selling costs, and paying off our loans, we recover our entire $67,000 in out-of-pockets costs, plus we generated a profit of $40,000.

Our ending value is our starting value ($67,000) plus our profit ($40,000), totaling $107,000.

From here, we can calculate our ROI:

ROI = (Ending value – Starting value) ÷ (Starting value)
ROI = ($107,000 – $67,000) ÷ ($67,000)
ROI = 59.7%

Sounds like a great ROI, right? Again, by itself, it doesn't tell the entire story.

Generating nearly 60 percent return on your investment seems great, but the time period over which you earned this return needs to be taken into account. For example, if it took twenty years to generate a 60 percent return, that's a lot less attractive than if it took a year (or less!).

ANNUALIZED ROI

This is where the concept of annualized ROI, which we discussed earlier, comes in. Let's review our annualized ROI formula:

Annualized ROI = ROI ÷ Years held

Annualized ROI allows us to massage our ROI into an annualized number. Basically, it tells us what our ROI would be over one twelve-month period for an investment with this ROI.

To determine annualized ROI, we need to know the holding period in years. In this example, the entire deal was completed in four months, which equates to one-third (0.3333) of a year.

So, our annualized ROI for our leveraged fix-and-flip example would be:

Annualized ROI = ROI ÷ Years held
Annualized ROI = 59.7% ÷ 0.3333
Annualized ROI = 179.1%

In other words, if we were to compress or expand (in this case, expand) this particular deal into a twelve-month period with the same level of returns, we'd see nearly 180 percent returns in that one year.

Using this example, if we were able to do three deals with the same level of return—each four months in length like this one—in that twelve-month period, we would see a growth of nearly 180 percent from our starting investment value.

This gives us a much better idea of how hard our money is working for us, and this annualized ROI number starts to allow us to compare this deal to other transactional investments that we might want to consider. Remember, with transactional investments, we are often limited by our time and energy, so choosing the highest-performing investment allows us to maximize our efforts.

Now, there is one more return metric that we often find useful when analyzing transactional deals, and that's internal rate of return.

INTERNAL RATE OF RETURN (IRR)

As we discussed back in our time value of money section (Chapters 8–11), IRR allows us to determine the compounded return of the investment. This metric not only takes into consideration the investment gain (like profit), the percentage gain (like ROI), and the time period of the gain (like annualized ROI), but it also allows us to factor in the timing of our money going out and coming back in.

Remember, money today is worth more than money tomorrow, so if we can hold on to our money longer and/or get our returns sooner, we will see greater growth in our net worth than if we have to invest sooner and wait longer for our returns.

In order to calculate the IRR for an investment, the crucial step required is to determine how much money is actually going out and coming in both at the initial investment and then during each regular time period. This investment is four months long, so it's reasonable to use a month as our time period (note that we can choose any regular time period, but shorter time periods require more work to break down when money goes out and comes in, and will thus give a more accurate compounded return metric).

Let's assume that money goes out and comes in for this investment as follows:

MONTH 1		
Purchase property		($100,000)
Loans received		$80,000
Purchase costs		($3,700)
Renovation costs		($10,000)
Holding costs		($825)
	TOTAL	**($34,525)**
MONTH 2		
Renovation costs		($15,000)
Holding costs		($825)
	TOTAL	**($15,825)**
MONTH 3		
Renovation costs		($15,000)
Holding costs		($825)
	TOTAL	**($15,825)**
MONTH 4		
Holding costs		($825)
Sale of property		$200,000
Pay off loan		($80,000)
Selling costs		($13,000)
	TOTAL	**$106,175**

Unfortunately, it's not easy to calculate IRR without a calculator or spreadsheet, but if we plug these values into an IRR calculator, we see that our compounded return is over 1,000 percent!

Jan-21	($34,525.00)
Feb-21	($15,825.00)
Mar-21	($15,825.00)
Apr-12	$106,175.00
	IRR: 1059.23%

That's a pretty hefty compounded return, and it tells us that if we could consistently do this exact deal over and over, with no downtime, and with our cash flow continually being reinvested as soon as it's earned, we could multiply our original investment more than ten times in a single year!

This still doesn't answer our question of how much using leverage has helped us with this deal, though. To answer that question, we need to revisit our unleveraged (no loan) scenario and see how those return metrics shake out.

REVISITING OUR FIX-AND-FLIP DEAL: UNLEVERAGED RETURNS

To recap from earlier, our profit in the unleveraged example was $43,750, and our expenses were as follows:

PURCHASE COSTS		
Appraisals		($450.00)
Loan origination costs		$0.00
Inspections/surveys		($500.00)
Closing costs		($1,000.00)
	TOTAL	-$1,950.00
REHAB COSTS		
Contractor/labor		($24,000.00)
Materials		($16,000.00)
	TOTAL	-$40,000.00
HOLDING COSTS		
Interest payments		$0.00
Property taxes during hold		($350.00)
Insurance		($500.00)
Utilities		($250.00)
Lawn care		($200.00)
	TOTAL	-$1,300.00
SELLING COSTS		
Commission to agents		($12,000.00)
Closing costs		($1,000.00)
	TOTAL	-$13,000.00
	TOTAL EXPENSES	($56,250.00)

Chapter 32

- What is the loan constant for a property with an annual debt service of $30,000 and a loan amount of $380,000?
  - **7.9 percent**
- What is the breakeven loan value of a property with an NOI of $25,000 and a loan constant of 7 percent?
  - **$357,142.86**
- What are some limitations of the loan constant?
  - **The loan constant is not useful for loans that don't have fixed interest rates or loans that are interest only.**

Chapter 33

- What is the concept of leverage?
  - **The concept of leverage is using borrowed capital for an investment with the intent that the return generated on the borrowed capital will be greater than the interest paid to secure the capital.**
- What are the two primary benefits of leverage?
  - **The two primary benefits of using leverage are: (1) using less of your own money for investments, and (2) boosting your investing returns.**
- What are the drawbacks of leverage?
  - **Leverage adds costs to your investments (in the form of interest), adds the risk of bankruptcy, and can lower your investing returns if used improperly.**

Chapter 34

- What is the difference between positive and negative leverage?
  - **Positive leverage occurs when the use of borrowed funds generates a higher ROI than would be generated with nonborrowed funds. Negative leverage is the opposite and occurs when the use of borrowed funds generates a lower ROI than would be generated with nonborrowed funds.**
- True or false: If your loan has positive leverage, it will be positive for a loan with any LTV up to 100 percent.
  - **True. No matter what proportion of a property you purchase using a positive leverage loan, it will provide positive cash flow.**

Chapter 35

- What is the Leverage (value) for a deal with a cap rate of 5.5 percent and a loan constant of 6 percent?
  - **−0.50 percent**

- How do you interpret the Leverage value?
  - **If the Leverage value is above zero, it will provide positive leverage. If the Leverage value is below zero, it will provide negative leverage.**

Chapter 36

- For a property purchased with a loan, what are the two types of financing?
  - **The equity put into the deal (typically known as the down payment) and the cash from the borrowed funds (debt).**
- What is the cash flow generated from equity on a property purchased for $300,000 with a 25 percent down payment, which has a cap rate of 6.8 percent?
  - **$5,100**
- What is the cash flow from borrowed funds for the same property if the leverage is 1.9 percent?
  - **$4,275**

Chapter 37

- What is the return on equity of an investment with cash flow of $12,000 per year and equity value of $135,000?
  - **8.89 percent**
- What is the equity value of a deal that sells for $475,000 and has liabilities of $366,000?
  - **$109,000**
- What are two strategies to improve your return on equity?
  1. **Sell and reinvest your profits**
  2. **Do a cash-out refinance**

Chapter 38

- What is the difference between transactional income and residual income?
  - **Transactional income is generated by trading your time for money (like a W-2 job or flipping houses). Residual income is generated by using existing money (investments) to generate additional income.**
- What are three examples of real estate–focused transactional income strategies?
  - **Three of the most common transactional income strategies are wholesaling, flipping houses, or becoming a real estate professional, such as an agent, property manager, or mortgage broker.**
- What are three examples of real estate–focused residual income strategies?
  - **Three of the most common residual income strategies are rental property investing, private lending, and note investing.**

Chapter 39
- What are the four ways you can generate returns from real estate?
  - **Cash flow, appreciation, amortization, and tax benefits**
- What is the difference between market appreciation and forced appreciation?
  - **Market appreciation is when the value of a property increases over time due to factors like the location of the property, demographic trends, the macroeconomic climate, and many other elements (often outside the investor's control). Forced appreciation is when the value of a property increases due to the actions of the investor, such as adding bedrooms or an ADU, renovating the kitchen, or adding bedrooms.**
- True or false: Cash flow is the most important of the four ways real estate generates returns.
  - **False. No means of generating returns is inherently superior to the others. It is up to each individual investor to determine for themselves what is the most important and best suits their financial goals.**

Chapter 40
- What are the three variables that impact your "compounding machine"?
  1. **How much is invested into the machine**
  2. **What rate of return is generated on your total investment**
  3. **How long you allow the investment to compound**
- If you make an initial investment of $25,000 and contribute $1,000 per month, with an estimated rate of return of 8 percent, what will your net worth be in thirty years?
  - **$1,611,711**

Chapter 42
- What are the four broad cost categories for transactional deals?
  - **Purchase costs, renovation costs, holding costs, and selling costs.**
- What is the profit on a fix-and-flip deal (no leverage) with a purchase price of $250,000, a sales price of $400,000, purchase costs of $5,000, rehab costs of $55,000, holding costs of $9,000, and selling costs of $24,000?
  - **$63,000**
- How does the analysis of a fix-and-flip deal change when leverage is used versus when leverage is not used?
  - **Generally speaking, there are more cost line items for a deal with leverage, including loan origination fees (purchase costs) and interest payments (holding costs). The rest of the analysis is very similar.**

Chapter 43

- In Chapter 42's "Hone Your Skills," you answered the following question: What is the profit on a fix-and-flip deal (no leverage) with a purchase price of $250,000, a sales price of $400,000, purchase costs of $5,000, rehab costs of $55,000, holding costs of $9,000, and selling costs of $24,000. What is the ROI of this deal?
  - **42 percent**
- What is the annualized ROI of the above deal if the project took four months to complete?
  - **126 percent**
- What is the IRR of a transactional deal that costs $150,000 out of pocket in Month 1, $20,000 in Month 2, $15,000 in Month 3, and then earns $240,000 in Month 4?
  - **217 percent**

Chapter 45

- What are the costs associated with a buy-and-hold rental property purchase?
  - **Purchase price, closing costs, improvements, and reserves**
- What is the best way to estimate capital expenses?
  - **To estimate annual capital expenses, you should take the average cost of the capital item and divide it by the life expectancy of that item. A roof that costs $20,000 and has a twenty-five-year life expectancy has an estimated average capital expense of $800 ($20,000 ÷ 25). Conduct this analysis for every capital item and add them together to get your total annual expected capital expense.**
- What is the cash flow before taxes of a property with an NOI of $30,000, annual debt service of $20,000, and capital expenses of $7,000?
  - **$5,000**

Chapter 46

- What is the total return for a property with $3,500 in cash flow, $2,950 in principal payment, and a total investment of $52,150?
  - **12 percent**
- What are your tax savings for a residential property with a structure value of $550,000, assuming you have a marginal tax rate of 32 percent?
  - **$6,400**

- True or false: Market appreciation and forced appreciation should be treated the same in your analysis.
  - **False. At least, we don't recommend it. Instead, we prefer to calculate the ROI of forced appreciation and omit market appreciation. While we hope market appreciation boosts our returns, it's difficult to predict and calculate, and should be treated differently than more predictable returns like cash flow, principal payment, and tax benefits.**

Chapter 47

- What are the two primary benefits of doing a BRRRR deal?
  - **First, BRRRR deals can boost returns by helping investors hold an appropriate amount of leverage. Second, BRRRR can increase deal volume, because it allows the investor to extract cash from an existing deal for use in a new deal.**
- How much cash could you take out using a cash-out refinance for a deal that has an ARV of $300,000, an LTV of 75 percent, closing costs of $4,500, and a current loan balance of $175,000?
  - **$45,500**

ACKNOWLEDGMENTS

The creation of *Real Estate by the Numbers* has truly been a team effort, involving countless individuals who have contributed incredible time and effort to this book.

In particular, we both would like to thank everyone from BiggerPockets Publishing who helped us take this book from concept to finished product, including Katie Miller, Kaylee Walterbach, Savannah Wood, Jamie Klingensmith, Melissa Brandzel, Peter Kranitz, and Wendy Dunning.

FROM DAVE

In addition to all the people named above, I would like to give special thanks to my partner, Jane, for supporting me in every way and always pushing me to be the best version of myself. My life is full because of you.

I would also like to thank my mom, dad, and sister, Elise, for a lifetime of encouragement and guidance. Without you all, this book, my career, and the rich and fulfilling life I lead would not be possible.

And, of course, I must thank all the people who have enabled the work I love at BiggerPockets. To Josh Dorkin for hiring me and teaching me so much about entrepreneurship, to Scott Trench for helping me build the career I enjoy so much, and to the dozens of amazing teammates I have had the privilege to work alongside over the years—thank you.

Lastly, I want to thank J Scott for inviting me to work with him on this book. I have learned so much from J over the course of this collaboration, and I am very grateful for the opportunity to work with such a kind and talented individual.

FROM J

Thank you to my amazing family, who, once again, were by my side throughout the process of writing this book. Thank you especially to Carol, who supports me in everything I do and who deserves all of the credit for everything we have accomplished together.

Most importantly, thank you to Dave Meyer, without whom you wouldn't be reading this right now. I couldn't have asked for a better coauthor, and I'm honored to have my name next to yours on the front cover of this book.

More from
BiggerPockets Publishing

The Book on Flipping Houses

Written by active real estate investor and fix-and-flipper J Scott, this book contains more than 300 pages of step-by-step training, perfect for both the complete newbie and the seasoned pro looking to build a house-flipping business. Whatever your skill level, this book will teach you everything you need to know to build a profitable business and start living the life of your dreams.

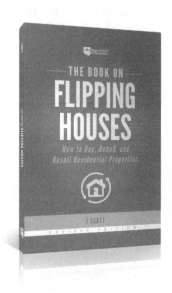

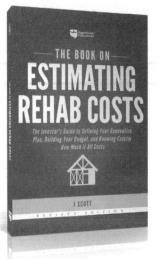

The Book on Estimating Rehab Costs

Learn detailed tips, tricks, and tactics to accurately budget nearly any house-flipping project from expert fix-and-flipper J Scott. Whether you are preparing to walk through your very first rehab project or you're an experienced home flipper, this handbook will be your guide to identifying renovation projects, creating a scope of work, and staying on budget to ensure a timely profit!

If you enjoyed this book, we hope you'll take a moment to check out some of the other great material BiggerPockets offers. Whether you crave freedom or stability, a backup plan, or passive income, BiggerPockets empowers you to live life on your own terms through real estate investing. Find the information, inspiration, and tools you need to dive right into the world of real estate investing with confidence.

Sign up today—it's free! Visit www.BiggerPockets.com
Find our books at www.BiggerPockets.com/store

Recession-Proof Real Estate Investing

Take any recession in stride, and never be intimidated by a market shift again. In this book, accomplished investor J Scott dives into the theory of economic cycles and the real-world strategies for harnessing them to your advantage. With clear instructions for every type of investor, this easy-to-follow guide will show you how to make money during all of the market's twists and turns—whether during an economic recession or at any other point in the economic cycle. You'll never look at your real estate business the same way again!

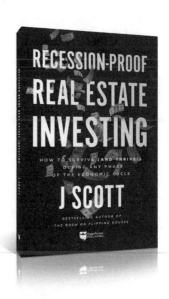

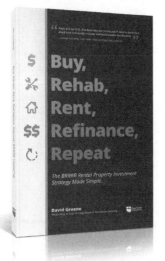

Buy, Rehab, Rent, Refinance, Repeat

Invest in real estate and never run out of money! In *Buy, Rehab, Rent, Refinance, Repeat*, you'll discover the incredible strategy known as BRRRR—a long-hidden secret of the ultra-rich and those with decades of experience. Author and investor David Greene holds nothing back, sharing the exact systems and processes he used to scale his business from buying two houses per year to buying two houses per month using the BRRRR strategy.

CONNECT WITH BIGGERPOCKETS

and Become Successful in Your Real Estate Business Today!

Facebook
/BiggerPockets

Instagram
@BiggerPockets

Twitter
@BiggerPockets

LinkedIn
/company/Bigger
Pockets

Website
BiggerPockets.com